Reproductive Justice

Reproductive Justice

The Politics of Health Care
for Native American Women

BARBARA GURR

Rutgers University Press

New Brunswick, New Jersey, and London

Library of Congress Cataloging-in-Publication Data
Gurr, Barbara Anne, author.
    Reproductive justice : the politics of health care for Native American women / Barbara Gurr.
       p. ; cm.
    Includes bibliographical references and index.
    ISBN 978–0–8135–6469–2 (hardcover : alk. paper) — ISBN 978–0–8135–6468–5 (pbk. : alk.
paper) — ISBN 978–0–8135–6470–8 (e-book)
    I. Title.
    [DNLM: 1. United States. Indian Health Service. 2. Reproductive Health Services—organization
& administration—United States. 3. Healthcare Disparities—United States. 4. Indians, North
American—United States. 5. Reproductive Rights—United States. 6. Women's Health—United
States. WQ 200 AA1]
    RG121
    362.1981—dc23
    2014014276

A British Cataloging-in-Publication record for this book is available from the British Library.

Visit our website: http://rutgerspress.rutgers.edu

Manufactured in the United States of America

This work is small and humble, but I dedicate it to the many strong and beautiful women in my life:
To my mother first,
and to my aunts, especially Aunt Patty and Aunt Kathy
—how lucky I am to have such women to guide me,
both here and there!
To my cousins and their daughters, and to all my sisters
To my grandmothers Anita and Edna, and to the many grand-mothers of my children
To Anita Garey, mentor, teacher, and friend.
To the women of Indian Country who shared their stories with me.
And to my own Hailey

This is for Charlie, so that you will know
and for Hailey, free to be.
This is for you both, together. Mine. Yours. God's.

Contents

Acknowledgments

My first thanks, always, go to Creator.

My partner, Steve, has been unfailing in his support for a long, long time. To paraphrase an Indiana Jones movie, "I chose wisely." Yes, honey, I would rather just sleep, but we have promises to keep and miles to go. My mother and father have stood behind me and beside me on every step of every journey I have ever taken, and that is a gift beyond measure. My sister-in-law Marylee has been the endless provider of dinners and babysitting, and this research simply could not have been completed without her constant support. My Pop still reminds me that I am loved. That's pretty cool. Thanks, Pop. But it was my Grandma who first opened this door for me, long before I was even born, in the way that Grandmas do. There is a longue durée here, too.

Dr. Nancy Naples introduced me to sociology and to institutional ethnography and ensured that I learned the skills and the knowledge to feel adequate to the job of this research. More importantly, her belief in me personally and professionally gave me the confidence to persevere with conviction. I will pay these gifts forward, as I can never pay them back. Dr. Anita Garey had the wisdom to slow me down and to assure me that slow was okay. These women continue to motivate me to be better, personally and professionally, even as they continue to guide me from near and far. I would like to also express my appreciation to my editor Peter Mickulas for his support, encouragement, and patience (especially patience!) throughout this process.

I am, always, indebted to John Around Him. The world is darker without you, *leksi*, but I am brighter for having known you. I am, always, grateful for the many gifts given to me by E. YMAOHH, even (especially) those I tried to reject. There is more here than I could have known then.

Tammy Lafferty and her family have been unstinting in their love and support. They welcomed me and mine into their home and their lives and kept me moving—literally—when I was ready to stop. I cannot tell you what your friendship means to me and my family. I am equally grateful for the love and support of all the women who helped me when I lived on the rez, and though I may not mention your names here, they are carved upon my heart. I remember.

I have met new relatives on this journey, and wish especially to thank Jerome and Nick, whose generosity and support of my family made all the difference when we were unsure and searching. To have a *tiospaye* is to know who you are. *Pilamayaye*, Thunder Valley.

I wish to also thank Lakota Harden, who continues from afar to provide wisdom through her words, her actions, and her sheer determination to *be*; and Katsi Cook, who inspired this work from the very first moment I heard her speak and who opened doors for me to learn more than I ever expected.

I did nothing to earn these graces in my life, and I owe debts of gratitude that are great. This work is my small *wopila*. It is not enough, but it is a beginning.

All profits from the sale of this edition go to Thunder Valley Community Development, Inc. (www.Thundervalley.org), a grassroots, community-driven organization making change on Pine Ridge Reservation.

Commonly Used Acronyms

ACLU	American Civil Liberties Union
ACOG	American College of Obstetricians and Gynecologists
AIM	American Indian Movement
AMA	American Medical Association
BIA	Bureau of Indian Affairs
CDC	Centers for Disease Control
CHRs	community health representatives
CHS	contract health services
EBM	evidence-based medicine
EC	emergency contraception
GAO	US Government Accountability Office
HHS	US Department of Health and Human Services
IE	institutional ethnography
IHCIA	Indian Health Care Improvement Act
IHS	Indian Health Service
MCH	Maternal and Child Health
NAWHERC	Native American Women's Health Education Resource Center
TLOA	Tribal Law and Order Act
USPHS	US Public Health Service
VAWA	Violence Against Women Act
WARN	Women of All Red Nations

Part I

Introductions

The Stories We Tell and Why

1

Introducing Our Relatives and Introducing the Story

In *Lako'l wicoh'an* (the Lakota way of being in the world), important things—prayers, ceremonies, the telling of stories, and the sharing of lessons—are marked with the phrase *mitakuye oyasin*. This phrase, which is commonly translated in English as "all my relations" or "we are all related," carries profound significance for Lakota and other Native people, reminding those who are gathered that all things are in relationship, and that our relationships define who we are and what our purposes might be. Our relationships carry responsibilities, sometimes joyful, sometimes challenging, sometimes tedious. Our relationships contour our lives in a thousand different ways.

The research discussed in this book emerged from my relationships in Indian Country, and from the often joyful, often challenging responsibilities of these relationships. I went to Pine Ridge Indian Reservation, home of the Oglala Lakota Oyate (People, or Nation) in South Dakota for the first time in the summer of 1999 to build wheelchair ramps with a service organization. In the year following, I returned to the reservation several times, meeting people, attending ceremonies and rodeos, and learning. My second trip there took me to the Rosebud Wacipi (dance, or pow-wow) and Rodeo; my third to the Black Hills Pow-wow in Rapid City, and to Emma, the director of the Badlands Bombing Range Recovery Project. On my fourth trip, I was invited to ride in the final day of the Sitanka Wokiksuye, the Bigfoot Memorial Ride held every year to remember and honor those ancestors killed at the Massacre of Wounded Knee in 1890.

I finally grew tired of paying the airfare from Connecticut to South Dakota, I suppose, and moved to Kyle, the "heart of the rez," in August of 2000. I worked as a teacher at Little Wound School from the summer of 2000 through the fall of 2001. During this time, I learned a great deal about the meaning of relationship as I was welcomed into the homes and families of my Lakota students, colleagues, and neighbors. We shared food and stories, prayed together, searched for lost calves in the springtime, danced together at pow-wow, and cheered together at basketball games. I knew that I had become a part of that community when an elder referred to me as *takoja* (grandchild), and that moment when she used the term so casually is one of my favorite memories from my time living in Kyle.

I also became pregnant with my son during this time. It is through him that I have learned my greatest lessons about being a relative, and perhaps particularly about being a relative to the Lakota people; his body, nurtured in my body, produced a physical fulcrum for my relationships on the reservation, a physicality that embodied the kinship already begun in the kitchens, classrooms, and prayer ceremonies of the community in which I lived. His body, through my body, is the material link of our web of kinship. Feminist sociologists frequently argue that notions of kinship that rely on blood are patriarchal in their essence. This may be so, as ideas of "family" that exclude relationship outside of genetics or marriage serve a heteropatriarchal function, for example by marginalizing other ways of creating family (queer families come to mind; foster and adoptive families; and the "fictive kin" that anthropologist Carol Stack [1974] so articulately discusses). In Indian Country, relationship is rarely restricted to biology or marriage. Nonetheless, for me and my relatives on Pine Ridge, my son provides tangibility to our attachment.

I am not Native American (my mother's people come mostly from Ireland and my father's from Germany), but I came to understand during my pregnancy that mothering a Lakota child produces particular responsibilities to my relatives through him. I say "I came to understand" this because although my Lakota relatives were always teaching me, they never preached at me; it was through their stories and the ways in which they lived their lives that I learned these things. I took classes at Oglala Lakota College on the reservation to learn more, and these classes were helpful, but I learned the most when I simply listened to the people around me, when they so generously shared their stories with me. In fact, it was some of these stories that turned my attention to reproductive health care as a subject of study, as I discuss below.

Our relatives on the reservation and elsewhere in Indian Country, for their part, also recognize their responsibilities to my son, and through my son to me and to the rest of our family. Since my son's birth in late 2001 I have returned to the reservation many times, sometimes with him, sometimes also with my husband and our daughter, and sometimes by myself. These visits, as well as the numerous phone calls, letters, and e-mails between my family and our Lakota relatives, have strengthened and broadened our relationships. My desire to provide my son with as strong a connection to his Lakota relatives as possible draws us back to them regularly, to visit, to pray, to learn, and more recently, to conduct research.

The Personal Is Political and Academic

I'm often asked by colleagues, peer reviewers, and friends why I chose to research reproductive justice in Indian Country, given the complexities involved: I am a non-Native sociologist trained in a department without Native Studies affiliations; I live two thousand miles from my field site and funded this research on a graduate assistant's salary; I needed not only my university's Institutional Review Board's approval, but also the approval of the Tribal Research Review Board, a process that took almost a year and needs to be regularly revisited. My response is always the same: I didn't choose this research—actually, I tried to avoid it. When I first set out to do my thesis in women's studies shortly after my son's birth, I chose Frida Kahlo's art as my first topic. Then I thought I'd look at the day care crisis in our country (if you're a working parent, you're probably familiar with that one). I didn't want to research Native women's lives because I didn't want to be yet another white scholar who thought she understood Indian Country and made an academic career out of that arrogance. But I have friends and family on Pine Ridge who shared their stories with me and took care of me when I was a little lost. When I left the reservation to return to Connecticut and give birth to my son, I also reentered a world of familiar resources, and academia has always been one of those. There was, perhaps, a sense of obligation. But there was also a burgeoning sense of responsibility, which is subtly but importantly different. I was aware that I had been treated like a relative by many community members on the reservation, and what kind of relative turns her back on those who have helped her—especially when she gains the opportunity to do research that might potentially help them in return, or at least shed light on some of the oppressions they survive? So I say I didn't choose it. I felt it was the right thing to do, and I hope I was right.

For this study, entry-level data focusing on the experiences of Native women who utilize the Indian Health Service (IHS) for their reproductive health care derives from participant observations and just over thirty interviews conducted between 2009 and 2011. But almost a decade earlier, when I lived on the reservation, I became increasingly aware of the health disparities between Native Americans and non-Natives as well as the efforts of IHS to address these disparities and the challenges in doing so. Native women's concerns about reproductive health care were particularly highlighted for me when I became pregnant and many of the Native women in the community in which I lived and worked, including students and colleagues in the school where I taught, reached out to support me in this pregnancy and help me prepare for my upcoming birth experience.

As Native women of all ages shared their stories about pregnancies, childbirths, child loss, and motherhood, I learned a great deal about their relationships with IHS. These stories and the knowledge these women shared with me prompted my research into reproductive health care for Native women, and particularly my interest in reproductive health care through IHS and on Pine Ridge Reservation. In fact, it was my interest in better understanding Native women's health needs that brought me to sociology.

When I entered graduate school, I carried the stories of my relatives from Pine Ridge with me into seminar rooms and research libraries and computer labs. It's a good thing I carried them in with me, because I would not have heard them otherwise. Native studies was conspicuously absent from my graduate program—a deafening silence, it seemed to me—and my insistence on "the indigenous question" in class after class grew tiresome for my peers, I'm sure. Although they had little direct experience in Native American studies to offer me, my professors were genuinely supportive of the project that drove me to graduate school, and encouraged me to take extra classes, read particular articles, write, write, and write some more about the intersections between race, gender, sexuality, and State regimes. I was fortunate to find those ivory tower relatives.

All of this led to my dissertation examining Native women's reproductive health care as this is coordinated, interrupted, informed, and mediated through what I understand to be imperialist medicine. I first began to think about this relationship between the State and the reproductive body during my pregnancy, when, as I have said, friends on the reservation shared stories with me about their own pregnancy and birth experiences. Those stories took me by surprise. They made me angry, and sad. They were not the same stories I tell about my own experiences, and I was acutely aware even before this research formally began that one of the reasons their stories and mine were so different had something to do with settler colonialism (although at the time I didn't have such fancy academic language to explain it). Those stories are the origin stories of this book.

In this research I look through those stories to the complex institutional organization of reproductive health care in the IHS and the consequences of this organization for Native women and their communities. My experiences on the reservation led me to wonder what the larger institutional forces are that organize Native women's experiences of reproductive health care, and how these extralocal forces—what Dorothy Smith (1999) has called the "relations of ruling"—actually accomplish this organization. How do dynamic social and political ideologies of race, gender, sex, sexuality, class, and nation inform the ways in which the State understands reproductive health care and organizes the delivery of this health care? In other words, why are my reproductive health-care experiences so different from those of Native women in general, and women in reservation communities particularly?

Thinking about Health Care Institutionally

Mainstream medical practice continues to seek solutions to disease and illness through evidence-based medicine (EBM), a model that relies on empirical evidence, clinical practice, and peer review but is increasingly criticized as acultural and inconsistently generalizable (see, e.g., Fitzpatrick 2001; Rogers 2004). At the same time, mainstream discourses around health care and reproductive health care in particular generally rely on notions of individual choice and agency: women "choose" their contraceptive method, they "choose" abortion, they "choose" their care provider. Evidence-based medicine has undoubtedly helped both care providers and their patients, and choice and agency are certainly integral to understanding health and well-being as well as disease and illness, but these do not tell the whole story. My questions interrogate the *social* aspects of reproductive health care; they emerge from the micro-level, personal stories of friends and relatives on Pine Ridge, but they focus on the macro-level and institutional processes behind their experiences. This research therefore centralizes some of the broader political, economic, and social forces that produce Native women's reproductive health-care experiences.

Dorothy Smith's conceptualization of the ruling relations provides an intellectual organization to the understandings that emerged from my time on the reservation and the research that followed. Smith (1999) argues that our lives are organized by institutional forces beyond our immediate purview, and that these institutional forces constitute relationships that shape our access to certain resources, our subjective experiences, and even our own understanding of these experiences. In thinking about Native women's reproductive healthcare experiences, it becomes clear that these ruling relations are, like all relationships, complex in both the underlying desires and expectations that inform them and in the material consequences that they produce.

The theoretical framework of reproductive justice developed by Sistersong, Asian Communities for Reproductive Justice, and others provides a space in which to consider the intersections of social structures such as poverty and institutional violence with social and political ideologies of race, class, gender, sexuality, and citizenship. My reliance on the frame of reproductive justice anchors this study in an intersectional perspective that allows room for the diverse experiences of Native women as they themselves understand them to guide the overall inquiry. However, my research questions are complicated by the extraordinarily complex and fractured bureaucratic organization of IHS as well as the multiple physical and ideological locations from which Native women seek health care. In this book, I focus specifically on three factors salient to Native women's health-care experiences: the function of race, class, gender, sexuality, and citizenship in reproductive health care as this health care serves the interests of settler colonialism; the organizational neglect and institutional control of reproductive health care within IHS (what I call the "double discourse" of imperialist medicine), which emerges from multiple locations; and the tensions between what Native women want and need and what they can access. These areas of focus allow me to trace the production of health care for Native people as a legal right emerging from seventeenth- and eighteenth-century treaty negotiations and illustrate the material consequences of decisions made by seemingly abstract forces elsewhere and elsewhen from Native women themselves. Additionally, the impacts of local and community structures on the health, health care, and care-seeking behaviors of Native women emerged as a theme in this research, and therefore, relying on a reproductive justice framework, I make note of the profoundly social nature of health for Native women as they navigate multiple marginalizations in their health care, but also call upon multiple resources to negotiate these marginalizations.

The forces that produce these tensions include not only the decisions of key elite parties (often based on competing interests), but also broad social, political, and economic processes. For example, because IHS is a federal agency that works throughout the contiguous United States and Alaska, the boundaries of IHS are frequently permeated by the national organization of health care as well as the government's relationship with Native nations. This is particularly relevant when considering reproductive health care, an often contentious area of political debate and one that is frequently used as a political bargaining chip. As well, the role of the government in organizing its own relationship with Tribal nations reflects a deep ambivalence about indigeneity, an ambivalence that leads to a double discourse in the political and cultural economies of sovereignty, dependence, assimilation, and resistance. It thus becomes necessary in this research to incorporate a deliberate interrogation of the State and its role in determining the shape and purpose of reproductive health care, particularly in marginalized communities.

However, the State itself must be understood broadly. Theorists differ widely in how they understand "the State" and particularly the varied powers and authorities of State apparatuses: many argue that the State is inherently racial, organizing racial formations and the exclusions and inclusions associated with it (Goldberg 2002; Omi and Winant 1994); others argue that the State is essentially patriarchal, producing and reifying structures of inequality which rely on binary, essentialist, and hierarchical constructions of sex and gender (Connell 1990; Eisenstein 1981). Still others focus on the role of capitalism and class inequalities in the production of a "welfare State" (Abramovitz 1996; Haney 2000). More recently, the State is understood from an increasingly intersectional perspective that attempts to understand the roles of race, class, gender, sexuality, and other social constructions of identity in the production or erasure of citizenship experiences (Cantu 2009; Rosen 2009; Smith 2006).

The State is, in fact, all of these things, and therefore is almost immeasurably variable, dynamic, and fluctuating. Although I acknowledge the necessarily porous nature of any definition of the State, when I refer to the State in this book I have in mind the diverse set of institutions subject to management by the ruling apparatuses located in the federal government. This understanding, already somewhat ambiguous, is further complicated by the changing motivations of these apparatuses, which are inherently fractured and often contradictory, directed by individuals, agencies, legislatures, and courts that are themselves frequently driven by competing interests and marked by poor communication. Nonetheless, despite the seeming inconsistencies often found in federal policy and practice, these multiple State parties both produce and mediate State interests, and ultimately serve State purposes. In the case of Native America, as I will argue, the State's underlying but driving aim is disappearance, either by extermination or through assimilation, into a (fictive) collective ethnicity (which is always already raced, gendered, and sexed).

Not only federal apparatuses, but also regional states (such as South Dakota, where Pine Ridge Reservation is located) and Tribal councils influence the reproductive health care available to Native women. The Indian Health Service is accountable in different ways to all of these. Further, IHS is institutionally linked to and deeply influenced by lateral organizations in the Department of Health and Human Services (HHS) where it is located, particularly the Centers for Disease Control (CDC), the National Institutes of Health (NIH), the commissioned corps of the US Public Health Service (USPHS), and the Centers for Medicaid and Medicare.

Additionally to these institutional complexities, Indian Country itself is a complex and dynamic location for study. (The term "Indian Country" was statutorily defined in 1948 by 18 U.S.C. 1151 as land within the limits of an Indian reservation, all dependent Indian communities within the United States, and all Indian allotments. The term "Indian Country" has also come to denote not only physical space but also the cultural and intellectual space predominantly influenced by Native America.)

In early 2014 there are 566 federally recognized Tribes, not all of whom have a federally recognized land base (known as a reservation in most of the contiguous United States). There are several dozen more recognized only on the level of one of the fifty states, and several dozen more than that seeking some level of recognition. All of these Tribes and nations, of course, have their own distinct cultures, languages, cosmologies, histories, and relationships with the United States.

Further complicating this dynamic is the imposition of political boundaries designating the "homes" of certain nations as here, or there, or somewhere in between. Additionally, approximately 78 percent of Native people do not live on a reservation land base, but reside in urban centers and other non-reservation communities (Norris, Vines, and Hoeffel 2012), although reservations continue to provide the controlling image of Native America in the twenty-first century.

Thinking about Settler Colonialism

Given these complexities, a degree of generalization becomes necessary in any discussion of Indian Country; as Native scholar and poet Paula Gunn Allen explained, "One of the articles of faith among people who write about and study Native Americans is their diversity" (1991, 205). Allen's work confirmed that "while the distinctions among native communities are many, and . . . the differences are vast, the similarities are far greater and much more profound" (205). She viewed the deliberate reification of separate Indian nations as a tool of colonization, for "united they resist conquest" (206). Choctaw scholar Devon Mihesuah presents a similar argument, contending that although "there was and is no such thing as a monolithic Indian woman . . . Indian women share the common context of gender and the 'common core' of struggle against colonialism" (1996, 15–16).

In this book I follow Allen's and Mihesuah's holistic perspective by examining settler colonialism through the development, organization, goals, and impacts of a single federal institution intended to provide health care to all Native Americans. However, I situate my discussion of reproductive health care primarily in the lives of Native women living on or near Pine Ridge Reservation in South Dakota. In this way, I trace the institution of IHS from its broadest and most abstract locations to a narrow focus on the lived experiences of Native women in a particular community. This trace brings to light structures of domination and control that uniquely target the reproductive bodies of Native women.

It is my hope that here I problematize settler colonialism, rather than indigeneity. Maori scholar Linda Smith argues that "problematizing the indigenous is a Western obsession" (2002, 91), and certainly a plethora of scholarship emerging from non-indigenous (and in some cases indigenous) locations attests to this, dating back to the era of salvage anthropology and even before. This focus on indigeneity as the problem shifts attention away from the profound violences of settler societies as they continually seek to create a "new world." The new world envisioned in settler colonialism necessarily requires the elimination of preexisting societies in order to justify its claims as distinct from the "old world." Settler colonialism therefore inevitably requires the elimination or continual subjugation of the already present indigenous body, which must be brought in line with the new regime or eliminated so that settlers can build a narrative of belonging. Conceptualizing indigenous peoples as incapable of surviving effectively in the "new world" (that is, in the collective ethnicity settler colonialism imagines) justifies their removal from it, a process I examine in this book.

Cherokee activist and scholar Andrea Smith (2005) and others have made clear that sexual violence is at the center of US settler colonialism (see Chapter 8). However, equally foundational to the structure of settler colonial societies are processes that produce, regulate, absorb, and eliminate various expressions of indigenous identity. These are processes of population control, or what Michel Foucault (1976) called biopower, and they are simultaneously raced, gendered, sexed, and nationalized, as the racial, patriarchal settler State seeks to produce and maintain a collective national identity. Native women's reproductive bodies are uniquely targeted in these processes, and imperialist medicine is just one of the technologies of subjugation, though it is neither clear-cut nor simple. This book considers how mainstream medical practice as it is institutionalized within IHS by the State serves as one mechanism to advance the goals of the settler colonialist State.

Organization of the Book

It is difficult to tell the story of Native women's reproductive health care without detours and sidenotes, because this is actually a collection of many interwoven stories. Those told by my informants about their experiences serve to center my research, but my role as an institutional ethnographer is to trace their stories to other origin points and make visible how they come to exist in the first place. I am aware that many readers who pick up this book will not have extensive knowledge of the history of Native-US relations or the professionalization of medicine and its impacts on women's reproductive bodies, and so those stories must also be told, at least briefly, in order to bring to light the complex cartography that organizes Native women's reproductive health care. In some ways, then, this book is a study of the longue durée—the long, durable history—of settler colonialism's relationship with Native American women's reproductive bodies, considering persistent patterns of race, gender, and sexuality that produce the complexities that organize all of our relationships in the twenty-first century.

Although these stories are complicated, I have tried to organize them in a way that highlights recurring themes. This book is divided into four uneven parts. Part I offers a brief introduction to Indian Country generally and Pine Ridge Reservation in particular, and considers the development of the reproductive justice paradigm and its relevance for Native women. Part II tells the origin stories of the ruling relations that govern Native women's reproductive health care in IHS. Here I map the role of the State over the last three hundred years, and particularly since the mid-twentieth century, in determining the form and function of its relationships with Native nations. I argue that medicine serves an imperialist purpose in the State's double discourse of care for and neglect of Native people, and that the reproductive body is a primary site for this imperialism through the State's exercise of biopower. The voices and stories of my informants organize Part III, which centralizes their experiences seeking and, occasionally, avoiding reproductive health care through IHS. Following the experiences of my informants, I conclude that the double discourse of care provided by the State is not only unjust but in fact has potentially genocidal consequences for Native communities. Finally, in Part IV, I examine some of the strengths that communities on Pine Ridge bring to the creation of their own reproductive justice, and consider the role of IHS in fostering these strengths as it moves forward in partnership with Native nations, yet remains indisputably a tool of the settler State.

I have heard that history is written by the victors, and many might argue that Native Americans are not the victors in the history of the United States. But settler colonialism is a never-ending process, not a foregone conclusion, and its stories have many tellers. Like relationships, stories contour our understandings of the world we inhabit, and teach us how to be people in the world, together, as relatives. This is a story about my relatives in Indian Country, and about how their relationships with the settler State that currently occupies this land organizes their health and health care, and even shapes their understanding of health and health care. It is also, though to a lesser extent, a story about the resistance of Native peoples to the settler State that seeks to dominate them politically, culturally, and economically, and about the accommodations made by Native people to this same domination. In some ways, it is my story. I am present in it, after all; as the researcher and the writer, I inevitably influence how you will read this story, and I should not be discounted. In most ways, however, it is not my story, and I am only the storyteller, though I weave in and out. This is a complicated story, just like the relationships that are centered in it.

2

Stories from Indian Country

On the wall of my office I have two maps, both of which are titled "Indian Country." One shows the contiguous United States, Hawai'i, and Alaska, with the locations of all reservations marked in red. The other shows the entirety of North America and Hawai'i, and the entire map is colored a solid red. Which one is correct? Both. Indian Country is complicated.

The Lakota people emerged from the womb of Unci Maka (Grandmother Earth) long, long ago. No one knows when, exactly. Before they emerged they were spirit, and some of their ancestors who chose not to climb to the surface remain spirit; you can hear them and feel them in what is now called Wind Cave National Park. For those who came to the surface and became human, hunger and cold awaited. They had to figure out quickly how to survive in physical bodies, but they had help: the *sunka oyate* (the puppy, or dog nation); *wanbli* (eagle); and of course *tatanka*, their relative the buffalo. Perhaps even trickster, who, along with Anog Ite (Double Face Woman), lured them to the surface in the first place, might have been helpful. It's hard to say with tricksters.

There were and are, of course, other two-legged beings on Turtle Island. Some of these the Lakota came to know, and others perhaps remained a mystery until the *wasicu* (the ones who steal the fat) came, and began to group them all together under the name "Indians," moving them about on Unci Maka like so many chess pieces: those to go there, these to stay here. It wasn't easy for the *wasicu* to do this to the Lakota or to the other Indians; there was a great deal of fighting and dying on all sides. Then there was negotiating and promising. Then there was theft. Theft of land, of children, of water. It was a terrible time. But the Lakota and other Indians survived.

In the early twenty-first century there are approximately three million people who identify as "American Indian" and "Alaska Native." There are another two million or so who identify as American Indian "plus"—Hispanic, African American, German, and so on (Norris, Vines, and Hoeffel 2012). "American Indian" and "Alaska Native" are terms used by the US Census and thus many other federal agencies (as well as many academics), and though many Native people also use these terms, it's really an invented language. This invented language that subsumes hundreds of different culture groups under one umbrella may seem no different from referring to "Europeans" or "European Americans," but in a white supremacist society there are indeed important differences, including the erasure of distinct cultural identities that potentially challenge the currently dominant paradigm. In this book, I tend to use the term "Native" because that's what I hear many Native people using when they refer to a collective identity, and because there is power in political unity. I also frequently refer to particular Tribal affiliations; this reflects my effort to distinguish different experiences for different people(s), and resist the potentially homogenizing effects of umbrella terms.

No one knows for sure how many people lived here before the arrival of European and other immigrants (so frequently, and incorrectly, marked by the voyage of Columbus in 1492; we do know that others landed on these shores before the Great Explorer, although Columbus's incursion marked the beginning of mass migrations). Scholarly consensus currently estimates around fifty million across the Western Hemisphere, but some estimates range much higher (Stiffarm and Lane 1992; Taylor 2002). These disparate numbers reflect ongoing data collection, but they also reflect the ongoing politicization of indigeneity and settler colonialism; some scholars argue that lower estimates derive from assertions of European superiority (following the false reasoning that Native Americans did not have the ability to produce or sustain large population centers, for example) and simultaneously serve to mitigate the horrors of genocidal extermination, while others maintain that higher pre-Contact numbers reflect a bias against Western civilization through the implication of mass genocide (Stiffarm and Lane 1992; Taylor 2002; see also Jennings 1993).

Thomas Jefferson was the first US president to propose a reservation system to provide land for Native Americans outside of the growing domain of the young United States. Jefferson enacted policies with the state of Georgia to remove members of the Cherokee Nation almost three decades before Andrew Jackson's infamous Indian Removal Act; his goal was to make more land available for purchase by the federal government, and specifically to separate Native Americans from the general population (Miller 2006). Today, Native people live on reservation homelands across the continental United States and Alaska, though the majority of reservations (and the largest) are west of the Mississippi River.* There are currently over 560 federally recognized Native nations, and approximately 300 of these have reservation homelands. Although reservations seem to dominate the public imagination of Native America (along with feathered head-dresses, tipis, and beaded moccasins), most Native people (almost 80 percent) live off-reservation (and wear sneakers). Some urban centers such as Chicago, New York, Minneapolis, Albuquerque, and Oakland have particularly high Native populations, due in part to the 1953 policies of termination and relocation, which offered Native people federal support to relocate off-reservation in pursuit of employment and education. So Indian Country is indeed everywhere, because Native people are everywhere.

Unemployment is disproportionately high for Native Americans. In 2011, national unemployment was 8.9 percent, but for Native Americans and Alaska Natives it was 14.6 (Solis 2012). Native Americans are statistically the poorest people in the country; Buffalo County (located on the Crow Creek Reservation in South Dakota) is the poorest county in the country, and Shannon County, which composes two-thirds of nearby Pine Ridge Reservation, is the second poorest. According to the 2010 US Census, seven of the ten poorest counties in the country are located on Native American reservations. Three of the five poorest are on reservations in South Dakota.

Native people are also statistically among the sickest in the nation, with diabetes, tuberculosis, and cardiovascular disease rates well above that of all US races combined (IHS 2008). Rates of sexually transmitted infections are high in Native communities, a disparity that the Centers for Disease Control correlates with poverty and restricted access to health care as well as, potentially, cultural mistrust in health-care–seeking behaviors (CDC 2011b). Native American women as a group have a higher rate of cervical cancer than non-Hispanic white women, although the rates vary by region (CDC 2012a). The disease is also most likely to be detected late in Native women, a direct consequence of limited health care among other factors. Although breast cancer rates for Native women are lower than all other race/ethnicities combined, survival rates are also lower (only African American women have a lower survival rate); survival is closely tied to access to diagnosis and treatment (American Cancer Society 2011–2012).

---

* Hawai'i is a somewhat different matter—its illegal annexation was acknowledged by President Bill Clinton in 1993, and Native Hawaiians fall into a distinctly different legal category than Tribal nations who signed treaties with the US government, whether under duress or not (not all Native peoples signed treaties that ceded land; the Western Shoshone, for example, located in what is now called Nevada, signed only a "Treaty of Friendship" and never ceded land). The Indian Health Service does not currently directly operate in Hawai'i, and therefore this study neglects Native Hawai'i.

The challenges of providing health care to Native people are directly linked to the social conditions that organize many reservations. Understanding the social contexts for health, health care, and health-care–seeking behaviors on Pine Ridge brings to light the broader conditions for health and health care centralized in a framework of reproductive justice. This contextualization also reveals the multiple ways in which the State exerts an organizing force on the lives of the Lakota people and illustrates how the State's permeation of the reservation, reflected as much in its absence as in its presence, demonstrates its ongoing double discourse of responsibility and neglect toward Native people. However, and importantly, close examination of health and health care on Pine Ridge, and probably on many other reservations, also reveals underconsidered community strengths.

On the Rez

The first time I went to Pine Ridge Reservation, I had little prior experience with Native people (at least, that I knew of). All I had to go on was what I had read—and I had read a *lot*. One of my favorite pieces was a chapter from John Fire Lame Deer's autobiography in which he essentially rebukes white people for living in boxes (houses) and watching boxes (television), using deodorants and perfumes, and sanitizing everything. It was co-written with Richard Erdoes, who also co-wrote Mary Crow Dog's biography *Lakota Woman*, another favorite, in which Crow Dog details her involvement with the American Indian Movement (AIM) and a debilitatingly racist federal government (as well as a Tribal government that may have been worse). So when I went out to the rez for the first time, I was determined not to be one of *those* white people. Taking seriously the chastising words of John Fire Lame Deer, I didn't even pack deodorant.

Well, let me tell you—those books set me up. I went with a service organization to build wheelchair ramps (my introduction to health disparities), and we camped on the property of a tradition-oriented Lakota man who allowed us to use his hot shower, watch his cable television, and sit in his air-conditioned living room. We didn't ride horses—we rode ATVs. And when it came time to check the wells on the property, Joe used bleach—bleach!—to clear them up. I was befuddled, but honestly, how's a white girl to know any better? All I had learned in school (in fact, all I had taught in school as an eighth-grade history teacher until I returned from that first trip) was the idea of the "noble savage," who certainly would never ride an ATV.

I came home from that trip just as Ian Frazer was releasing his book *On the Rez*. I really enjoyed Frazer's previous book *Great Plains*, but I was deeply disappointed by his depictions of Pine Ridge Reservation in *On the Rez*. Was this really the same place I had just gone to? Frazer's stories were full of addiction, isolation, and depression, with a few inspirational moments thrown in (like the story about SuAnne Big Crow, an amazing athlete from the town of Pine Ridge, and the community center built in her memory). But I had seen generosity, prayer ceremonies, and school pride. I had been invited to share meals punctuated by teasing laughter. I had been awed by the illimitable vastness of sky and plain, the comforting roll of the Black Hills in the distance, the starkness of the Badlands. I was angry at Frazer at first—his story was not mine, and it felt like a lie. I came to discover over the following years, however, that his book was not a lie, exactly—it was one story, or one collection of stories, with their own truths. Just as this one is.

Pine Ridge Reservation, located in the southwest corner of South Dakota, is the Tribal center of the Oglala Lakota Oyate, one of the seven council fires of the Lakota nation. Reservation boundaries are difficult to determine. The original treaty-ceded lands extend well beyond the boundaries currently recognized by the US government and, as confirmed by the Black Hills Treaty Council (2011) as well as numerous informants for this study, the Oglala Lakota do not formally recognize as legal or binding the loss of land now considered off-reservation or "in trust." The US Census currently recognizes roughly 3,500 square miles of reservation land area (about the size of Connecticut and Delaware combined), making Pine Ridge the eighth largest reservation in the United States. According to census measurements, the reservation consists of part of two counties (Jackson and Bennett), and the entirety of a third, Shannon County. Additionally, there are off-reservation lands that have a high Native population held in trust by the federal government for the Lakota people. There are few paved roads on the reservation other than BIA Route 2, making travel difficult at certain times of the year, and most communities are built in a cluster model to better centralize services, which means there may be vast distances between one community and the next.

Counties and many villages on the reservation are named after past Bureau of Indian Affairs (BIA) agents, reflecting an incursive sense of ownership on the part of the settler State and its representatives. However, reservation residents commonly rely on Lakota names to describe geographic areas of the reservation; for example, the town of Kyle where I lived and worked is named after a BIA agent, but it is also commonly referred to as Pejuta Haka, Medicine Root district, because of the particular plants available there. Which name you use—Kyle or Pejuta Haka—may vary with whom you are speaking to, and it may also depend on what you mean to say; names carry meaning, after all. The layering of dominant culture names atop indigenous references and the occasional simultaneous existence of both speaks to the complexities of settler colonialism and indigenous resilience.

It is extremely challenging to determine accurately the number of people who live on the reservation. This is due to several factors, including misreporting of race, migratory patterns among Native families, local distrust of government agencies such as the US Census, and a relatively small population. Despite the challenges of data collection, it is clear that the federal government has failed to investigate, document, and disseminate reliable information about the extreme conditions found on most reservations, and many Native people view the lack of reliable information as an example of neglect (see, e.g., Faircloth and Tippeconnic 2010; Kraus 2001; US Commission on Civil Rights 2004; see also Chapters 7 and 8 and Appendix A below). The 2010 US Census claims the reservation is home to approximately nineteen thousand people, roughly seventeen thousand of whom are Native American (though not all are enrolled members of the Oglala Sioux Nation). Other sources, however, indicate the number of residents to be as high as forty thousand (McGreal 2010; Nieves 2004; Schwartz 2006).

The Native American Housing Assistance and Self-Determination Act of 1996 provides funds to support the construction of homes for Native people through the Department of Housing and Urban Development. However, Oglala Sioux Tribal President Theresa Two Bulls testified in 2010 during a joint hearing of the Senate Committee on Indian Affairs and the Senate Committee on Banking, Housing, and Urban Affairs that funding has been inadequate and has "not satisfied the treaty and trust responsibilities or obligations of the United States government, nor has it resulted in a majority of our low-income Tribal members living in decent, safe and affordable housing" (quoted in Woster 2010). There is a severe housing shortage on the reservation, and approximately one-third of the homes are substandard, without regular access to water, electricity, adequate insulation, and sewage systems (FEMA 1999; McGreal 2010; Oglala Oyate Woitancan 2008; Steele 2007). Additionally, approximately 55 percent of the homes on Pine Ridge are infected with Stachybotrys, also known as black mold, a potentially lethal infestation (Schwartz 2006; Shaw 2004). Although the majority of my interviews occurred in public spaces or outside, four of them occurred in my informants' homes. One of these homes had so much black mold in one of the two bathrooms that my informant's family of six no longer uses it.

Since Mari Gallagher's 2006 study on the effect on public health of food deserts (areas with limited access to affordable, nutritious foods), there has been some debate about the links between health and regular access to nutritious foods. The majority of studies considering these links find that better access to a large grocery store is associated with healthier food intake as well as reduced risk of obesity and its associated health concerns (Larson, Nelson, and Story 2009). Many of these studies also indicate that increased access to *all* foods, not just healthy foods, is most strongly linked with reduced obesity and related disease. Of course, the interactions between diet and health are complicated by numerous factors, and to date no studies have found a conclusive causal link between high rates of obesity and lack of access to nutritious foods, but the strong evidence in support of access to a wide variety of food choices indicates the importance of food access as one aspect of healthy living. On Pine Ridge Reservation, as on many reservations, there is a dearth of grocery stores; there are only two, although there are many more convenience stores, which offer fewer healthy options and are often more expensive.

Recently, other food options have begun to appear on the reservation; for example, Native American Natural Foods was formed on the reservation in 2005, and currently provides a range of products based on traditional Lakota foods, including Tanka Bars (made with cranberries and dried buffalo meat). In 2009, Native American Natural Foods partnered with Thunder Valley Community Development to open the E-Tanka Café, one of few Native-owned businesses on the reservation, and the only public Internet access location. The E-Tanka Café not only provides nutritious foods (the Tanka Dog, a hot dog made from buffalo meat, is one example), but also provides paid internships to local youth. However, the news is not all good: in May 2012 the Sioux Nation Shopping Center, the larger of the two grocery stores on the reservation, was closed for several days due to allegations they were selling outdated meat. This left residents with two options: leave the reservation to purchase groceries (if transportation was available) or shop at a convenience store.

Additionally, potable water can be scarce on the reservation, as contaminants from mining and other industrial wastes have polluted local water sources throughout western South Dakota and impacted the health of many of the state's residents, particularly those in communities that do not have water treatment facilities (Matthiessen 1991; Owe Aku 2011). Lack of access to potable water is not uncommon in reservation communities. In 2010 the Environmental Protection Agency released a report analyzing water access on Diné'tah, home of the Navajo people, which covers twenty-seven thousand square miles across the states of Arizona, New Mexico, and Utah (Diné'tah is the largest reservation homeland in the United States). They found approximately 56 percent of homes lacked regular access to adequate water and sewage facilities.

Although the Diné and their indigenous neighbors have long dwelled in desert areas, historically effective methods of obtaining water have been disrupted by the actions of the settler State, inhibiting access to food and water for Native peoples across the southwestern United States. For example, in 1960 the US Army Corps of Engineers completed construction of the Painted Rock Dam on Tohono O'odham land in Arizona, after assuring the Tribal government there would be minimal impact on Tribal agricultural practices. The purpose of the dam was to redirect some waters to surrounding communities and to control seasonal flooding, but continuous flooding in the decades following the dam's completion rendered almost ten thousand acres of agricultural land unusable, and curtailed the Tohono O'odham's ability to provide for themselves, as well as costing Tribal revenues from the loss of a large family-owned farm. Residents of flooded communities were relocated to a forty-acre parcel of land. For the Tohono O'odham, this has increased reliance on government-provided and commercially accessed food, and has been linked to increasing rates of diabetes (Joe and Young 1994; Reader 2010). In 1986, the federal government reached a settlement with the Tohono O'odham that included thirty million dollars and the Tribe's right to purchase up to ten thousand acres, which will be considered part of their reservation. The lake and reservoir that resulted from the dam have been closed to the public since 2009 due to heavy contamination from pesticide runoff.

In the late-1980s Congress approved funding for the Mni Wiconi Water Project (*mni wiconi* means "water is life" in Lakota), which will eventually bring clean water as well as water treatment facilities to the communities on Pine Ridge and several other reservations in South Dakota. The project had not been completed when I lived on the reservation in 2000–2001 and numerous community members warned me not to use the water for any purpose other than bathing. Most homes I visited during that time had water coolers in them, although many families could not afford the large water bottles for the coolers and instead relied on tap water despite their concerns. The Mni Wiconi project stalled in 2005 due to defunding by President George W. Bush, but in 2009 the Department of the Interior was granted Recovery and Reinvestment Act funding to complete construction. At the beginning of 2014, thirty years after its initial approval, it is not yet complete.

Violence is rampant in many reservation communities, and this is certainly the case on Pine Ridge. When I worked at the school there were regular fights between students, sometimes with weapons and sometimes without (it is amazing how much damage one adolescent body can do to another). Journalist Erik Eckholm (2009) estimates that there are approximately five thousand young men involved in over thirty-nine gangs on the reservation; he offers no estimate of young women's involvement, although I am told anecdotally it has been increasing over the last decade. Many homes and buildings on the reservation bear the graffiti tags of local gangs. Rates of sexual violence are particularly high across Indian Country, and the legal, medical, and social resources needed to address these crimes and serve the survivors and their families are sorely lacking, due in part to federal and regional state underfunding and judicial policy (see Chapter 8). During a research trip to the reservation in 2010 I learned that the only domestic violence shelter on the reservation had been closed by the Tribal council due to allegations of corruption, leaving survivors with no ready access to services.

The statistics on Pine Ridge are daunting, to say the least. However, they are not uncommon on reservations across the country. Forget what you think you know about "Casino Indians"—very few Tribal nations have achieved financial stability through gambling ventures, and Pine Ridge, though it has invested considerable resources in its Prairie Wind Casino, is no exception to this rule. Most reservation residents, on most reservations in the country, live at or near poverty level in homes that are overcrowded and substandard. Most reservation residents attend schools that are outdated and poorly staffed. Most reservation residents travel long distances for groceries, health care, and gas for a car—if they have one. Most reservation residents struggle with addiction, either their own or a family member's, and depression. And with boredom: on Pine Ridge, as on many reservations, there is no movie theater, no mall, no bowling alley. Talia, a twenty-two-year-old Lakota mother of two whose older sister was one of my students when I taught on the reservation, told me she thinks teenagers on Pine Ridge have unprotected sex because "there's nothing else to do," and if there's no condom in the house, they'll take their chances. Transportation is difficult and at some times of the year impossible, although the Tribal council has recently approved a public transportation system.

So Frazer didn't lie, after all. But perhaps he didn't tell the whole story.

"Indian People Are Strong": Identity and Community Capital

As developed by Pierre Bordieu (1977, 1986), the concept of social capital refers to the benefits that accrue to individuals or families by virtue of their ties with others. Importantly, social capital is frequently linked with the strategic investment, and thus availability, of material resources (see also Portes 1998). Political scientist Robert Putnam (1993) broadened this sociological concept to consider social capital as it is possessed and exercised by whole communities, with a focus on the effectiveness of political systems. Community capital is often understood from this framework as consisting of certain measurable resources produced and utilized by a common group of stakeholders, thus linking (individual) social capital to the well-being of larger groups who may be understood to share certain defining characteristics such as geographic location or even national identity. However, communities, of course, are complex and dynamic systems and more than the sum of their parts, which can include material resources and political systems but also include history, community-wide and individual goals and needs, and diverse cultural behaviors such as religious or spiritual practices, language knowledge and practice, expectations around gender and sexuality, family structures, and other factors.

On Pine Ridge Reservation, the dynamic interplay of all of these is organized in some way by two overarching structures: the political production of a geopolitical "reservation" space marked by ongoing legacies of settler colonialism, and various shifting historical and contemporary meanings of Lakota identity and the ways these meanings are enacted and embodied by Lakota people. These can be difficult to measure, but they may be linked to widely held community values and the meanings given to these values in the context of surviving settler colonialism. Many scholars argue that such shared meanings of identity serve as sources of strength and resilience for indigenous peoples, including the Lakota (see Anderson 2000; Brown et al. 1974; Crow Dog 1991; Brave Heart 1999; LaDuke 1999; St. Pierre and Long Soldier 1995; Trask 1993).

I am told by friends and relatives on the reservation that back in the "buffalo days" (prior to extended contact with non-Natives), the Lakota people valued four particular virtues above all others: *woksape* (wisdom), *woohitika* (bravery), *wowacintanka* (fortitude, or strength), and *wacantognaka* (generosity). These values historically organized social and spiritual life for Lakota communities, and they continue to be held in high regard today (Goodman 1992; Young Bear and Theisz 1996; see also Castle 2003; Mohatt and Eagle Elk 2002). At the school where I taught they are mentioned regularly in classes, painted as murals on school walls, and advocated at school gatherings. They are built into some courses in the same way that many schools adopt other character-building curricula. They are frequently invoked during prayers and prayer ceremonies across the reservation, and in fact the performance of these virtues is required for many ceremonies. The heroes of the Lakota people—Tasunka Witko (Crazy Horse) and Tatanka Iyotanka (Sitting Bull), for example—are remembered in part for their embodiment of these values and held up as role models for their descendants who inhabit the reservation today. Those who exhibit these traits regularly are understood to be leaders in their communities who can be depended upon for guidance and support in a variety of matters, thus imbuing these individuals with a degree of cultural and symbolic capital. At the same time, the Lakota emphasis on wisdom and generosity, which earned individuals this quality of social or political influence, may also work to curtail abuse. Of course, it may not; the Lakota are no more immune to corruption and abuse of power than anyone else.

Trevor Hancock (2001) describes healthy communities as those that have high levels of social, ecological, human, and economic capital, but I would argue that any understanding of the strength and well-being of whole communities must include far less tangible factors as well, particularly in the case of communities dominated by settler States. As the values of wisdom, bravery, fortitude, and generosity contribute to admired and socially sanctioned performances of Lakota identity within and beyond the geopolitical space of the reservation, they produce an admixture of community, social, and symbolic capital. Value performance becomes a kind of group identity marker at the same time that it produces expectations of particular behaviors from individuals. These expectations and behaviors contribute to a sense of shared identity: the Lakota have historically valued certain behaviors; Lakota individuals may be encouraged to behave in these ways because they are Lakota; because the Lakota behave in these ways, they remain Lakota. Embodiment of these virtues therefore produces a sense of belonging that has deep historical roots. These core values and the ways in which they help to define Lakota identity thus contribute to community capital as the community is understood to be culturally specific, and that cultural specificity exists in opposition and even defiance of the dominant culture. The community continues to survive as such, both physically and symbolically, in part through the enactment of these values.

Not all Lakota people exhibit these virtues or are interested in developing them, and not all Lakota people will enact them in the same ways or perform them consistently. They remain, however, as core values claimed by the Lakota people and imbued with a degree of social appreciation and social and symbolic value. As with Bordieu's (1986) conceptualization of cultural capital as acquired through effort over time, these virtues are never completely mastered, but must be practiced regularly—what many of my informants refer to as "walking the red road" and others refer to as *Lako'l wicoh'an* (the Lakota way of being in the world). Although enactments and encouragement of these values exist across the reservation, they do not exist in isolation. Pine Ridge is a large reservation, and the Lakota people are diverse in their beliefs and behaviors. As well, Pine Ridge, like other communities in the United States, experiences generational differences, the impact of technology and media access, and shifts in cultural norms; all of these shape Lakota identity in the twenty-first century.

In the summer months on Pine Ridge, there are community pow-wows every few weeks, held outdoors under the sky. Not everyone goes and not everyone dances or sings, but it's a fun time, with elders sitting in the shade chatting and teenagers stalking the perimeter in small groups, searching each other out to snag (make out). Usually, the drum groups who perform at these pow-wows are locals, and it's not uncommon to see young children standing around the drum and even taking a turn singing. Pow-wows are traditionally opened by veterans, who enter the circle carrying the American flag and the flag of the Oglala Nation. When I lived on the rez, most of these veterans were elders, and male. The last few years, they've been younger, and there have been women, looking smart with medicine wheels beaded onto their uniforms. The Lakota are proud of their warriors.

There are prayer ceremonies all year long; Wednesday and Sunday nights are popular for *inipi* (a purification ceremony). When I lived there I frequently attended *inipi* at the home of *leksi* (uncle) John, a well-respected and beloved *wicasa wakan* (medicine man) who taught in the Lakota language department at Little Wound School. After ceremony, we would gather in his tiny kitchen and share a meal, and I learned quickly to bring meat to his table rather than baked goods—diabetes is common on the reservation, and the Lakota people, generally speaking, are big meat eaters. Meatloaf went over well, banana muffins did not. Once a month, Leksi made the seven-hour trip across South Dakota to the men's prison in Sioux Falls to bring prayer ceremony to the prisoners there, and when I told him how great I thought that was, he looked surprised. I don't think he had really considered that bringing prayer ceremony to prisoners a day's drive away was optional; it was simply necessary. When I was pregnant with my son, I brought Leksi some tobacco and asked him to pray for my child (offering tobacco when one is asking a favor is common, as tobacco is sacred and often used in prayer ceremonies). He took the tobacco, but told me they were already praying for us in *inipi* (which I had to stop attending once I was pregnant—too hot!). Leksi died of cancer a few years ago. I miss him terribly. I miss just knowing he's there, praying and teaching.

Not everything went smoothly during my pregnancy. My son's *ate* (father) decided not to be involved, lines were drawn, and people chose sides. But many of my neighbors and colleagues didn't care about the gossip; they recognized that I was far from my own home, and scared, and that I missed my family. One elder told me, "Your mom must be worried about you. Tell her I'll take care of you until you bring that baby home." Although some shunned me, many of these relatives rallied around me, visiting me at home, taking me for walks, and bringing me food. One of these was a *hunka* brother (adopted, a relative in the Lakota way) of my son's *ate*, and he made a point of checking in with me regularly at the school where we both worked, even offering to set aside an eagle feather for my son's naming ceremony. I'll never forget that. A few years ago his daughter was in a terrible car accident, and when I went to visit her in the hospital, one of the first things he asked me was how my son is. He's a good man. In the end, though, we didn't use the eagle feather he set aside—we used another on the day my son got his Lakota name, given to us by different relatives who recognized that my family needed their help. But that's a story for another time.

Basketball games, football games, and local rodeos are well attended by students and community members. I coached the cheerleading team with a colleague one fall, and they won the cheer division at the Lakota Nation Invitational, one of the biggest basketball tournaments in the state (it's also a wrestling tournament and hosts Lakota language and knowledge bowls, an art show, and a hand games tournament; it's a big deal). Believe me, their skills were not due to my coaching—they were due to the fact that their previous coach, a deeply tradition-oriented woman who had since taken an administrative position at the high school, never really stopped working with them, and the cheerleaders themselves were committed to doing well for their school. One of them was a young woman who was also a student of mine. Valerie was quiet but intense, and we spent a lot of time together. She would occasionally drop by my apartment behind the school for a visit, or we would hang out after class and just chat about the things that teenage girls chat about with their teachers. On a research trip to the rez in 2009, I drove by a small billboard on the side of the road with her picture on it—only a few months before, she had been killed in a car accident. This is an all-too-common occurrence on the reservation; the roads are dotted with public safety signs that say, "Think! Why die?"—a sign for every vehicular death. So many signs. There's a sign for Valerie now. I miss her, too.

The school where I worked was one of the first Tribally-run high schools in the country, and has a strong Lakota language and culture curriculum, taught by tradition-oriented teachers who are deeply committed to their students' success. One of these was a woman I'll call Tara. Tara woke up every day and got her son and herself ready for school. During the day she checked in with him regularly, as well as checking in with his teachers to make sure he was doing his work and being polite. After school she ran an extra Lakota language class for students. Then she would go home and do the things that wives and mothers often do for their families—clean a bit, probably, and cook and serve dinner and make sure her children did their homework. Then she would help her husband prepare for *inipi*. After the ceremony, she would feed everyone who came, and probably get to bed around midnight or so. Next day, she would do it all again. Tara taught me a lot about activism, which I'm sure she never called any of this. But her determination to survive as a Lakota woman and to raise her son as well as the sons and daughters of her neighbors to be strong in their Lakota identity taught me that "activism" is not just what we see on the streets or on the Internet or in the news; sometimes, "activism" is the simple act of doggedly, determinedly surviving. Sometimes fortitude and bravery are spectacular, as they are in Sundance ceremony; sometimes they are mundane, as in the simple acts of taking care of your family and your community day after day. Sometimes resilience is really resistance, and survival is defiance.

Prairie fires are fairly common on the reservation in the summer months. When this happens, people come from miles around to help out. When there's a memorial service to commemorate someone's passing and wipe the tears, people come from all over the reservation, bringing food and gifts and stories to share. One evening on my way to one of these my truck got stuck in the mud. I started walking, my skirt hiked up and my boots sticking with every step. Someone must have seen me and called for help, because before I had gotten very far Harold came rumbling along in his pickup. Harold was one of the shop teachers at the high school, a quiet man who smiled a lot and joked quietly with me whenever I saw him. The students loved him. He hopped out of his pickup and attached some chains to my truck and had it pulled out before I got back to it. I tried to pay him—cash or cookies, I had both—but he just waved me off and followed me back to my apartment to make sure I didn't get stuck again. Later that year the students in his class fixed my brakes for me, and *they* accepted some cookies.

Homes are overcrowded, and part of the reason for this lies in inadequate housing, but it also indicates the strength of family ties as siblings, grandparents, and cousins keep their doors open to those who need a bed or a place at the table. One of my students, Michael, joined Leksi John's household mid-year, trying to escape a gang in nearby Rapid City. Leksi's house was already crowded, and even had temporary additions built in the back, tarp-covered lean-tos for the most part. "That's how it is when you're a medicine man," Tara told me when I marveled at how they could find room for one more. "You can't turn anyone away." Michael was tough, skipped class a lot, and sometimes got into trouble. He also wrote me just about the most beautiful poem I've ever read. Then he called me a white bitch one time when he was angry about a quiz grade. When he, Leksi, the dean of students, and I sat down to talk about it, all four of us cried. I hear Michael has several children of his own now. I think about him often, and that beautiful poem he wrote.

On my second trip to the reservation, a friend took me for a ride around his ranch to look for lost calves. We rode without speaking, listening to the sounds of KILI radio (one of the first Tribally run radio stations in the country, and the only radio station on Pine Ridge). He found calves while I was less than helpful, still enraptured by the prairie land of Pine Ridge that is so different from the suburbs of Connecticut where I grew up. Finally, he pointed to the Black Hills in the distance and asked, "See those hills?"

"Beautiful," I replied immediately, hoping for a story.

He answered only, "Crazy Horse said, 'When you see the Black Hills, think of me.'"

I replied in my wisest voice, "Ah. Crazy Horse."

We were silent for a while and I waited. Finally, thinking that perhaps he needed prompting and that perhaps silence needs to be filled with words, I asked, "When you think of Crazy Horse, what do you think of?"

We drove on. I was beginning to think there would be no story after all, just that brief comment. When Joe finally spoke, he curled his fingers into a fist and said simply, "I think Indian people are strong."

There was a wealth of stories in that simple reply, and those stories, like the relationships I first found on the reservation, continue to unfold. For example, thirteen years after that second trip to Pine Ridge, a white buffalo calf was born on a small dairy farm in Connecticut, two thousand miles away from Joe and the Black Hills. *Tatanka* (buffalo) are a sacred relative of the Lakota and other Native peoples, and a white buffalo is particularly important, a gift from the Creator that reminds us of Pte San Win, White Buffalo Calf Woman, who brought the sacred pipe to the Lakota. In the month following that calf's birth, hundreds of people traveled to the farm to pray and to celebrate our relationship with the *Tatanka oyate* and with each other. My parents took my children, and they met Lakota, Mohawk, Pequot, Cherokee, and other Native and non-Native relatives. The farm's owners welcomed everyone, and even hired extra security to make sure the calf and her visitors remained safe; they are also now a part of this community, and a part of its "capital." We are all related, after all.

Indian Country, like most communities, is a place of complexity and contrasts: grief and violence jostle with faith and strength, people fight and hurt each other, and people help each other. People get sick. Some people work hard, and some people don't. Some people are brave and some people are generous, though maybe not every day. But Indian Country is different from other communities as well, due in part to the politics of its manufactured nature (discussed in Chapter 5), and due in part to the persistence and resilience of Native people. It's the rez, certainly—many reservations. But it's also in the cities. And it's in the prison system. It's in poetry, at the pow-wow, and on a small New England farm. It's in the enactment of certain virtues, and even in the failure to enact them. And it's in my home, where two maps tell two different stories, and a young boy with an eagle feather knows his name.

3

Whose Rights?
Whose Justice?

Reproductive Oppression,
Reproductive Justice, and
the Reproductive Body

In the United States we rely on a liberal ideology that locates responsibility for health and wellness in individual choices. Similarly, the language of "rights" and "justice" tends to promote a legalistic, objective standard that protects the individual. When mainstream conceptualizations of objectivity are coupled with this individualist ethos, the social environment is potentially neglected. As medical sociologists and others recognize, however, health is profoundly social. The fundamental role of race, class, sex, and gender inequalities in contemporary societies, and the histories from which these inequalities derive, necessitate the careful and deliberate consideration of social relations in any effort to understand health and wellness. Scholars of women's health and health care must therefore not only consider reproductive rights from a legal perspective but also investigate the interactions between social, economic, and political forces and women's reproductive experiences. This requires a broad conceptualization of the ways in which women's well-being is shaped by these interacting forces to produce various reproductive experiences. It also means that we must question not only how but also why women's reproductive bodies are used as mechanisms of oppression against whole communities.

The Racial Patriarchal State

As a political structure and through State-endorsed social practices, patriarchy seeks to control women's bodies and opportunities around sexuality, parenting, and even labor based on presumptions about the female reproductive body. Many scholars assert that the State is essentially patriarchal, producing and reifying structures of inequality that rely on binary, essentialist, and hierarchical constructions of sex and gender (see Connell 1990; Eisenstein 1981; Haney 2000). In the patriarchal State, they argue, sexuality, and particularly women's sexuality, is regulated by the State through its policies, laws, and allocation of resources, and reproduction becomes a primary defining characteristic of women. However, the State's interest in producing a collective national identity assigns different values to different reproductive bodies, reflecting and producing different reproductive experiences.

Other theorists argue that the State is inherently racial, producing and organizing racial identities and the exclusions and inclusions associated with them (Goldberg 2002; Omi and Winant 1994). Critical race theorist David Goldberg argues that race is integral to the emergence and development of the modern nation-state and that "the apparatuses and technologies employed by modern states have served variously to fashion, modify, and reify the terms of racial expression, as well as racist exclusions and subjugation" (2002, 4). Race therefore becomes a tool in the efforts by modern nation states to produce a collective national identity either by excluding or forcibly including certain people on the basis of produced racial categories. In this logic, diversity and heterogeneity are perceived as a challenge to security, to cultural normativity, and to the availability of resources, and the racially constructed "other" must be eliminated, managed, or contained. Goldberg argues that the "homogenizing logic of removal, extermination, and assimilation is internal to administration and governmentality" (2002, 30), and in fact inseparable from institutionalization. The State thereby becomes "the institutionalization of homogeneity" as racially configured others are removed or contained, marked by physical and symbolic boundaries that demarcate their bodies from the national collective.

Sociologist Joanne Nagel presents a more intersectional understanding of the State, asserting that racial boundaries are also sexual boundaries that produce "a kind of . . . cartography . . . in which we can chart the ethnic landscape by tracing lines in the geographic, legal, cultural, social economic, political, or sexual sand" (2003, 45). These boundaries may be spatial, as they are in the case of reservations; they may be legal or political, such as those created by the mass of legislation and court decisions that shape (albeit ambiguously) the contours of Native sovereignty; and they may, of course, be boundaries that provide for the inclusion or exclusion of certain people based on racial/ethnic/

nationalist identity, as is the case with IHS eligibility criteria. However, they are also, inevitably and always, sexual boundaries. These boundaries, variably understood, coordinate the specific inclusion of Native women in the bureaucracy of the federal government (for example, as recipients of federal funding for reproductive health care) while simultaneously enforcing a racial barrier of exclusion by differentiating Native people legally and politically from other US citizens, reflecting the diversion of resources that simultaneously produce and negate Native identity.

Andrea Smith takes up the complicated intersections of race, gender, sexuality, and the State specifically for Native women, asserting that "Native women, whose ability to reproduce continues to stand in the way of the continuing conquest of Native lands, endanger the continuing success of colonization" (2005, 79). Native people cannot be effectively contained if Native women continue to physically and culturally reproduce Native children. To address this and to contain the potential pollution Native identity presents to the (fictive) collective ethnicity, State interests organize the embodied lives of Native women in particularly regulatory ways.

Biopower and Settler Colonialism

Historian Patrick Wolfe (1999, 2011) describes settler colonialism as the elimination of indigenous peoples through various measures including extermination, physical relocation, and assimilation. Yet at the same time, Native people can never be fully eliminated; while settlers seek to replace the Native as the "natural" collective proprietors of the land, the original indigenous must remain present in the margins as the State's apparatuses work to produce the nation in part by marking who the nation is *not*. The settler State *requires* indigeneity, at least ideologically and in the terms it dictates.

This double discourse of production and elimination, organized by the settler State's drive to imagine the nation as a homogeneous collective, relies on its exercise of biopower, the set of techniques used by governmental apparatuses to administer and manage the bodies residing within the borders of the State (Foucault 1976). Such management may call for the removal of transgressive bodies through physical marginalization or even death, but it more commonly works to domesticate them, producing docile bodies that do not challenge the dominant paradigm but may serve to mark its borders. This docility is produced in part through dependence on the very apparatuses that regulate the transgressive body, such as reproductive health care as it is and provided and regulated by the State through IHS.

The imperialist history of the United States reflects its use of biopower through its manufacture of socially and politically raced, classed, and sexed bodies. As Native Hawaiian scholar and activist Haunani Kay Trask reminds us, the United States was "created out of the bloody extermination of Native peoples, the enslavement of forcibly transported peoples, and the continuing oppression of darkskinned peoples" (2006, 82). The violent origins of this creation, enacted through a process of "othering" the nonwhite body, reflect the assimilationist drive of the nation as it seeks to create a collective ethnicity. This collective, however, can only be always a fiction; nation making is a temporal process, not a teleological one, and "race," "gender," even "sexuality," so frequently used as the markers of inclusion or exclusion, are dynamic social constructs. For example, what counts as "white" or "black" or "indigenous" is ever-dependent on social processes, including the political economy of any given moment. Thus in a white supremacist society such as the United States, race does not merely have an impact on the nation; it serves as an ideological mechanism through which the nation is both produced and subjectively experienced.

In a patriarchal society such as the United States, the production and experience of the nation is equally reliant on social and political constructions of gender, sex, and sexuality that are most frequently understood (and reified) through a hierarchical, binary framework that privileges dominant conceptualizations of masculinity over femininity, hegemonically embodied sex, and heteronormativity. Thus nation building, the production of a (fictive) collective ethnicity, is always already gendered; patriarchy is not merely a social system, it is the very idiom through which the racialized State is constructed. Because patriarchy relies on the control of women's bodies, motherhood, as a site of physical and cultural identity, is targeted for control in the production of the nation. The links between race, class, gender, sexuality, and citizenship are essential to understanding the threat presented by Native women's reproductive bodies. The fiction of a collective ethnicity—e pluribus unum—is built and sustained on homogeneity, "one nation, under God, indivisible." Women's reproductive bodies challenge the production of a unified national identity, and they therefore become a site of both active and passive regulation by the State. Fatherhood, which certainly has its own set of cultural ideals and restrictions, is nonetheless left in a position of relatively unregulated embodiment (although fatherhood certainly warrants a closer examination than I give it here).

Reproductive Oppression

Consider, for example, the enslavement of African and African American women and the sexual violence perpetrated against them. The rape of black women by white men in the antebellum South served the goals of white supremacy, capitalism, and patriarchy by producing a future slave labor force through the bodies of enslaved women, and was coupled with the manipulation and destruction of African American families by slave owners. These and other legacies of the trans-Atlantic slave trade continue to reverberate in the twenty-first century through ongoing reproductive oppressions in African American communities, including the hyper-sexualization of African American women's bodies and ongoing controversy over contraception and abortion access, as well as high rates of poverty for African American families and continued segregated housing and educational opportunities: all forms of marginalization which symbolically and materially remove African Americans from the collective. Similarly, the forced removal of Native American women, their families, and their communities from traditional homelands as well as from public discourses about the collective nation provides the legal and social foundation for Native-US relations in the twenty-first century. The violent oppressions enacted on Native communities in the ongoing project of "disappearing" Native peoples—from land, from history, from contemporary stories about the nation—are enacted in part through the bodies of Native women, including Native women's sexuality and reproduction, as indigenous communities continue to be targeted in particular ways under a heteropatriarchal, white supremacist settler colonial regime.

The population control efforts embedded in these histories are further evident through legislative actions such as the passage of the 1875 Page Act and the Chinese Exclusion Act of 1882, which severely restricted the entry of unmarried Asian women into the United States as part of an effort to limit the growing Asian and Asian American population; the passage of anti-miscegenation laws throughout the United States; the sterilization of women of color as well as people deemed medically unfit during the twentieth century; increasingly restricted access to abortion counseling and services following the passage of *Roe v. Wade* in 1973, particularly through class-based policies such as those enacted by the Hyde Amendment beginning in 1976; welfare "reform" such as President Clinton's 1996 Personal Responsibility and Work Opportunity Reconciliation Act, which tied women's fertility to welfare eligibility; and targeted immigration policies that continue to effect the exclusion of certain communities from the rights and protections of full citizenship, including health safety. These official policies must be understood as not only race- and/or class-based but also, in their essence, patriarchal, for it is the reproductive bodies of women that are primarily marked for management. In the United States, the drive to curtail reproduction of the unwanted, the "other" (read: nonwhite, or poor, or atypically abled, or . . .) has not landed with equal force on the reproductive bodies of men, though the reproductive lives of men are certainly inextricably entwined in the consequences, and masculinity is configured in ways that allow for inclusion or exclusion from the national body.

These attacks on women's reproductive bodies continue into the twenty-first century. In recent years, numerous states have passed some of the most restrictive anti-choice legislation since 1973 at the same time that race is increasingly inserted into pro-life propaganda. In-vitro fertilization and other forms of assisted reproduction remain financially out of reach for most women in the United States, and are socially and politically complicated for lesbian women and gay men, who are also denied access to legal marriage in most parts of the country. Emergency contraception is unavailable in many hospitals, and pharmacists retain the right to refuse to dispense it. Cesarean sections are at an historic high (currently 33 percent); and so on.

Although these institutionalized oppressions impact all women, they land with particular force on the bodies of *some* women—namely, women of color and poor women—in unique ways. Across the country, women of color and poor women suffer disproportionately high rates of cervical cancer, sexually transmitted infections, HIV/AIDS, unintended pregnancies, diabetes, and other health concerns (Kaiser Family Foundation 2009; Krieger et al. 2005). Overexposure to toxic environmental conditions in poor communities, limited access to healthy foods and safe housing, welfare policies that effectively restrict family forms as well as access to community resources, violence against women and children, and a myriad of other social, political, and economic forces contribute to these disparities. They are not natural, nor are they entirely the result of individual lifestyle choices. They are structurally produced, and they are produced along different axes of identity and social location. In this country, all women experience reproductive oppression, but we don't all experience it in the same ways.

Reproductive Justice

In response to this diversity of needs, increasing numbers of community-based organizations began to emerge in the late 1970s that specifically addressed the health needs of women of color and low-income women. These organizations, such as the Committee for Abortion Rights and Against Sterilization Abuse (CARASA), the National Black Women's Health Project, Sistersong: A Women of Color Health Collective, and Asian Communities for Reproductive Justice recognized that the mainstream reproductive rights movements, largely dominated by white, economically advantaged women, did not adequately address the needs of all women. Additionally, the prominence of abortion rights in US-based reproductive rights movements—a prominence produced in part as reaction to unrelenting attacks on abortion access—has left little social and political space in which to consider other reproductive health needs, including the resources to parent with dignity. Conceptualizations of reproductive justice coalesced in response to the perceived lack of consideration in mainstream reproductive rights movements of the multiple causes of reproductive oppressions identified in and by marginalized communities.

Reproductive justice is broadly understood as "the complete physical, mental, spiritual, political, social, environmental, and economic well-being of women and girls" (Sistersong 2006, 5). This expansive definition recognizes the wide range of issues that impact women's true reproductive freedom and links this freedom to community wellness. The reproductive justice framework centralizes intersectional and locally grounded examinations of women's embodied experiences, seeking to explicate and address oppressions that are produced along multiple institutional dimensions and experienced across multiple social locations. Reproductive justice emerges from and retains important ties to other reproductive rights and reproductive health movements, but it simultaneously works from an expanded conceptualization of health, justice, economic security, and self-determination that includes community needs and institutional structures and rejects narrow formulations of reproductive health as an individual experience. Reproductive justice thus takes into consideration the conditions for health as well as access to health care and freedom from disease-producing contexts.

The model of reproductive justice continues to be elaborated upon by numerous local, national, and transnational organizations to reflect diverse identities, needs, oppressions, and ambitions, including labor rights, healthcare access, and the rights of gay, lesbian, and transgender people. Organizations such as Spark Reproductive Justice Now, which organizes queer youth in the Atlanta, Georgia, area; the National Asian Pacific American Women's Forum; Woman Is the First Environment Collaborative; the Alliance for Reproductive Justice in Alaska; Voces Latinas in New York, and others coordinate local, national, and transnational efforts for change predicated on building comprehensive reproductive health and safety for all communities. The diversity of social and political issues represented by these and similar organizations reflect the efforts of activists and scholars working to address a multitude of community needs through the rubric of women's reproductive health. In this way, by centralizing the lives and health needs of women within multiple agendas for freedom, reproductive justice mirrors (brightly?) the tactics of State regimes that utilize women's reproductive bodies as the mechanism for enacting broadly oppressive policies. Whereas the State has historically used women's reproductive bodies as a means of population and community control in its quest to build an exclusive national collectivity, reproductive justice relies on women's reproductive bodies to address the diverse health needs of whole communities. Though for vastly different reasons, women's reproductive bodies and freedoms remain in the center of both agendas.

Reproductive Justice and Human Rights

The fundamental right to health and the conditions for health has been recognized in numerous international human rights instruments. For example, the International Covenant on Economic, Social, and Cultural Rights (ICESCR) specifically recognizes "the right of everyone to the enjoyment of the highest attainable standard of physical and mental health" and asserts that States hold responsibility for "the creation of conditions which would assure to all medical service and medical attention in the event of sickness" in Article 12. The Convention on the Elimination of All Forms of Discrimination against Women (CEDAW) specifies reproductive health care as a human right by requiring in Article 12 that "States Parties shall ensure to women appropriate services in connection with pregnancy, confinement and the post-natal period, granting free services where necessary, as well as adequate nutrition during pregnancy and lactation."

The wide recognition of these rights does not guarantee, however, that they will be honored. The United States has signed but not ratified both the ICESCR and CEDAW, thereby simultaneously acknowledging the fundamental rights they espouse and potentially reducing its own accountability for providing and protecting these rights. The United States has both signed and ratified the Universal Declaration on Human Rights, which defines the fundamental right to the conditions for health and notes in Article 25 that "motherhood and childhood are entitled to special care and assistance." In addition, in 2009 the United States supported Resolution 11/8 of the Human Rights Council, which outlined in detail the responsibilities of States to address maternal mortality and morbidity and, importantly, situated these health concerns within the broader contexts of reproductive health and reproductive rights.

The reproductive justice framework, which is both a theoretical paradigm and an activist model, brings together in cogent ways theories of human rights and inequality with intersectional examinations of women's embodied experiences, and locates these in local social contexts. This grounding of international human rights law in locally driven conceptualizations of women's health needs expands understandings and applications of the fundamental right to health. By situating women's fundamental right to health in the broad social contexts of spiritual, environmental, and economic well-being, reproductive justice asserts the links between all of these areas and resists false isolation of the right to health from the conditions for health.

Further, the reproductive justice paradigm's focus on marginalized communities also recognizes that women's reproductive rights are meaningless without addressing the social contexts in which these rights are exercised, including historically oppressive structures of racial, economic, and sexual inequality.

Therefore, while reproductive justice incorporates human rights in its organizational framework, it simultaneously complicates prevailing liberal ideologies of "rights" and "choice" in reproductive health. As many feminist theorists have noted, liberal approaches to reproductive rights rely on an understanding of equality as equivalent to and productive of sameness between men and women, without adequately interrogating sexual and gender differences (see, e.g., Bloodsworth-Lugo 2007; Grosz 1994; Spelman 1988). These approaches rely on and reproduce notions of citizenship that are individualist, acultural, heteronormative, and presumptively male, neglecting analyses of gender, race, class, and sexuality as well as structural constraints imposed by social, political, and economic inequalities.

Reproductive justice scholars and activists argue against such readings of citizenship. For example, Loretta Ross, one of the founders of Sistersong, contends that the limited notion of legal rights which adheres to this construction of citizenship "ignores the intersectional matrix of race, gender, sovereignty, class and immigration status that complicates debates on reproductive politics in the United States for women of color" (2006, 62). Reproductive justice scholars and activists therefore centralize the ways in which intersecting social and political forces impact women's lives in differential and consequential ways (Ross 2006, 62; see also Davis 1983, 1990; Luna and Luker 2013; Roberts 1997; Ross et al. 2002; Smith 2006). This evolution from a liberal approach in which "rights" are individualized to a more comprehensive incorporation of social, economic, and political structures and histories that necessarily includes community needs expands local, national, and transnational conceptualizations of reproductive health as a human right.

This broader analytical framework also produces theoretical space for the consideration of group rights, in conjunction with individual rights. This shift is particularly relevant to many Native American women, whose group identity has been historically targeted for removal and assimilation by the US government. Additionally, it is this very group identity that provides Native Americans access to health care through the Indian Health Service. Treaties between Native nations and the United States as well as numerous pieces of legislation such as the Snyder Act of 1921 and the Indian Health Care Improvement Act (IHCIA) of 1976 produce and recognize a responsibility on the part of the federal government to provide health care specifically for Native people, as discussed in Chapter 5. However, access to this health care is legally contingent on enrollment in a federally recognized Tribal nation. The State is thereby further implicated in protecting and providing for the basic right to health, as this health care is legally reserved for those Native people who can satisfy Tribal requirements of cultural identity, and this cultural identity is further located within a larger racial identity that has been approved by the State. Thus the complex and unique relationships between

Native nations and the federal government synthesize both individual human rights and group rights to health and the conditions for health, including health care. The Indian Health Service acts as a fulcrum between the fundamental right to health and the rights of Native Americans as outlined in treaties between the United States and Native nations. Ultimately, the failure of IHS to meet the reproductive health-care needs of Native American women reflects the failure of the federal government to meet basic human rights obligations to Tribal nations; this failure is locally particular, but when contextualized within the international framework of human rights, it reflects the neoliberal policies of the United States' nation-building project and its own assumption as the ultimate sovereign within its political borders.

Reproductive Justice and the Role of Health Care

Health care is an integral aspect of reproductive justice, and concerns over access to care and quality of care must be articulated in ways that highlight, rather than mask, the links between health care and social, economic, and political environments. As sociologist Ana Clarissa Rojas Durazo argues, "medicine, as a tool of social control . . . bears the interests of the MIC [medical industrial complex]—the relationship between medicine, capital, and the State" (2006, 181). She further asserts that "medical care is structured for whites to access it earlier . . . whereas people of color often cannot access care until the disease is too advanced for successful treatment" (186; see also Belluck 2009 and IHS 2006 for a discussion of delayed care in Native American reservation communities). Thus although in some ways the concept of reproductive justice moves past a limited focus on health-care delivery, it simultaneously requires an acute understanding of the role of health institutions, particularly in marginalized communities, in providing for or even directly inhibiting women's well-being.

My informants primarily associated reproductive health care with prenatal care, but reproductive health care is necessary throughout women's lives. It can include, among other things, contraception, abortion counseling and services, prenatal care, childbirth, postpartum care, breastfeeding, testing and treatment of sexually transmitted infections, various types of cancer care, menopause care, and other aspects of care, including, as discussed in Chapter 8, care for survivors of sexual assault. Yet these regularly reproduced health-care interactions cannot be taken for granted. Access to adequate and competent health care can be limited in many communities of color, economically disadvantaged communities, and rural areas, and Pine Ridge Reservation is no exception. In this book, I follow the leads of my relatives and informants in centralizing certain forms of reproductive health care (namely, prenatal care, childbirth, contraception, abortion services, and sexual assault care); however, the very means by which we readily recognize "reproductive health care" as including some things and not others reflects the ruling relations of knowledge construction, particularly around medicine and the linked roles of medical institutions, policy makers, and academics.

Although the existence of the Indian Health Service can be understood as an affirmative effort on the part of the federal government to address the reproductive health needs of Native women (as well as the health needs of the general Native American population) and meet its obligations to ensure Native peoples' right to health, the continual failure of the president and Congress to provide sufficient resources to IHS as well as wider ongoing struggles over sovereignty and self-determination undermine these goals and ultimately contribute to the reproductive oppression of Native women who cannot access adequate health care. Further, the failure of IHS to respect the basic human rights of Native women to exercise choice and freedom in their reproductive experiences directly contradicts its mission to provide for the health and well-being of Native people. Durazo refers to this contradiction as the "double discourse" of care: "expressed interest in the provision of care, while making people of color sick" (2006, 183). From a reproductive justice perspective, the double discourse of IHS is revealed through the tension between its expressed intent to provide adequate, culturally competent health care to all (federally recognized) Native Americans while it both actively and passively inhibits Native women's basic human right to health care and the conditions for health.

Although my research centralizes the production and consequences of this double discourse as it relates to reproductive health care specifically, this double discourse in fact permeates State relations with Tribal communities and reflects an ongoing national ambivalence toward heterogeneity, and particularly indigeneity. Health care provides a mechanism for the racial, patriarchal State to regulate the reproductive bodies of Native American women as part of a settler colonialist agenda. The Indian Health Service, therefore, can also be understood as an instrument of the settler colonialist drive of the State toward conquest and assimilation, despite its declared intention to provide health care, and in spite of its frequent success in caring for communities and individuals who are racially and economically marginalized in the broader national body.

Part II

Tracing the
Ruling Relations

Health Care, the Reproductive
Body, and Native America

4

The Ruling Relations of Reproductive Health Care

The biomedical model of reproductive health care in the United States today has developed over the last two centuries from heteropatriarchal assumptions about women as reproducers, assumptions that centralize and privilege the experiences of economically advantaged and white women. The practice of mainstream medicine continues to rely on a narrow construction of health care in which women of color, women who are economically disadvantaged, differently abled women, and women who do not identify publicly and/or privately as heterosexual may not be able to access the care that they need, or may be required to negotiate health-care structures that do not fully recognize their embodied experiences (ACRJ 2005; O'Hanlon 2006; Philips and Philips 2006). Additionally, women who choose to remain childless stand outside of a reproductive health-care system, which privileges the production of babies as the social objective of women's biology (Kelly 2009; Rothman 2000). For example, it took the American College of Obstetricians and Gynecologists (ACOG) until late 2011 to issue a formal statement urging its members to acknowledge and address the specific reproductive health-care needs of transgender clients, which can include hormone therapies and various surgeries but is currently less likely to include baby making. Similarly, the continuing prominence of abortion access in debates around health-care and reproductive rights emphasizes legal access to abortion over the right to have and keep one's children and raise them in culturally appropriate ways.

The ruling relations of reproductive health care solidify these ideologies in particular ways through funding streams, policy development, and government-sponsored research, as well as through the active provision of certain health-care modalities to specific populations. The historical development of reproductive health care as a medical specialty and the strong hand of the State in organizing its foci, particularly for specific populations, have resulted in ideologically complex and differential systems of care for women and rendered a comprehensive understanding of reproductive health care challenging to distinguish from political and social constructions of gender, race, class, sexuality, and citizenship. Because IHS relies on a biomedical model of care that is derived from mainstream medical practice and its partnerships with the research community and the State, these relationships prove particularly salient when considering reproductive health care for Native women.

Childbirth and the Ruling Relations of the Medical Profession

The medicalization of reproduction in the United States can be traced back to the end of the seventeenth century with the incursion of male doctors into the birthing room. Prior to this, childbirth and women's reproductive health was largely the province of women, usually family members and lay midwives and healers (Leavitt 1986; Wertz and Wertz 1989; see also Ulrich 1982, 1991). The inclusion of midwifery (later gynecology and obstetrics) in the practice of university-educated doctors was, in fact, incidental to the agendas of these early male professionals, as their primary motivation was not to attend childbirth itself, but rather to assert their professional value in a relatively new field.

For most of the eighteenth century the use of doctors was limited geographically to large cities and economically privileged (predominantly white) women, who increasingly sought out the services of university-educated male physicians in their efforts to ensure a safe and painless birth experience. Immigrant women, who might be economically limited to local midwives, were often also more culturally conservative in their approach to birth and generally preferred women attendants (Leavitt 1986; Wertz and Wertz 1989). Slave women in the antebellum southern states, of course, had no choice in the matter; even after emancipation, African American women continued to rely primarily on the services of local midwives, or "grannies," well into the twentieth century due to several factors including racism, poverty, and isolation in rural areas (Fraser 1989; Schaffer 1991; Wilkie 2003). Poor and rural women, including Native women, who could not afford or access professionally trained doctors, continued to rely almost solely on a dwindling number of increasingly persecuted midwives, although Native women in reservation communities may have also had the occasional use of army physicians and later physicians who worked for the Office of Indian Affairs.

Childbirth became increasingly important to the practice of professional medicine as gynecology and obstetrics developed into specialty areas and physicians increasingly sought out pregnant women as a gateway into more general family practice. However, the professional stability doctors sought was threatened by the variety of lay healers practicing during the nineteenth century, and medical professionals trained in universities (and thus from the social elite) developed several strategies to narrow the field of competition for patients and increase the social and professional status of medically trained doctors. One such strategy was the formation of professional associations. Several regional states formed local professional organizations throughout the nineteenth century, but it was not until the American Medical Association (AMA) was formed in 1848 that a national organizational structure for doctors coalesced. By the end of the nineteenth century, organized medicine, led by the AMA, was able to implement laws that restricted who could practice what types of medicine, and what criteria were necessary for licensing.

The founding of nonproprietary medical schools was another measure intended to separate elite educated doctors from lay healers. Paul Starr (1982) argues that the standardization of medical education through the founding of medical schools and their eventual reorganization along roughly universal lines proved essential to the legitimation of professional doctors. The Medical College of Philadelphia, King's College Medical School (later Columbia), and Harvard Medical School were all founded before the nineteenth century. Midwifery was the first medical specialty at each. Johns Hopkins University established its medical school a century later, in 1893, and offered the most demanding and rigorous curriculum, including the new requirement that all students entering hold at least one prior college degree. The early emphasis at Johns Hopkins on integrating research and practice with education was instrumental in forging the union between science and research within clinical hospital practice, linking the three as inextricable measures of a quality medical education.

Despite the growing standardization of medical education, many doctors still considered obstetrics, as it was known by the beginning of the twentieth century, to be poorly taught and poorly practiced. One of the AMA's primary goals in the second half of the nineteenth century was to further systematize medical education and eliminate schools that failed to offer a rigorous theoretical and clinical experience (Beck 2004; Starr 1982). Nonetheless, medical education was not effectively regulated until the Flexner Report, a professional self-study in 1910, led to stricter state laws and universal standards. Following release of the Flexner Report, in 1912 the Federation of State Medical Boards was formed and agreed to base its accreditation policies on academic standards determined by the AMA, thus imbuing the AMA's decisions with considerable authority over health-care regimes. By the 1930s, the combined efforts of state licensing boards and the AMA resulted in an increasingly narrow range of medical schools and the standardization of medical education the Flexner Report had advocated.

As medical researcher Andrew Beck (2004) points out, however, while reforms improved the quality of medical education in the United States, they also reduced the number of doctors serving disadvantaged communities, as many small, rural medical colleges, including African American medical schools, were forced to close. Additionally, more stringent admission requirements and the extended course of study now required to become a physician inhibited economically disadvantaged students from pursuing careers in medicine, a problem with which IHS continues to struggle as it seeks to increase the number of Native American medical students through grants and scholarships. Thus diverse types of knowledge about health, wellness, and the body were increasingly marginalized and discredited, as a single model, emerging from an exclusively elite education, became progressively established.

By the late eighteenth century, the use of a private physician who could attend birth at home had become a mark of social status that separated the elite classes from the economically disadvantaged, including immigrants and women of color (Ehrenreich and English 1973; Wertz and Wertz 1989). Hospital maternity wards, originally constructed as charity hospitals for poor women and women of color, also proved integral to the development of obstetrics into a profession. Maternity wards served as the location of knowledge production and reproduction as future generations of doctors learned from more advanced colleagues and from the bodies of poor women. This is strikingly true in the development of gynecological surgery; for example, J. Marion Sims, often called the father of modern gynecology, developed a surgical cure for the vesica-vaginal fistula in 1849 through experimentation on slave women and taught it to new doctors and medical students also using the bodies of slave women (Cassidy 2006; Litoff 1978). These women were not afforded anesthesia, and Tina Cassidy (2006) asserts that they most likely became addicted to opium, a much cheaper narcotic. The race, class, gender, and sex ideologies that informed and allowed such work as that performed by Sims and his students and colleagues have uncomfortable echoes in Indian Country, where contraceptive technologies such as Quinicrine (approved by the FDA only as an antimalarial treatment) and Depo-provera have been tested and heavily marketed (see Lopez 1999; NAWHERC 2003; A. Smith 2002, 2005).

At the same time, the Fordist model of production, itself reflective of newly emerging industrial technologies, fostered a cultural preference for efficiency that still organizes hospital care today (Martin 1989; Starr 1982; Wertz and Wertz 1989). The first decades of the twentieth century reflect the widespread efforts to systematize not only medical education but also birth itself, which was increasingly viewed as a pathological process from which only a small number of women escaped permanent damage. Birth moved further into the controlled setting of the hospital as the effort to systematize what was perceived to be an essentially unpredictable and dangerous process resulted in the increasingly regular use of interventions such as sedation, episiotomy, and forceps. Locating childbirth in the hospital made these interventions more readily available to the trained practitioner, thus still further implicating technology (and the training required to wield it, training that was available only to medical students and doctors) and allowing doctors increased control over the process. The hospital became increasingly viewed by medical professionals as the most efficient site for labor and delivery, and economically privileged women increasingly turned to the hospital as the only location where they could effectively access technological interventions. As more and more women sought hospital care for their childbirth experiences, the hospital itself became a privileged site from which economically disadvantaged women, including many women of color, immigrant women, and women in rural locations, were excluded.

In these ways, the practice of medicine became further implicated in and even productive of different class- and race-based statuses, as economically advantaged women (who were predominantly white, married citizens) retained a measure of choice and agency over the birthing process that was not necessarily available to women in other social locations. By the mid-twentieth century, homebirth and birth without a licensed physician had become an anomaly for all but the most socially disadvantaged, as popular understandings of women's role in childbirth evolved to accommodate increasing medical interventions and authority, and the medical management of childbirth came to dominate the experience (Ehrenreich and English 1973; Leavitt 1986; Wertz and Wertz 1989).

Producing Prenatal Care

The development of prenatal care as a medical specialty requiring the expertise of university-trained doctors emerged during the second half of the nineteenth century and both followed and aided the establishment of professional medicine's legitimacy. Medical care, itself ever-improving, undoubtedly saves lives and ameliorates suffering, but the professionalization of prenatal care has also led to an increasing assumption of authority over women's reproductive bodies by professional associations such as ACOG. This growing investment of authority in professional medicine in both pregnancy and childbirth potentially divests women and diverse communities of agency as it limits what knowledge is available, how it is available, where, and to whom.

By the beginning of the twentieth century, as birth itself was increasingly located in the hospital, prenatal care from a physician had become established as a regular aspect of pregnancy care, and folk or lay medicine, though still practiced, was increasingly eschewed in favor of care from a doctor by those who could afford it (Ehrenreich and English 1973; Wertz and Wertz 1989). This relocation of pregnancy care from lay and folk medicine communities to professional medicine was encouraged by early medical studies in eclampsia and complications of toxemia, which linked lack of adequate prenatal care with low birth weight and premature birth. The development of a specific regimen of prenatal care was also encouraged by the Children's Bureau, an agency within the Labor Department that was formalized in 1912. Several studies conducted by the Children's Bureau found a strong correlation between poverty and infant mortality; at the same time, the Children's Bureau determined that poor women received little to no formal prenatal care, and in response US officials launched public health programs in which specially trained nurses conducted home visits with poor urban- and rural-dwelling expectant women. This was largely funded by the Shepperd-Townsend Act, which provided just over one million dollars to states in matching grants for the training of midwives to provide maternal and infant health care.

Throughout the twentieth century, medicalized prenatal care became increasingly established as a prerequisite for healthy birth outcome (Alexander and Kotelchuck 2001; see also Davis-Floyd 2004; Ginsburg and Rapp 1995; Rapp 1994). For example, in 1969 ACOG issued standards of care that recommended regular visits to a gynecologist every four weeks for the first twenty-eight weeks, followed by visits every two to three weeks until thirty-six weeks, and then every week until parturition (Hemminki 1988). This continues to be the preferred schedule of care in the early twenty-first century, reflecting a close monitoring of the pregnant body by medical authority, despite recommendations by the National Institutes of Health in 1989 that eight to eleven visits were sufficient for women in their first pregnancies, and fewer for women who had already given birth if there are no complications (NIH 1989).

The early ACOG standards were followed in 1985 by a report issued by the Institute of Medicine, which recommended the enrollment of all pregnant women into a system of prenatal care as a matter of federal policy. Shortly thereafter a series of legislative initiatives was enacted by Congress to expand prenatal care for poor women. Prior to these expansions, low-income pregnant women were covered by Medicaid during pregnancy only if they were single, already received welfare benefits, or met very low medical-need income thresholds. The Medicaid eligibility expansions extended coverage to pregnant women living below 133 percent of poverty level, effectively covering most low-income women and their infants through pregnancy and the postpartum period and leading to the further establishment of prenatal care as a population-wide public health intervention. In this way, the roles of multiple parties such as medical and social researchers, Congress, professional medical associations, states, and federal agencies have contributed to the organization of medicalized prenatal care for women generally, and specifically economically classed women in particular. This increasingly strong linkage between professional medical organizations, the State, and women's reproductive health, though challenged by many feminist health activists (see, e.g., Morgen 2002; Rothman 1982; Ruzek 1979), continues to organize women's embodied experiences.

Importantly, there have been several studies questioning the benefits of medicalized prenatal care (see Fiscella 1995; Strong 2003). Andrew Healy and his colleagues (2006) found that racial disparities in perinatal mortality persist despite early and regular access to prenatal care. Greg Alexander and Milton Kotelchuck conclude in their study of prenatal care in the United States that "our current prenatal care approaches are not particularly effective and cannot be given wholehearted endorsement" (2001, 309). As they further point out, prenatal care became an established standard of practice without randomized clinical trials; currently, researchers struggle with how to control for various variables ethically, thus complicating adequate understanding of prenatal care in a medicalized context. Several studies that question the efficacy of medicalized prenatal care in addressing low birth weight, premature birth, and infant mortality point to social disparities such as poverty, racism, and unequal access to lifetime health care as important determinants in infant health (see, e.g., Fiscella 1992; Healy et al. 2006).

Although there is some question about the precise mechanisms of success, adequate prenatal care continues to be strongly linked in the medical literature to healthy birth outcome and lowered rates of infant mortality, particularly through the prevention of premature births and low birth weight. However, in the United States there are stark disparities in prenatal care access and utilization. According to a report of the Pregnancy Risk Assessment Monitoring System, a surveillance project sponsored by the CDC and state health departments, in 2002 only 75 percent of pregnant women who had live births received adequate prenatal care (Kim et al. 2008). In 2007, 16.2 percent of all live births in the United States were preceded by no prenatal care or late prenatal care (Kaiser 2009). These disparities exist along several dimensions, including socioeconomic status, race, and low levels of education. Native American women are the least likely to receive adequate prenatal care, and non-Hispanic white women are the most likely to receive regular, timely prenatal care; adolescents are less likely to initiate care in the first trimester than are older women; multiparous women are less likely to receive early prenatal care than women with no previous births; and women whose pregnancies are unintended are less likely to receive early prenatal care than are women whose pregnancies are planned. Rectifying the disparities in prenatal care access and utilization is a goal of Healthy People 2020, a decade-long initiative sponsored by the CDC designed in part to reduce overall health disparities in the United States, as it was in the previous program, Healthy People 2010.

One emerging effort to address the infant health disparities that may result from inadequate prenatal care is the model of preconception care. According to the CDC, the main objective of preconception care is to reduce risk factors that might affect healthy birth outcome through "a set of interventions that identify and modify biomedical, behavioral, and social risks to a woman's health and future pregnancies. *It includes both prevention and management, emphasizing health issues that require action before conception or very early in pregnancy* for maximal impact" (CDC 2006, my italics). Importantly, while the CDC notes that preconception care can alleviate human suffering by helping to avoid fetal and infant death and illness, it is also emphasized as a way to alleviate "the burden on the health-care system" as "each child born with an intellectual disability or a comparable condition leads to direct and indirect societal costs over his or her lifetime of more than $1 million" (ibid.). This emphasis on cost reduction reflects ongoing State concerns over the cost of health care, particularly the cost of health care for the poor and atypically abled.

The developing rhetoric around preconception care is important for several reasons. It is also complex. With its emphasis on screening and interventions, preconception care potentially inserts medicalized care with a focus on reproduction into the lives of women at younger and younger ages. The presumption of future pregnancy assumes a heteropatriarchal role for women as reproducers; young women who are encouraged to take up "preconception" as a model of care are concurrently, though invisibly, encouraged to consider themselves as reproducers, thus placing primacy of health and well-being on their future potential as mothers. They are also thus invisibly encouraged to consider themselves potentially linked to men. In these ways, their health care becomes organized around assumptions about their sexuality, and their social futures are organized by hegemonic notions of womanhood as linked to motherhood. As well, the CDC's emphasis on individual interventions that "identify and modify biomedical, behavioral, and social risks" and further insert medical regimes into women's health care through "prevention and management" (CDC 2006) completely neglects social aspects of health and wellness such as poverty, lack of access to health care, and violence.

At the same time, and importantly, preconception care does offer potential health benefits to young women, regardless of actual reproductive outcomes. Preconception care may also strengthen public health agendas and provide support for the alleviation of social disparities such as inadequate access to clean water and nutritious food if it can be adequately expanded from its current individual-oriented biomedical conceptualization. This is particularly important in Indian Country, where these resources are often scant or even unavailable. As well, the high rate of adolescent pregnancy throughout Indian Country and on Pine Ridge Reservation (see Chapter 9) indicates that "preconception" care must, indeed, start early, particularly if it can offset potential risks from delayed entrance into prenatal care by adolescents. Thus, preconception care can be of genuine benefit to women's and infants' health; it can also potentially be used to justify demands for social and economic resources for whole communities. This approach, however, is complicated by its reliance on a heteronormative model of womanhood, which potentially restricts Native women's subjective experiences of reproductive and sexual freedoms.

Obviously, healthy babies are important to Native women and their communities; however, healthy women are surely important as well, regardless of their reproductive choices and potentialities. The linkage of women's health and well-being to their presumed reproduction and the potential use of this presumed reproduction as a bargaining chip for improved public health reflects in complicated ways both the work of the State as it relies on women's reproductive bodies to produce structures of oppression, and reproductive justice efforts as they rely on women's reproductive bodies to argue for community well-being. At the same time, the limited, heteronormative assumptions embedded in the preconception model ideologically restrict women's access to a full range of reproductive and sexual freedoms and potentially produce and impose community as well as national expectations for the function of women's reproductive bodies.

Evidence-Based Medicine: Standardization and Knowledge Production in the Twenty-first Century

The fundamental assumption that physicians well trained in both clinical and academic settings could and would make the correct diagnoses and choose the correct methods of treatment became fairly common in the first half of the twentieth century, due to the diligence of organizations such as the AMA and highly respected schools such as Johns Hopkins. However, by the early 1970s some professionals were beginning to question this assumption, arguing that physicians by themselves might not be an adequate final authority (Eddy 2005; Wennberg 1998). Prompted by an increasing realization that wide variations in practice continued to exist, the intense standardization of knowledge and practice over the previous century came under close scrutiny. At the same time, the rising cost of health care during the 1980s encouraged efforts to streamline clinical practice into an increasingly efficient model. A new form of standardization evolved, beginning in the early 1990s. Through partnerships between clinical practitioners, medical researchers, and the insurance industry, evidence-based medicine (EBM), predicated on empirical analyses of diagnoses and treatments, emerged as a means of providing resources to physicians in the form of collected and professionally validated knowledge. It has also increasingly served as a means of reducing costs (e.g., through evidence-based coverage). In the early twenty-first century, the evidence-based model is the dominant organizational form of both clinical practice and health-care management technologies (Eddy 2005; Mykhalovskiy and Weir 2004).

According to medical researcher David Eddy (2005), EBM provides general guidelines to address the needs of patients and influence the decisions of health-care providers primarily through rigorous methods of review. The collected knowledge made available through EBM is intended to augment clinical experience, not replace it, and ensure that clinical practices do not fall out of date with emerging research. It is also intended to be generically applied to a class or group of patients defined by some clinical criteria, and therefore offers a seemingly objective standard of care in which all patients similarly clinically identified are subject to the same care modalities.

Evidence-based practice thus relies on a generalized form of knowledge. The knowledge mechanisms of EBM—including clinical studies, extensive literature reviews, and analyses of previous studies—produce certain relations of power in health care by their reliance on particular understandings of science and knowledge as empirical, replicable, and generalizable. In this framework, other ways of knowing can be devalued or dismissed, and the diverse social contexts produced by race, class, gender, sexuality, and citizenship potentially disappear. At the same time that EBM produces and validates a particular kind of scientific knowledge to be applied to the body, it must ultimately gather that knowledge from the body; the reliance of EBM on clinical trials not only privileges a certain kind of knowledge over other kinds, but also produces that knowledge from the bodies of patients in ways similar to those which fostered the growth of obstetrics through the research site provided by maternity wards.

However, and unlike early maternity wards, evidence-based medicine may exclude vulnerable and disadvantaged groups. Marginalized groups historically have limited participation in clinical trials and even less of a role in the commissioning of new research, both of which have increased since the advent of EBM. Without specific consideration of disadvantaged populations, treatment based on evidence-based medicine runs the risk of inadequacy, as generalized information does not necessarily sufficiently consider social contributors to health and disease, such as poverty and racism. Additionally, patients' cultural practices may inhibit both diagnosis and treatment, and distrust of State institutions (such as IHS) may further inhibit care. Thus the very generalization of care that EBM seeks to produce, although it unquestionably improves care for many, may not only fail to improve care for others but actually impede care for some to whom it is applied. EBM also raises the question of power and visibility in medical decision making: some critics argue that it limits the power of individual physicians to diagnose and prescribe treatment (see, e.g., Rappolt 1997; Rodwin 2001); others that EBM disempowers patients and produces a doctor-centered or even research-centered paradigm (see, e.g., Frankford 1994; Rogers 2002); others express concern over the limitations it imposes on care for marginalized populations who may not be adequately included in research and whose social contexts may remain unaddressed in the very conceptualization of evidence that organizes EBM (see, e.g., Goldenberg 2006; Kravitz, Duan, and Braslow 2004).

Like the development of professional medicine itself, EBM has its origins in reproductive health care. The first large-scale attempt to systematically review practice and care options was the publication *Effective Care in Pregnancy and Childbirth* (Chalmers, Enkin, and Kairse 1989), and the Cochrane Library, one of the largest clearinghouses in the world for EBM analyses, began as the Cochrane Pregnancy and Childbirth Database. As EBM continues to grow in authority, its organizing influence on perinatal care also grows, and "the woman in the body" (Martin 1989) continues to disappear. Diverse types of knowledge, including women's own subjective experiences, are increasingly invalidated by the systemization of medical authority.

For example, in her analysis of the links between evidence-based practice and rising cesarean section rates in the United States, the anthropologist Claire Wendland (2007) found that three key studies released between 1996 and 2001 have contributed significantly to the rise in cesarean sections since the mid-1990s. However, as Wendland points out, these studies in fact reflect a bias toward empirical knowledge that neglects women's subjective experience of their birthing bodies. Similarly, a study published in 2000 known as the Term Breech Trial concluded that when a baby presents as breech at labor, the best course of action is cesarean; vaginal breech birth cannot statistically be considered safe. This study, too, has contributed to rising rates of cesarean section around the world, as well as a significant decrease in breech delivery training for obstetricians. Although the Term Breech Trial has come under intense scrutiny and criticism for the ways it has contributed to ongoing efficiency measures that potentially overmanage childbirth, dissent has not been powerful enough to counteract the overall organizing effects of the study. Other aspects of perinatal care from prenatal care through the early postpartum period have been similarly organized by EBM, further standardizing women's subjective experiences to fit the findings produced by the medical-industrial complex through randomized clinical trials, meta-analyses, and academic reviews (see, e.g., Davis-Floyd 2004; Martin 1989; Wagner 2008).

The Indian Health Service, like its lateral institutions in the Department of Health and Human Services, increasingly relies on EBM to serve its patients. For example, IHS offers an online submission, consultation, and reporting system (nicknamed OSCAR) for the collection and dissemination of "Best [i.e., Evidence Based] and Promising Practices" (OSCAR 2013); care practices can be submitted by any IHS health-care provider, but will be evaluated by subject matter experts before being disseminated. IHS also recommends that its practitioners consult the CDC Community Guide, an online resource for evidence-based practices reviewed by the CDC. In many ways increasing reliance on evidence-based practices has improved the delivery and efficacy of health care for Native people, particularly for chronic diseases such as diabetes (Roubideaux 2012). Yet at the same time that it is increasingly adopting standardized practices, IHS is formally committed to honoring the diversity of the over 560 Native nations it serves. Translating EBM into culturally and locally relevant practices presents unique challenges for IHS as an institution as well as for IHS practitioners in individual areas. One way IHS seeks to meet these challenges for chronic disease care is through the development of culturally relevant practices and education materials, as well as Tribal consultations (Roubideaux 2012). Similar efforts for reproductive health care have not been as consistent.

The historical development of professional medical care, which originated with the treatment of women's reproductive bodies, continues in the twenty-first century to organize mainstream conceptualizations and practices of health and wellness. At the same time, increasing reliance on empirical measures and peer-reviewed evidence potentially precludes and even discredits other ways of knowing about women's bodies and their reproductive needs. These processes have always been not only sexed and gendered but also raced and classed, and thus cannot be extricated from social and political drives toward homogenization and assimilation, masked as efficiency. Even as women's bodies have served as a primary resource for knowledge construction and professionalization, women's diverse needs and experiences—and especially those of women of color and poor women—have been marginalized and neglected. There is no question that rigorous standards, access to broad knowledge, and the continuing pursuit of better knowledge improve care for many, perhaps ultimately even for most. However, without careful consideration of both the process of reaching these goals and the very meaning of "improved health care," the social contexts of health and wellness will remain under-considered, and the subjective experiences of women not only in IHS but also other health-care systems will be further neglected in favor of maximized efficiency. The increasing institutionalization of health care by itself is neither a good nor an evil; but the ruling relations that organize the move to improve health care also drive what that improvement looks like, as well as whom it serves and how. These ruling relations must be carefully examined if the goals and the outcomes of health care are to be better understood.

5

Producing the
Double Discourse

The History and Politics of
Native-US Relations and
Imperialist Medicine

As numerous historians and other scholars assert (see, e.g., Deloria 1970; Smith 2006; Veracini 2010; Wolfe 2011), conquest does not happen in a teleological or totalizing way. Colonizers who seek to settle "new worlds" must first and continually manage the preexisting inhabitants, addressing multiple forms of resistance and the stubborn persistence of sheer existence. Tactics of control, negotiation, assimilation, resistance, and management evolve on all sides. The complexities of Indian Country and Native-US relations today did not develop through a natural course of social evolution; they were produced through a labyrinthine and unfinished history of treaty negotiations, local and national tactics of assimilation and self-determination, local and national economic structures, and other factors, as these all intersected with and were intercepted by Native people themselves.

Ultimately, the complicated relationship between the United States and Native American nations is heavily informed by changing and often conflicting understandings of sovereignty and dependency. The provision of health care for Native Americans theoretically and historically moves somewhere in between these two concepts; these shifting locations depend heavily upon the national political and economic climate, as well as national changes in health-care priorities. They also depend heavily upon changing ideologies of race, class, and nation. Understanding the double discourse of IHS, therefore, necessitates consideration of these factors as they have manifested in and organize Native-US relations.

Sovereignty and Dependence:
The Double Discourse of Settler Colonialism

The unique relationship between Native Americans and the United States has received scant attention from State theorists, perhaps because the complex nature of this relationship challenges State theory to find a satisfactory theoretical framework. However, the concept of sovereignty is essential to understanding the historical and continuing development of this relationship. The meaning of sovereignty for Native American nations is widely debated and often misunderstood. From a Native perspective, sovereignty derives from occupation of the land and self-government, rather than the proclamations and decisions of US government apparatuses. It is rooted in continuous cultural epistemology (see Champagne 2005), historical and dynamic in nature but also variable because the diversity of Native nations leads to a necessarily flexible conceptualization of sovereignty and what is now called "self-determination"; sovereignty is not "one-size-fits-all."

Sovereignty and land ownership, concepts originally understood from the framework of English law, mark the origins of Native-US relations. British colonization of North America was marked by the Doctrine of Discovery, which extinguished Native title to land and reconceptualized non-Christian inhabitants as merely occupants. The young United States, however, initially rejected this doctrine in favor of treaties that recognized various Indian tribes as political entities with sufficient sovereignty to enter into binding legal contracts. This political move was probably precipitated by the need for allies in the US war for independence and later military conflicts. It is in this sense that the very notion of "nationhood" was first applied to Native peoples, and sovereignty became codified in the dealings between Native peoples and the United States.

This original conceptualization of sovereignty for Native nations has undergone myriad changes and continues to evolve in response to the needs and dictates of multiple parties, including Tribal nations, individual states, and the federal government. Many Native scholars question the very notion of sovereignty, noting that in its current iteration it largely reflects European notions of hierarchy and statehood and neglects indigenous conceptualizations (see, e.g., Alfred 1999; Deloria and Lytle 1984). Nonetheless, and despite the limited application of the sovereignty encoded in numerous treaties and other legal documents, the ongoing development of sovereignty as a concept and as a practice continues to organize the relationships between Native peoples and the settler State.

Removal and Its Costs

The role of treaty making between the United States and Native nations is important both for what it reflects symbolically and for what it means materially to both parties. Many early treaties were written to codify trade relations, but relations between the United States and Native nations took on a new dimension after the trade in beaver fur began to decline, reflecting US prioritization of geographic expansion. Hostilities between the United States and Native nations grew more prevalent as the settler State and its citizens sought increasing access to land occupied by Native people. Treaties after the early 1800s primarily served as a means of resolving armed conflict and negotiating for land cession. Agreements between the federal government and Native nations increasingly reflected offers on the part of the United States to provide certain services, including food, education, and health care, for Native nations that signed treaties ceding land and for Native people who remained within their reservation borders.

By the late 1800s, treaty making had become considerably more expensive for the United States. The 1868 Fort Laramie Treaty, one of the last signed and ratified by the United States, is very specific in terms of payment of cash, services, and goods, and mentions several times the provision of a physician to agency Indians (those who lived on the newly formed Pine Ridge Reservation, referred to at the time as Red Cloud Agency). The wealth of capital invested in this treaty reflects the negotiating skill of those Lakota leaders engaged in securing it, including Mapiya Luta (Red Cloud), Tasunka Kokipapi (They Are Afraid of His Horses), and Tasunka Milahanska (American Horse). It is also indicative of the United States' concern over continuing strife with the Sioux Nation and its allies and the impact of this strife on the increasing number of white settlers as well as on the transcontinental railroad, still under construction at the time.

It is in this respect that federally funded health care can be framed as a "trade" for land, as it often is by Native people, including several of my informants. Christina, a Lakota elder who does not utilize IHS services, was adamant that Native people are fortunate to have "prepaid" health insurance, noting that "we're the only group of people in America who have that." She also expressed strong support for the work of IHS health-care providers, praising several by name. Donna, a sixty-one-year-old Lakota woman who has lived on Pine Ridge Reservation her entire life, was less supportive of IHS's work but nonetheless echoed a similar sentiment, exclaiming, "They owe us! If they don't want to provide health care, then why don't they give the land back?"

The conceptualization of health care as a commodity for which Native people have already paid is echoed in the national ideology of health care in the United States as a purchasable commodity rather than a right, and has particular implications for Native nations. Treaties between the United States and Native nations serve as legally binding documents, which, though unevenly applied, nonetheless outline the positive obligations of the federal government toward the well-being of Native people. However, the framing of these obligations as a prepaid market transaction rather than a standing legal obligation restricts the abilities of Native people to further negotiate the quality of the health care they have already "purchased." Further, as the federal government purports to avoid active involvement in the free-market system in which health care in the United States is located, its legal obligations to provide health care to a specifically demarcated population outside of the market system are resisted financially and ideologically, although the Supreme Court's 2012 decision to affirm Congress's right to impose tax penalties on Americans who are not eligible for public assistance but do not purchase private health insurance counteracts the federal government's claim that it does not actively influence commerce. In 2010, approximately 29 percent of Native Americans had no health insurance (Denavas-Walt, Proctor, and Smith 2011); the Affordable Care Act of 2010 requires them to either purchase health insurance, pay a fee (known as the shared responsibility payment), or apply for an exemption. The larger impact of this requirement in Indian Country remains to be seen.

For the most part, treaties served to remove Native populations from the national body, relocating them in managed spaces on the edges of American society. Once it safely contained the Native populations within the borders of treaty-defined homelands, Congress turned to other legislative maneuvers to assimilate Native people and organize Native sovereignty. To begin with, the 1871 Indian Appropriation Act specified that no Tribe thereafter would be legally recognized as an independent nation for the purposes of treaty making. Since this time, Indian policies have been determined by congressional statute or executive order. Rather than codifying a nation-to-nation relationship, however, this move served to impinge on the sovereignty of Native nations in determining the shape and form of their relationships with the federal government by asserting the authority of Congress and the president and limiting the negotiating and management powers of Tribal leaders. Native nations were thus entered into the pluralist form of democracy organized by the United States, in which their needs are often in direct competition with the needs of other interest groups such as regional states and federally funded programs such as Medicaid, the federal prison system, and the Veterans Administration.

This location counteracts the unique status of Native nations as sovereign nations with legal rights, and serves assimilative purposes as Native nations and their members were further integrated into the bureaucracy of US politics.

At the close of the Civil War, the United States turned its war machinery westward and intensified its military engagement with Native peoples for the following two and a half decades. These years were marked by fierce resistance from Native nations, but also by tremendous loss, as the US Cavalry not only had greater and more advanced weaponry but also continued its history of assaulting unarmed Native communities (for example, the tragedies of Sand Creek in 1864, Washita in 1868, the Marias Massacre of 1870, and the Big Hole Massacre of 1877). For their part, many Native people, particularly on the Plains and in the Southwest, also ambushed and attacked noncombatant white settlers in an increasingly bloody exchange as the United States pushed inexorably westward. In 1890, after the Massacre of Wounded Knee in which over three hundred unarmed Lakota women, children, and elders were killed by the Seventh Cavalry on Pine Ridge Reservation, the violent policy of extermination that marked the second half of the nineteenth century shifted to one of assimilation. Boarding schools and churches, supported structurally and financially by the federal government, became the primary means of integrating Native people into the American mainstream, and often the means of providing health care. The government continued its active pursuit of assimilation through legislative policies, as well.

For example, the Dawes Allotment Act of 1887 imposed heteropatriarchal land ownership on Native people as part of the effort to transform traditional collective relationships with land into a more individualized model consistent with the US conceptualization of private ownership. Native families were required to register a male head of household in order to be allotted a segment of agency land, which was then to be inherited through male primogeniture. These registration lists continue in the early twenty-first century to inform Tribal enrollment criteria for many Native nations, as they provide an early census of Tribal membership. The Dawes Act also furthered the national production of a collective ethnicity by releasing Native land previously held in trust by the federal government to be settled by white settlers and developed by growing industrial business interests, further fracturing and reducing Native landholdings originally guaranteed by treaty. According to the historian Judith Nies (1996), between 1881 and 1900 Native landholdings were cut in half, from 155 million acres to 77 million. By the end of the nineteenth century, official policy had not only severely reduced Native lands, it also allowed for federal control of Tribal resources in trust for Native peoples, further eroding notions of Tribal sovereignty and inaugurating a formal status for Native nations as wards of the government rather than citizens of their own Tribal communities or even the US as a whole.

Ironically, political moves such as the Dawes Act, intended to further assimilate Native Americans into the American mainstream, also further implicated the federal government in a paternalistic role unique to its relationship with Native people. The status of Native nations as wards of the government whose land is held in trust is certainly a direct rejection of political sovereignty for Native nations; simultaneously, however, this paternalistic relationship furthers the responsibilities of the federal government to care for its Native citizens. This increasingly demonstrated federal conceptualization of Native nations as a type of subnation within the larger collective, similar to a special interest group but with quasi-sovereign status. This view was reinforced by the 1924 Indian Citizenship Act, in which Congress granted US citizenship to all Native people. As citizens of the United States and of their state of residence, Native people became eligible for all benefits of US citizenship, including social welfare programs; however, the act further complicated concepts of Native identity by essentially imposing a tripartite citizenship, as Native people became de facto citizens of their regional state and the United States as well as their Tribal nation. The control over Native identities assumed by the US government has encouraged reliance on formalized blood quantum rules to validate claims to Native identity and increasingly restrictive mechanisms for achieving federal recognition of Tribal status, as discussed further below and in the next chapter.

Imperialist Medicine

Along with treaties and war, medicine and health care also served the goals of the settler State's ambitions. The origins of sustained efforts to utilize Western medicine in Indian Country began in earnest in the late 1700s with the use—and testing—of smallpox vaccines among Native American Tribes, most notably the Arikara and Mandan. Diane Pearson (2004) argues that these vaccinations were an essential aspect of the imperialist agenda of American expansion, as medical treatments were used as trade items and to generate goodwill among Native communities. Western medicines were not offered universally to Native groups; availability of vaccinations was limited by geographic isolation as well as limited funds (Brown 2006; see also Pearson 2003). Significantly, they were also withheld from those groups occupying valued territory or presenting a possibly hostile resistance to American expansion (Pearson 2003; Rockwell 2010). This was particularly apparent with the Indian Vaccination Act of 1832, the first piece of legislation specifically targeting Native American health. Rockwell argues that "vaccinations were less an example of generous social policymaking and more an example of a means to facilitate removals and broader policy" (2010, 152), noting that decisions about whom to vaccinate and when aided Native American allies, bolstered economic partnerships, and excluded Natives seen as enemies.

The growing prevalence of medical care as an enticement in treaty negotiations throughout the nineteenth century is linked to the emerging health needs in Native communities at this time. Contact and interactions with European and European American social, political, and military forces produced social chaos for many Native communities as well as introducing what David Stannard refers to as "microbial pestilence" (1992, xii). The strategic availability of Western medicine to certain communities, particularly through treaty negotiations, thus became a tool of medical imperialism as it was increasingly sought by Native communities but its distribution was dictated by State interests. For example, in the 1836 treaty between the United States and the Ottawa and Ojibwe peoples (the first time health care in exchange for land was explicitly offered in a treaty between the United States and Native nations), the federal government promised to provide annual payments for vaccines and other medicines as well as the service of a physician as long as the Ottawa and Ojibwe remained on their treaty-allotted land. Thus access to health care was contingent upon meeting State-mandated conditions, and these conditions specifically included a physical containment of Native bodies, separate from the general population.

By the beginning of the twentieth century, the indigenous population, which had numbered in the millions in the mid-sixteenth century, had been reduced by wars, starvation, epidemics, forced relocations, and numerous massacres to approximately 228,000 (Snipp 1991). Confined to reservations, often denied access to resources such as nutritious food, traditional ceremonies, and adequate housing, the health conditions of Native people were truly dire. The most visible victims of the widespread health crisis in Indian Country were children and infants. In an attempt to curtail the near-daily deaths of Native children across the country, in 1912 Commissioner of Indian Affairs Robert Valentine ordered all Bureau of Indian Affairs (BIA) field agents to "take immediate steps to greatly reduce infant mortality. Save the babies!" (quoted in Emmerich 1997). The entire BIA was mustered in service to the health of Native children, though it was field matrons in particular, the white women who provided health care and education in reservation communities, who served on the front lines of the campaign.

The focus on the well-being of Indian children presented a strategic opportunity to further assimilate Native families through the doctrine of scientific motherhood, an ideology that combined European American gender roles (particularly around femininity) and European American valorization of empirical science. The concepts that formed the foundation of scientific motherhood were predicated on racial and ethnic divides that presumed Northern European superiority. Indigenous practices were devalued and displaced as Native women were encouraged to adopt the European American tenets of female, heteronormative domesticity that dominated the late Progressive era.

Field matrons, baby clinics, mandatory educational sessions, and even baby festivals and competitions promoted European American notions of hygiene and disease prevention for babies and children, while Native parenting practices, such as the use of cradle-boards, were actively discouraged. Native mothers, in particular, were framed by the Bureau of Indian Affairs as incompetent and even dangerous to the well-being of their children, and many children were removed, often permanently, from their homes and families during these years (see Emmerich 1997).

Indian Agent Walter West, the superintendent on the Southern Ute Agency during the campaign era, wrote that

> a special effort has been made to impress upon the . . . Indian mothers, the necessity of taking proper care of children, and to teach them . . . the better methods of caring for and feeding the young [by] showing the advantage of vaccination of children . . . daily bathing for baby, children sleeping alone, offering the baby frequent drinks of boiled water, etc. . . . also the disadvantages of . . . putting babies in tight bound native containers, lack of proper care of person and clothing of child. (Department of the Interior 1917)

Specially designed education sessions and festivals were often held on "pay day," the day when enrolled members of a Tribe could obtain from government agents the commodity supplies (most often food) promised in their treaty agreements. Access to resources was often linked to programs such as these as well as church attendance (Powers 1986). The coerced attendance at such events was not always entirely successful, but many Native women embraced these efforts as traditional subsistence practices, family forms, and healing modalities were increasingly distorted or destroyed through the reservation system, or simply could not be accessed, or were no longer effective in meeting the new challenges brought on by colonization. Many European American practices undoubtedly benefited the health of Native children, although their value was contingent on the distortion of previous ways of living and the simultaneous move to a poorly resourced reservation system. The promise of better health thereby became further entrenched in assimilation efforts by progressively displacing indigenous knowledge and practices and linking access to treaty rights such as commodities to the assimilative efforts of churches and the BIA's education sessions.

In some ways, the preconception care model of the early twenty-first century is reminiscent of the Save the Babies campaign of the early twentieth century: the ultimate goal is healthy babies, not necessarily healthy women, and the strategies embedded in each approach reflect heteropatriarchal assumptions about women's roles as mothers, while relegating their health (as mothers, as women, as adolescents) to a secondary status in relation to potential or real children. At the same time, just as the Save the Babies campaign provided genuine relief to at least some degree, preconception care may also work to reduce maternal and infant morbidity and mortality. As well, both campaigns incorporated or have the potential to address longstanding social contexts that contribute to poor health conditions.

The infant mortality rate did indeed decrease through the efforts of the Save the Babies campaign, but the overall health of Native people continued to deteriorate. Health facilities on reservations in the early twentieth century were poorly equipped and poorly staffed, despite high rates of tuberculosis, trachoma, smallpox, and other infectious diseases as well as ongoing high rates of infant mortality. The majority of health care was provided in off-reservation facilities, requiring Native patients to be removed, often for long periods of time, from their families and communities. At the same time, Native peoples' access to their traditional healing practices was increasingly curtailed. The criminalization of Native spiritual practices through the 1883 Indian Religious Crimes Code and the 1892 Rules for Indian Courts limited the ability of Native people to seek tradition-oriented healing modalities, thus increasingly restricting them to the poorly articulated health-care model offered by the federal government. For Native women, restrictions were further imposed by the ongoing social dislocation of lay midwives, brought on by the professionalization of medical practice in the nineteenth and early twentieth centuries.

In response to the ongoing health crisis in Indian Country, Congress enacted the Snyder Act in 1921, which formalized federal involvement in Native health care. The act specifically authorized the BIA to "direct, supervise, and expend such moneys as Congress may from time to time appropriate, for the benefit, care, and assistance of the Indians," including "relief of distress and conservation of health" (Snyder Act 1921). The Snyder Act thus recognized a special status for Native people, at least in terms of public health. However, it established only discretionary programs rather than entitlement to specific services and did not adequately define eligibility or identify levels or goals for funding. These aspects remained under the control of Congress, which has historically resisted adequate appropriations for Native health care.

The dire health conditions that led to the Snyder Act also prompted many Native organizations to lobby for a presidential commission to review Indian policies, and in 1926 the secretary of the interior authorized an economic and social study of Indian conditions. Social scientist Lewis Meriam led the study for the Institute for Government Research (now the Brookings Institute), with financial support from the Rockefeller Foundation. The Meriam Report (officially titled *The Problem of Indian Administration*), released two years later, provided extensive evidence of the failure of assimilation policies and documented the urgent health needs of Native communities, including high rates of tuberculosis, infant mortality, and trachoma. Additionally, the report noted that the health work of the Indian Service fell markedly below the standards maintained by the Public Health Service, the Veterans Bureau, and the military. Almost a century later in 2003 and again in 2004, the US Commission on Civil Rights issued nearly identical findings regarding health and health care for Native Americans (see US Commission on Civil Rights 2003, 2004).

The Double Discourse in the Twentieth Century

At the same time that specifically designated health campaigns seemingly solidified a unique status for Native people, legal maneuvers such as the Dawes Allotment Act and the Citizenship Act were designed in part to eventually remove from Native people any unique status derived from treaty agreements, thus incorporating them into the American polity and removing federal responsibility for health care and other federally funded programs. The work to legally assimilate Native people into American society was furthered in the 1950s with the official policy of "termination," designed to (finally) end the federal trust relationship between Native nations and the US government and fully integrate Native people into the broader society. This policy must be understood within the political and economic context of the post–World War II era. Previous to World War II the Bureau of Indian Affairs, under the leadership of John Collier, had been widely recognized as protective of Indian rights, but postwar debt led Congress to a close examination of all federal expenditures, and the costs for improvement of Indian welfare, carried almost exclusively by the federal government, were frequently challenged. Several legislators began to argue for the dismantling of the BIA and the complete termination of the federal government's relationship with Indian Tribes. Western Republicans were particularly keen to dismantle the reservation system completely after it became clear by the late 1940s that over a third of the US's mineral resources were located under reservation land, and that the bulk of these reservations were in western States.

In 1949 the Hoover Commission's Task Force on Indian Policy argued that "assimilation must be the dominant goal of public policy" and that "the basis for historic Indian culture has been swept away." The task force recommended that "pending achievement of the goal of complete integration, the administration of social programs for the Indians should be progressively transferred to state governments" (Graham et al. 1948; see also Freeman 1954). Regional states, however, resisted the shift, fearing the added economic costs of providing health care, education, and other social services to reservation communities, as did many Tribal leaders, who feared the loss of both services and sovereignty.

Despite these protests, in 1953 the House of Representatives passed Resolution 108, inaugurating an era of termination policies that eventually ended federal services for over one hundred Tribes. The same year, Public Law 280 transferred criminal jurisdiction over Tribal lands to state and local governments in six states and made such transfers available to all states, without Tribal consultation. These policies dissipated federal responsibility for the well-being of Tribal communities and disbursed it to those regional states that chose it or were assigned it by Congress. The decentralization of services for Native people was furthered by the 1954 passage of Public Law 568, which transferred responsibility for Indian health care to the US Public Health Service (USPHS), thus formally removing responsibility for the health and well-being of Native peoples from the BIA and incorporating it into the broader-based USPHS.

At the time of the transfer, studies indicated tremendous health disparities between reservation Indians and the rest of the American population: the infant mortality rate was 53.7 (per one thousand) compared to 27.1 for all Americans combined; the average life expectancy was just under forty-two years, compared to just over sixty-two for all Americans combined; and leading causes of death included high rates of preventable causes such as accidents, influenza, and pneumonia (Brophy and Aberle 1966). It was clear that the Bureau of Indian Affairs had failed in its responsibility for the health and well-being of Native communities, a task greatly complicated by ongoing poverty and isolation. The USPHS had better professional and technical resources, was better able to attract professional staff, and was organized around managing public health crises and public health services, which were badly needed on most reservations at the time.

However, improved access to resources was not the sole reason for the transfer, which was resisted by the BIA, the USPHS, and individual Tribes. The removal of Native American health care from the Bureau of Indian Affairs (a federal agency intended to represent the interests of Native American peoples) to the US Public Health Service (a federal agency intended to serve the public health needs of all Americans) reflected changing political notions of dependency and ongoing assimilation objectives, which were in turn influenced by changing national priorities. For example, during World War II, 10 to 25 percent of Native Americans drafted into the military were discharged due to active tuberculosis; similar problems plagued those Native people who left the reservation to work in defense plants (Bergman et al. 1999). The scandal of returning wartime active duty personnel and defense workers to their reservations due to egregiously high and largely unchecked tuberculosis rates was cited almost a decade later during the debates on the transfer. President Dwight D. Eisenhower's budget bureau felt the transfer of Native health care to the USPHS was not economically justified and would not substantially improve the efficiency of care on reservations; on the other hand, Senator Arthur Watkins, a Republican from Utah and one of the architects of termination policy, viewed the transfer as a way to end federal responsibilities to Native nations as distinct groups. Ultimately, PL 568 was passed, and the health-care crises in Indian Country, including high rates of tuberculosis, infant mortality, and preventable diseases, abetted the opportunity to mitigate the unique status of Native nations as their health care was subsumed under the aegis of US public health.

The Turn Back to Sovereignty

Following the removal of health-care responsibilities from the BIA, the Indian Health Service became increasingly centralized under the auspices of the USPHS. However, growing demand for community control throughout the 1950s and 1960s, encouraged in some respects by the Economic Opportunity Act of 1964 as well as by American Indian and other civil rights activism, resulted in a growing regional pattern of service that continues today. This regionalization was further encouraged by President Richard Nixon's policy of self-determination. The policy of termination had proven an abysmal failure, and in 1970 President Nixon shifted the focus from termination to self-determination for Tribal nations. Nixon's description of the relationship between the US government and Tribal nations as one of "solemn obligations" based on written treaties as well as legislation once again shifted national conceptualizations of Native American health care. Emery Johnson, director of IHS from 1969 to 1981, asserts that Nixon's Indian policy statement "gave credibility to our position that the Tribes had purchased a prepaid health-care plan in perpetuity" (quoted in Bergman et al. 1999, 588). Political scientist David Wilkins (2002) goes still further by asserting that although Indian policy continues to suffer today from congressional vacillation and even outright attack, the results of Nixon's policies, particularly the Indian Self-Determination and Education Assistance Act of 1975, have included a readier recognition that Native peoples are nations, not ethnic minorities. Thus once again the political pendulum swung in Indian policy, from early investment of political sovereignty through extermination, to assimilation and termination, and finally a return of (limited) sovereignty through self-determination.

The Indian Self-Determination and Education Assistance Act continues to form the backbone of much federal policy and has provided for economic and social development in reservation communities as well as varying levels of federally recognized sovereignty. For example, Title I of the act established procedures by which Tribes could negotiate contracts with the BIA to administer their own education and social service programs. It also provided direct grants to help Tribes assume responsibility for social programs. Subsequent amendments in the 1980s and 1990s included block grants from IHS and the BIA to cover a number of programs independently of direct federal control. These aspects have been crucial to the delivery of health care for Native people, allowing reservation communities to assess their own needs and determine the means by which those needs are met on the local level.

Tribal Participation in Health Care

In fact, health care became an immediate focus for Tribal nations seeking block grants through the Self-Determination and Education Assistance Act. The first Tribally contracted program was for Community Health Representatives (CHRs) on Pine Ridge Reservation in 1965, four full years before IHS requested funds for the specific purpose of training CHRs, who are employed by individual Tribal governments. The CHR program has proven to be one of the most successful grassroots efforts of IHS's partnership with local Tribes; in the early twenty-first century, it has grown to over fourteen hundred CHRs representing over 250 Tribes in all twelve IHS service areas (IHS 2012).

One of the earliest forerunners of the CHR program was the Lakota TB and Health Association on Pine Ridge Reservation, also known as the Lakota Grandmothers, a small group of women who organized Tribal health committees and managed numerous health programs. Because these women were not employees of IHS (although they were supervised by an IHS public health nurse), they could operate outside of federal structures. In the 1960s, they did this by disseminating information about birth control, and later providing access to birth control at community meetings and outside of the official purview of IHS, which avoided contraception because it feared it would be accused of fostering genocide in the increasingly politically charged climate of Pine Ridge Reservation (Bergman et al. 1999, 582). The work of the Lakota Grandmothers provides important insights into the advantages of community-driven efforts to identify and address women's health-care needs outside of, but in partnership with, the federally organized health-care system of IHS. Similar grassroots work is currently underway on Akwesasne Reservation in upstate New York and Canada through the development of a prenatal program led by local Mohawk women (see Chapter 7).

Tribal nations' use of block grant funding to contract with non-IHS facilities as a means of providing health care has also increased. Contract health services (CHS) and compacts (provided under Title V of the Self-Determination Act) constituted approximately 40 percent of the IHS budget in 2008, reflecting the growing interest and efficacy of Tribal nations in managing their own social programs, including health care. Tribal nations have exerted increasing control over their health care in other ways, as well; for example, in 1998 control of the Alaska Native Medical Center was officially transferred from IHS to the Alaska Native Tribal Health Consortium in partnership with the Southcentral Foundation (an Alaska Native–owned, nonprofit health-care organization); it has since won numerous awards and recognitions, including a Magnet designation for excellence in nursing in 2003, recognition as a Center of Excellence in Evidence-Based Practice in 2006, and the 2012 Excellence in Patient Care Award for customer satisfaction. Since the mid-1990s the Gila River Indian Community, home of the Akimel O'odham (Pima) and Pee Posh (Maricopa) in Arizona, has increasingly taken over the administration of health care from IHS, and its operations include a Tribally run Department of Public Health. Other reservation communities, including Pine Ridge Reservation, have developed similar mechanisms which range from fully staffed Tribal health departments to Tribally operated clinics as well as facilities and programs run in partnership between Tribes and IHS.

In 1976, Congress passed what is arguably the single most important piece of legislation pertaining to Native health care. The Indian Health Care Improvement Act (IHCIA) represented the first legislative development of specific goals for Native health care, intended to provide "the highest possible health status to Indians and to provide existing Indian health services with all resources necessary to effect that policy" (Indian Health Care Improvement Act 1976). Whereas the Snyder Act had previously allowed for Congress to provide funds for Native health care "from time to time," the IHCIA required the appropriation of funds. It also mandated the inclusion of Native people in planning and managing health programs, created a scholarship program to assist in the training of Native health-care providers, and authorized services for Native people in urban areas. Like other key pieces of legislation, the IHCIA required regular updates to address changing needs. After it officially expired in fiscal year 2001, Congress granted continuing one-year extensions until it was reauthorized and rendered permanent as Title X of the Patient Protection and Affordable Care Act in 2010. The latest version of the IHCIA includes specific mention of long-term health care for Native elders, increasing attention to mental health services, and the improvement of outdated facilities, among other needs. Specific to Native women's reproductive health, the 2010 IHCIA specifically makes note of the rising rate of cervical cancer (all cancers combined are the second highest cause of death for Native American women and leading cause for Alaska Native women); the low incidence of prenatal care; and the egregiously high rate of infant mortality in Native communities (see Chapter 7).

Changing Political Opportunities

The ideological shift from assimilation policies and termination to self-determination and self-governance owes much to the social and political demands of various constituents of the late 1950s through the mid-1970s. The agitation for legally protected civil rights by racial-ethnic groups, women, gays and lesbians, students, migrant workers, people with disabilities, and the poor resulted in a morass of legislation and social programs that reverberated throughout the lives of Native people. Legislation such as the Economic Opportunity Act and the Civil Rights Act of 1964 and, more specific to Native people, the Self-Determination and Education Assistance Act of 1975, the Indian Child Welfare Act, and the Indian Religious Freedom Act (both passed in 1978) as well as increasing Tribal control over health care, resulted from a confluence of factors, including the shifting political landscape.

The commitment of numerous Native scholars, lawyers, and activists is largely responsible for changes in the political and social statuses of Native nations both locally and nationally. In the early 1960s, young Native activists in cities and college campuses became increasingly interested in a growing sense of Tribalism through the work of Native organizations such as the National Indian Youth Council and the indigenous theories being developed and promulgated by thinkers such as legal scholar Vine Deloria Jr. Numerous informants in my study also credited the work of the American Indian Movement (AIM) for positive changes on Pine Ridge. Joe, who was forty-eight when we first met in 1999 and was living on the reservation during AIM's 1973 occupation of Wounded Knee, told me, "They made it good to be Indian again." AIM was not the only Native organization working on Pine Ridge and elsewhere in Indian Country; Women of All Red Nations (WARN) and the National Congress of American Indians were both active in the 1960s and 1970s, and their work continues today. WARN, which began as a sister organization to the American Indian Movement, has been particularly focused on the needs of women and children, including health-care needs.

However, despite the success of Native activists and scholars as well as certain federal legislations such as the Self-Determination Act, social and political backlash from non-Natives in the 1980s eroded some of the political gains of Native people. In the years immediately following the passage of the Indian Self-Determination and Education Assistance Act, per capita spending on all Native American programs was higher than spending for the general population. However, President Ronald Reagan's election in 1980 signaled a reversal for Native programs as his administration sought to reduce federal fiduciary responsibilities. After 1985, per capita spending on Native American programs was less than on the general population, resulting in a wide gap that persists today. The Reagan and George H. W. Bush administrations oversaw a growing period of neofederalism in which regional states increasingly exerted sovereign rights, including over the Tribal nations within their borders. Perhaps more immediately devastating to Native people were the steep cuts in social service programs for the poor, such as food stamps and the public service employment portions of the Comprehensive Employment and Training Act, as well as emerging federal policies aimed at further reducing federal financial support and incorporating Native nations into the private sector. National and local Native rights organizations such as the National Indian Health Board, the Native American Rights Fund, the White Earth Land Recovery Project, Running Strong for Indian Youth, and others continue today to work for progress in Indian Country, but the shift in Native-US relations precipitated by the Reagan-Bush era has certainly altered, and narrowed, the political opportunities available to Native people. The legislative and fiduciary record of the Obama administration reflects a generally stronger, though somewhat mixed, support for Native sovereignty, as discussed further in Chapters 6 and 8.

The United States' drive toward absorption of Native people into the broader national body—an ongoing effort to "disappear" them through assimilation—has been interrupted by the development of self-determination policies, which seemingly reject assimilation by recognizing the sovereignty of Native nations. Yet at the same time, self-determination institutes only a limited sovereignty as the United States continues to interpret and enforce its various meanings through the judicial system, some financial control, and ongoing policy development. Michael Omi and Howard Winant (1994) offer some insight into the simultaneous structural integration and structural exclusion of Native Americans into the political system of the United States by arguing that racial projects reflect continuous efforts to reorganize and redistribute resources along particular racial lines; this division of resources reflects neither outright exclusion nor full inclusion, but rather a mix of both insider and outsider statuses for Native nations and Native people, similar to what the political scientist Kevin Bruyneel (2007) refers to as "the third space of sovereignty."

Federal Indian policy in the early twenty-first century continues to organize much of Indian Country, and these policies in general remain poorly articulated and often contradictory. In large part, this has been due to the lack of clear exposition between the creation of these policies and the means of their implementation. The fragmented nature of Indian policy and changing notions of sovereignty and dependence are reflected in the evolving structure of the Indian Health Service, which seeks to serve Native people but is largely directed not only by tribal needs but also by multiple non-Native parties including members of Congress, regional states, other federal agencies, and even the changing nature of health care in the United States. The Supreme Court, as well, has been heavily involved in shaping Indian policy, including health-care policy (see, e.g., *Scholder v. United States* 1970, in which the Supreme Court determined that congressional appropriations for Native health care do not belong to Native people, but rather to the public). Additionally, the competing needs of uniquely identified groups such as veterans and federal prisoners impact the funding available for social programs in Indian Country. Thus, although there is general acknowledgment of a federal obligation to provide health care to Native Americans, the scope and limitations of this obligation remain poorly defined. The influence of these multiple and often ambiguously defined points of authority on the delivery of health care to Native peoples imposes convoluted restrictions, and complicates the mission of IHS both externally and internally.

6

"To Uphold the Federal Government's Obligations . . . and to Honor and Protect"

The Double Discourse of the Indian Health Service

To raise the physical, mental, social, and spiritual health of American Indians and Alaska Natives to the highest level . . . to assure that comprehensive, culturally acceptable personal and public health services are available and accessible to American Indian and Alaska Native people [and] . . . to uphold the Federal Government's obligation to promote healthy American Indian and Alaska Native people, communities, and cultures and to honor and protect the inherent sovereign rights of Tribes.
—Indian Health Service
Mission Statement

The fragmented nature of Indian policy creation and implementation is clearly reflected in the organization and structural challenges of the Indian Health Service. Historically IHS follows a fairly linear trajectory of development. However, its increasing institutionalization has progressed during a period when State-produced concepts of self-determination, coupled with social movements for community control, encourage locally oriented service. As a result, its structural integration into the bureaucracy of the United States produces convoluted and multiple locations of authority and complicates IHS's unique mission and its emphasis on comprehensive community-based care.

The management of IHS operations and resources is accomplished through a decentralized organizational structure and hierarchy that includes a central headquarters located in Rockville, Maryland and twelve area offices (based in twelve geographic areas, which often cover hundreds of square miles and several states). Each of the regional areas is further divided into local service units, which are operated by either IHS or a contracting Tribe. This decentralized structure allows individual IHS areas and Tribal nations to better address the unique needs of Native people, but it also complicates oversight and accountability within the hierarchy of IHS and perpetuates uneven delivery of services among different areas.

This complexity is further exacerbated by the placement of IHS in the Department of Health and Human Services (HHS). This nested location produces IHS's reliance upon Congress and the president for its budget, for the appointment of its director, and even for the actions it takes to realize its mission, as much of its medical agenda corresponds to the initiatives emerging from the Centers for Disease Control and its funding structure is increasingly tied to the Centers for Medicare and Medicaid Services. This structure also provides IHS with a broad federal level of support as many of its employees, for example, are commissioned officers in the Public Health Service. The close relationship between IHS and these as well as several other divisions within HHS is reflected in the adoption of mainstream medical practices as well as its overall organization of medical care through an evidence-based model. Importantly, this accountability and management structure has significant consequences for Native women's reproductive health care, as described more fully in the following chapters.

The institutional complexities that govern IHS and organize its ability to "promote healthy American Indian and Alaska Native people, communities, and cultures" also, at times, impede its ability "to honor and protect the inherent sovereign rights of Tribes." This reflects the deep double discourse of health care for Native people as it is provided by a settler State that wrestles with the tensions between meeting its obligations and eliminating indigenous challenges to its (fictive) collective ethnicity. Many of my informants are aware of the failings of IHS, but few of them understand the multiple and convoluted mechanisms that influence the form and functions of IHS. Like most people, they are largely unaware of the bureaucratic intricacies that shape their health-care experiences; they only want decent health care in a timely manner. Their frustrations with what is available to them often leads them to a simplistic blame game in which "IHS" or "the government" or sometimes just "they" simply fail to do what is needed. The irony, of course, is that whether or not they understand the complexities of IHS's mission and the structural obstacles that prevent it from fully meeting this mission, my informants are correct: ultimately, and despite notable successes, IHS *is* failing, and perhaps particularly failing Native women. This failure is not unmitigated, however. For example, IHS is justly proud of its success in reducing infant mortality as well as maternal mortality (Brenneman 2000), and six of its hospitals have been officially designated "Baby Friendly" by the World Health Organization and the United Nations, reflecting strong and ongoing efforts to encourage breastfeeding. (It is important to note the gendered calculus of exclusive breastfeeding, which presents important challenges to women who must work for a living in a nation—the United States—that does not universally offer paid maternity leave. Emphasis on the "breast is best" model may also produce added anxiety for women who have trouble breastfeeding, even with support, or who simply do not wish to for a variety of reasons.)

Nor is IHS's failure simple: there is no single cause to be identified and addressed, but rather numerous reasons for numerous failures, many of them deriving from the sheer complexities of providing health care to the poorest, sickest people in the country. Certainly, fault can be found with IHS and its personnel, as I discuss below and in the following chapters; but responsibility for the failure of IHS to provide adequate health care to Native people, and particularly adequate reproductive health care, also derives from the multiple sites of authority and control that direct the mission of IHS and determine the resources available to meet its mission.

Indian Health Service Funding

As the IHS Budget Workgroup asserts, "The federal budget is a moral, as well as a fiscal document. The nation's budget priorities are a demonstration of its core values and, in the case of the Indian Health Service, of its commitment to addressing the health needs of American Indian and Alaska Native people" (HHS 2011). Yet one of the greatest limitations imposed on IHS by Congress and the president is its persistent and stark underfunding. The annual budget appropriation for IHS is consistently below identified levels of need, and in fact is consistently below that of other, similar federal programs such as the Veterans Administration and the federal prison system (Harvard Project on American Indian Economic Development

2008; NPAIHB 2009). Federal appropriations for Tribal nations are deeply influenced by the broader political economy in which they are determined; they also reflect shifting conceptualizations of the relationship between the State and the Native nations within its borders. To date, this relationship has been one of dominance, control, and neglect, wherein assimilation of Native people into the collective of the national body serves both the cultural and economic goals of the State.

The Indian Health Service was granted formal agency status in 1988, following declining social service appropriations during the first half of Reagan's presidency. The US Commission on Civil Rights found in 2003 that IHS has never been adequately funded, and that "the anorexic budget of the IHS can only lead one to deduce that less value is placed on Indian health than that of other populations" (US Commission on Civil Rights 2003, 49). The commission's findings in 2004 assert unequivocally that "the federal government has failed to satisfy explicit trust obligations" to Native people, specifically in the provision of health care (US Commission on Civil Rights 2004, 95). Given the much lower rate of budgetary growth for IHS in comparison with other federal health programs such as the Veterans Administration and the federal prison system, the commission concludes that the failure of Congress to fund Native health care adequately while other, similar programs experience slightly greater growth rates is attributable at least in part to either "intentional discrimination or gross negligence" (2004, 96).

Although decreasing appropriations for Native health care in the late 1980s and early 1990s can be attributed in part to the fiscally conservative Reagan-Bush years, Congress's lack of understanding about the capacities and purposes of IHS information management and billing systems are also responsible. Appropriations during these years were made with the assumption that IHS would bill Medicare, Medicaid, and private insurance when Native patients were eligible for these. However, IHS systems were not designed to generate billing, as IHS was not originally intended to serve as a paid provider. Therefore these funds could not be accessed in the ways Congress imagined, and IHS was forced to operate with increasing budget shortfalls. Not only have allocations been insufficient, but IHS's ineffective billing system has resulted in a further loss of revenue on the other end, as well; a recent Government Accountability Office (GAO) study reported that IHS has been paying a majority of their contracted health services at billed rates rather than the mandated Medicare rates, resulting in overpayment of millions from an annual budget that is already too small (GAO 2013). Upgrading and updating these billing systems continues to be a priority for IHS, and constitutes a varying but consistently substantial portion of the annual budget. However, lower budgetary appropriations and reliance on reimbursement through billing continue to create significant funding uncertainties, particularly in light of recent congressional cuts to Medicaid, increasing needs in the Veterans Administration since 2002, and inaccurate billing systems.

Increasing reliance on third-party payers by both Congress and thus IHS echoes earlier legislative mainstreaming of Native identity and potentially serves to reduce federal responsibilities to Native people as a distinct collective interest. Donna, a sixty-one-year-old enrolled member of the Oglala Lakota Nation, described IHS's reliance on private insurance and Medicare to cover the cost of medical care as "totally unfair. The government is supposed to be paying for this, not us. They're just trying to find ways not to pay for us." Donna understands that reliance on Medicaid compromises her status as an enrolled member of a federally recognized Native nation and instead inserts her into a class-based, rather than Tribally based, collective identity. She also offers an accurate assessment of the State's fiduciary relationship with Native nations, which has been marked by regular and ongoing efforts to reduce the financial cost to the State of indigeneity within its national body. Other informants shared this view, both in formal interviews and informal conversations, and it is well known on the reservation that IHS is underfunded, as patients are frequently directed to make an appointment with a contracted facility in order to access certain tests, or must endure long wait times due to understaffing.

The Obama administration has demonstrated a strong commitment to improving the delivery of health care to Native people through increased funding. For example, the American Recovery and Reinvestment Act of 2009 included close to $500 million for IHS to complete needed construction projects as well as update its health information technology system. Additionally, in one of his earliest acts in the Executive Office, President Barack Obama included just over seven million dollars for IHS to further develop its outreach advocacy programs in Native communities in the Omnibus Appropriations Act of 2009. Importantly, a major portion of the funds were intended to expand domestic violence and sexual assault projects already in operation, including further training and the purchase of forensic equipment to support the Sexual Assault Nurse Examiner program (see Chapter 8). This funding is essential to providing care and services to survivors of sexual assault, which is egregiously high in Indian Country, and will potentially have an impact on the reproductive health care of these women. The president's consistent proposed budget increases for IHS reflect the Executive Office's overall commitment to health care as well as recognition of the specific needs of Native communities, and Native organizations such as the National Indian Health Board continue to praise Obama for his commitment to Native health care. However, the Affordable Care Act's requirement that Native people purchase health insurance or pay a fee is likely to affect IHS's upcoming budget appropriations in ways that are reminiscent of Congress's uninformed budgetary justifications in the late 1980s and early 1990s, as public or private health insurance will be expected to pay a portion of expenses.

Although the budget increases, coupled with additional funding from the 2009 Recovery and Reinvestment Act and 2009 Omnibus Appropriations, were necessary (and in fact represent the greatest increase in real terms allocated to Native health care since the late 1970s), they were not sufficient to fully meet accumulated and ongoing needs in Indian Country. Additionally, the allocation and use of some of these resources by IHS itself has come under scrutiny by Congress as well as nongovernmental organizations such as Amnesty International and the American Civil Liberties Union, as discussed below and in Chapters 7 and 8. Lateral offices in the Department of Health and Human Services have also noted fiscal mismanagement in IHS; for example, in the fall of 2009 the Department of Medicaid and Medicare threatened to withdraw funding from Pine Ridge Hospital due to noncompliance involving both medical treatment and administrative issues. At that time, Pine Ridge Hospital received approximately 66 percent of its funding from the Department of Medicaid and Medicare. A satisfactory plan was submitted by IHS, and funding has continued.

No Money, No People, No Service

The accumulating impact of this underfunding and mismanagement is sharply felt at every level of IHS, and ongoing funding uncertainties extend beyond direct care through IHS; the consequences for contracted health services were noted by IHS Director Robert McSwain in his opening remarks to the National Combined Councils annual meeting in early 2009, when he explained that payments to contract health services (CHS) facilities "are strictly limited by law to available CHS funds, which results in thousands of patient referrals without any source of payment. CHS funds regularly run out before year end. This produces hardships for patients and undermines relationships with hospitals and other providers" (McSwain 2009). Contract health services are particularly relevant to Native women seeking reproductive health care, as IHS spending on direct care is often channeled toward emergency services and chronic disease treatment, and its medical staff is often limited. Many Native women living on Pine Ridge rely on contracted services through the Native Women's Health Center of Rapid City and Rapid City Regional Hospital, both of which can be over two hours away from their place of residence. At both of these facilities Native women must use private insurance if they have it and apply for and use Medicaid if they are eligible to offset anticipated loss through delayed IHS payment, which can take up to a year.

According to Charles Grim, director of IHS from 2002 to 2007, these ongoing budgetary shortfalls render IHS a program of "universal eligibility but limited availability" (quoted in US Commission on Civil Rights 2004, 47), resulting in a severe shortage of health-care services. Former director McSwain (2009) asserts that this situation continues to worsen, rendering essential services unavailable: "if available, limited staff, equipment, and facility space often result in deferring services. These deficiencies contribute to backlogs that result in more severe health problems over the long run." IHS acknowledges that its system "explicitly rations care, deferring and denying payment for medical services that are thought to be of lower priority" (US Commission on Civil Rights 2004, 48).

Reproductive health care is, apparently, a lower priority than other health concerns. My informant Sarah, who previously worked for IHS in an administrative capacity, explained that on Pine Ridge Reservation the number-one funding priority is emergency services, followed by diabetes treatment and cardiovascular health. She felt these budget areas required so much funding that the amount remaining for nonemergency care, including reproductive health care, was entirely inadequate. This neglect of reproductive health care was confirmed by Donna, who scoffed, "Reproductive health care? Oh, no, not in IHS. They don't pay any attention to that." Informants who have experience with IHS as care providers and/or health advocates agreed that reproductive health care in IHS is generally inadequate, despite efforts by both IHS and the Public Health Service (and some successes, particularly around perinatal care).

This rationed system of health care results not only in prioritizing certain health services to the detriment of others, but also in differential funding to IHS areas, resulting in some areas receiving greater allocations while others remain relatively neglected. For example, despite the fact that almost 80 percent of Native Americans live off reservation (Norris, Vines, and Hoeffel 2012), health care for Native people living in urban communities remains underfunded and underdeveloped. IHS estimates that funding for urban health programs is currently at 22 percent of need, and that an estimated 25 percent of Native Americans who live outside of reservation communities must travel from an underserved urban area to an IHS or Tribal health facility to obtain health care (UIHP 2009).

According to Rose Pfefferbaum et al. (1997), the greater provision of health-care services to Native people in reservation communities than to those in urban centers or rural, nonreservation communities is based on two principles: isolation versus access, and the impact of federal recognition on eligibility and self-determination. Reservation communities tend to be isolated geographically, and access to non-IHS service providers limited if not nonexistent. Although IHS recognizes that the potentially greater proximity to health-care providers in urban centers does not ensure access to these providers, theoretical access nonetheless serves as justification in budget decisions. Additionally, IHS services are reserved for members of federally recognized Tribal nations; changing notions of sovereignty increasingly emphasize Tribal control of resources and, with few exceptions, Tribes continue to be reservation-based. Therefore, IHS focuses its efforts on these areas. This institutional organization of resources based on assumptions of access and conceptualizations of sovereignty produces challenges to health-care access for many Native people who reside off reservation or who migrate between reservations and nonreservation locations.

The greatest complaint informants had about IHS was difficulty accessing the services they wanted when they needed them, although many also expressed dissatisfaction with the way they were treated by care providers and office staff, and with long wait times for appointments. Nancy explained, "You can just never get what you need, you know? I mean, it takes forever." Other community members on Pine Ridge described IHS as "a mess" and "a joke." Donna expressed great anger when sharing her experiences at IHS, particularly over clinic wait times, telling me, "I have a job, I can't just take a whole day off to get to the clinic. We're supposed to be getting real health care! They just don't have enough people, or I don't know, maybe all these doctors don't want to work on the rez. I guess we need more Indian doctors, is IHS doin' anything about that?" She further explained that she delays seeking health care because she can't afford to take the time off and gets too angry at the long delays. Other informants shared stories of waiting for months to see specialists (including oncologists), and as long as a year for eyeglasses or dental work. Sarah laughed and said, "It's like those signs they used to have in stores that said 'no shoes, no shirt, no service,' only with IHS it's 'no money, no people, no service.'"

Donna's and Sarah's understanding of one of IHS's key challenges is accurate: delays in care are caused in part by inadequate staffing, an ongoing problem in the IHS system. There are many reasons for this; for example, the majority of IHS facilities are found on reservations that can be isolated and poorly resourced. For non-Native health-care providers who may be far from home and unfamiliar with Native and reservation cultures, this isolation, combined with the often complex health problems of Native people and inadequate resources to address these problems, make working for IHS challenging, as Donna notes when she says, "Maybe all these doctors don't want to work on the rez."

Donna's assertion that "maybe we need more Indian doctors" is equally salient. Approximately 70 percent of all IHS employees are Native, but IHS literature does not indicate exactly which positions these employees fill; anecdotally and from my own experiences in IHS facilities as well as at the 2009 Maternal and Child Health (MCH) conference sponsored by IHS, the majority of direct care providers seem to be non-Native. Yet racial identification may be salient for Native people in their health-care interactions; as Joseph Cooper-Patrick et al. (1999) found in their study of almost two thousand adults, patients in race-concordant relationships with their doctor rated their health care as significantly more participatory than patients in non-race-concordant relationships, even after adjusting for other factors such as age and gender.

Patients are not the only ones frustrated by inadequate staffing. Betty, a former midwife with IHS on Pine Ridge, listed "paper-chasing" as her number-one frustration and the long work hours as her second. She described six- and seven-day work weeks, averaging well over fifty hours a week, in order to meet the clinical needs of the reservation's residents, and added, "then when they come in you have so little time with each of them, because you know there are more in the waiting room. You just feel like you're always falling behind." At the 2009 MCH conference, many health-care providers expressed frustration with their work conditions, although they universally expressed a strong commitment to providing quality care to their patients. Many providers were particularly discouraged by IHS regulations, which often require them to refuse service or send patients elsewhere because they simply do not have access to the equipment, personnel, or time to meet their needs. Thomas Sequist et al. (2011) found similar responses in their study of IHS: 32 percent of responding physicians reported inadequate access to high-quality resources, and only 29 percent reported access to high-quality specialists. Betty and other care providers also expressed frustration with Native clients who wait too long to seek care, although they were quick to acknowledge obstacles such as lack of transportation, geographic isolation, and lack of information. However, not all care providers are so understanding; at a clinic on Pine Ridge I overheard two physician's assistants discussing "these people with all their problems"; in fact, everyone in the waiting room overheard this conversation, as it occurred just behind the receptionist's counter. Nonetheless, among care providers it seems that frustration is directed more toward what they described as a well-intentioned and essential but overworked, inefficient system than toward individual patients or administrators.

Addressing the continuing shortage of health professionals was a major component of both the director's Strategic Vision for 2006–2011 and the Indian Health Care Improvement Act of 2010. Recruitment efforts in recent years have improved to include loan repayment plans and more competitive salaries, as well as increasing scholarship dollars for Native students entering medical training. In addition, IHS has expanded its Community Health Representatives program. These CHRs serve a valuable function by filling in some of the gaps left by inadequate staffing, for example through home visits and community education on diet and nutrition. They are not classified as health professionals, although they are required to complete extensive and ongoing training and are paid employees of the Tribal nation they serve (funds are provided through IHS in adherence to the Indian Self-Determination Act).

In 2003 approximately 95 percent of IHS health professionals and engineers were commissioned officers in the USPHS, including 45 percent of IHS physicians. Thus, a high number of medical professionals who serve Native people are not directly employed by IHS or Tribal nations, but by the separate federal agency of the USPHS. This poses potential problems for Native people, as USPHS officers are available for deployment elsewhere as needed. For example, over twenty-four hundred USPHS officers were deployed to the Gulf region in the months following Hurricane Katrina, including many serving in IHS. The removal or potential removal of health professionals who provide service to Native Americans creates further uncertainties about the quality and continuity of care in an already overstrained system, as noted by several of my informants.

When I asked Anne, a twenty-six-year-old mother of two, about her experiences with IHS, she sighed in frustration:

> You just never know who you're gonna see, or how long it's gonna take. IHS is just a pain, y'know? I mean, you wait all that time, and then you barely get to talk to them. They just don't care. I never felt like they cared what happened to me. Even when I was pregnant and they would talk to me about breastfeeding and stuff, I felt like it was all about the baby and nobody cared about *me* [laughing]. But I guess it's supposed to be about the baby, right?

Anne is thus made invisible twice in her health-care interactions; she is unable to develop any kind of relationship with her care provider because she may not see the same person twice and doesn't have enough time with them to develop a rapport, and during her pregnancy her care focused on "the baby" rather than her own needs.

Anne's understanding that "it's supposed to be about the baby" is a common one both on the reservation and in mainstream society, echoing dominant discourses about the primary function of women's biology, which is to produce babies; her laughing reference to this maxim justifies the neglect of her own needs because after all, pregnancy is "about the baby," not the pregnant woman. Popular pregnancy books such as the ubiquitous *What to Expect When You're Expecting*, breastfeeding support groups such as La Leche League, and even medical school educations reinforce this ideology by neglecting sustained considerations of women's personal needs in favor of providing information on the medical needs of the fetus, the physical changes wrought during pregnancy, or the health benefits of breastfeeding for infants (see Bobel 2001; Martin 1989; Soliday 2009; Strong 2003). Similarly, pro-life discourses that value the future life of the unborn over the life of the pregnant woman ignore the broad array of social contingencies in which women experience pregnancy and motherhood. This elevation of the health of fetuses, babies, and children over the health of women, even women as mothers or potential mothers, echoes the Victorian sentimentality that framed the "Save the Babies" campaign (see Chapter 5) as well as the twenty-first-century move toward preconception care (see Chapter 4). It also speaks to the construction of reproductive health care as primarily about the body, as opposed to a holistic understanding of health and wellness such as that developed in reproductive justice framings, which insist on sustained consideration of the intersections of physical health with economic, spiritual, mental, and emotional health in community contexts.

Unlike Anne's dissatisfaction with IHS, Christina, a Lakota elder, was adamant about the good work being done by IHS on Pine Ridge and blamed any faulty care within IHS on the federal government's failure to provide adequate funds. However, Christina does not use IHS services herself, but has relied on private insurance through her employment for the last several decades. Nonetheless, she insisted that "people need to take care of themselves. They need to get to the clinic, or whatever. The government can't do everything for us." She is right, of course; the government (or IHS) can't do everything, and there must be some individual responsibility for health and health care. At the same time, Christina's failure to consider the obstacles that may impede access to health care reveals the strength of two dominant discourses on the reservation: the individualist ethos that shapes mainstream discourses around health care, and the role of an abstract "government" that Native people understand is not fulfilling its obligations, even if they are unsure of the exact details. For Christina, responsibility for poor health *care* resides with the "government," which must provide better funding; responsibility for poor *health* resides with the individual, who must make better choices. Structural limitations or institutional obstacles are not a part of this nexus. Yet as this research reveals, the institution of IHS often mediates the relationship between the abstract "government" and the individual, and its role cannot be discounted.

Eligibility: Producing "Indian-ness"

The chronic underfunding of IHS has resulted not only in long delays and decreased services to Native people, but also in increasingly restricted and complicated eligibility requirements. Some scholars and Native activists argue that the eligibility requirements of IHS are too restrictive and unfairly limit access to services, particularly in urban areas (see, e.g., Forquera 2001; Sanderfur, Rindfuss, and Cohen 1996). From the perspective of IHS, however, limiting eligibility is necessary in light of severely restricted resources. More broadly, eligibility requirements also reflect the ongoing efforts of the settler State to eliminate the indigeneity within its borders through what Ward Churchill has described as "statistical extermination" (2003, 222).

A claim to Native identity is essential in order to receive services from IHS, in every case except when a non-Native woman is carrying a Native child (in which case the non-Native woman is entitled to prenatal and neo-natal care as well as birth services), or when a medical officer determines that care for a non-Indian member of an Indian household is necessary to prevent a public health hazard. In direct-service IHS facilities (as opposed to contracted facilities), Native identity is generally understood liberally to include not only direct descent and formal enrollment, but also family and community standards of acceptance. Contracted facilities generally adhere more strictly to formal eligibility criteria, which often obstructs the care Native people who live off reservation can receive. However, even formal criteria are at times highly ambiguous; over thirty legal definitions have been proposed and developed by various apparatuses within the federal government in efforts to determine who is and who is not eligible for federal services. These definitions have frequently served an exclusionary purpose as the State has sought to curtail the extent of indigeneity within its borders. The most common criterion put forth continues to be that of blood quantum, a means of measuring racial authenticity reminiscent (and reproductive) of nineteenth-century eugenics.

The practice of measuring the quantity of Indian blood an individual possesses began in the early twentieth century as a way to reduce federal expenditures for Indian education and has continued as a way to determine inclusion into or exclusion from Tribal and federal services. Although the Bureau of Indian Affairs asserts that it in no way requires Tribes to rely on blood quantum in determining their membership, in 2000 it published regulations outlining the standards necessary for Native people to receive a Certificate of Degree of Indian Blood (CDIB) card. Applicants for the card are required to submit a completed genealogy with supporting legal documents such as birth certificates or proof that an ancestor was listed on the Dawes Allotment rolls to demonstrate their direct descent from an enrolled member of a federally recognized Native nation. The CDIB, which impacts eligibility for a number of federal services, thereby proves sufficient indigeneity by relying on blood quantum measurements to validate genetic inheritance of race.

The assumption that race can be biologically quantified, aside from simply being erroneous, ignores the social and political constructions of race as these shift and evolve to reflect State needs in the production of a (fictive) collective ethnicity. For example, the biological construction of race inherent in blood quantum measurements was legally and socially codified in the antebellum period to produce more Black bodies through the assertion of the "one-drop" rule, which dictated that any measure of African ancestry—even "one drop" of blood—marked one as black, and thus enslaveable. For Native Americans, blood quantum is used for opposite purposes: one cannot be legally considered Native American without *enough* Native ancestry. Further, this biological assertion of race reflects a deeply held heteropatriarchal conceptualization of family, which excludes nonbiological relatives; one cannot obtain the prescribed degree of properly authenticated blood through adoption, marriage, or other social rites of family making. Queer relationships are rendered virtually invisible in this matrix, and virtually unproductive of family.

An additional complication to Tribal enrollment derives from the increasingly complex heritages of many Native people whose blood quantum may cross racial and Tribal boundaries. According to Matthew Snipp (1991) and Kenneth Payson (2003), Native people have had a high outmarriage rate (approximately 50 percent) for several decades; the result is an increasing number of Native people who claim multiple heritages, whether these are all Native or include non-Native descent. The 2010 census found that almost half of all Native Americans are of mixed heritage, and this sector of the Native population is the fastest growing (Norris, Vines, and Hoeffel 2012).

The courts have repeatedly recognized the rights of Tribes to determine their own membership, and this right remains arguably the most essential component of self-government. The rules for this membership, which vary widely by Tribe but nonetheless generally continue to rely on blood quantum measurements, are encoded in Tribal constitutions that are varyingly influenced by the federal government. With the growth of self-determination, however, community standards are increasingly considered as a measure of eligibility for Tribal services. These often eschew formal enrollment requirements in favor of community involvement; one's status in the community, language ability, and even long-standing residence can often lead to recognition as "one of us" regardless of enrollment or even racial/ethnic identification (IHS n.d.; Pfefferbaum et al. 1997). As Louis, a forty-four-year-old *wicasa wakan* (medicine man) on Pine Ridge told me, "It's not about a number [Tribal enrollment number issued to enrolled members] . . . it's about how you were raised. It's about how you treat your relatives." In Louis's calculation of belongingness, identity is produced through the social performance of relationship—"how you were raised . . . how you treat your relatives"; the number of Tribal ancestors or how far removed they are from the Dawes allotment rolls is not relevant to him.

Given increasingly community-driven understandings of membership that often work outside of or even reject federally derived criteria for enrollment, many Native nations have been reluctant to fully equate formal Tribal membership with eligibility for services. However, while some Tribes are eliminating formal blood quantum criteria, others are adopting stricter blood quantum rules to determine eligibility; this excludes Native people who may be actively involved in their communities but whose blood quantum is not high enough to meet descent requirements for a particular Tribe. The need for recognition based on blood-borne or even community-based identity and the fact that such recognition almost always privileges one or more identities over others produces political and epistemological complexities that reflect the slipperiness of political constructions of race. For example, my informant Nancy has enough blood quantum to enroll as Oglala Lakota, but not enough to enroll as Hopi. She feels "shut out" of her Hopi community. She told me, "I mean, I feel like they accept me and all, but it's just easier up here [on Pine Ridge] 'cuz I'm enrolled here, so I spend more time here and then I lose touch with my family down there." Nancy's need to reside where she can access services is driven by her blood quantum, but the result is that her cultural identities must also be differently valued and enacted.

Additionally, Tribal membership does not provide for federal services unless the Tribe is federally recognized. Historically this recognition was conferred through treaties, acts of Congress, presidential executive orders, and federal court decisions—settler State apparatuses. In 1978 the BIA issued regulations governing any further instances of federal recognition; these include historical and continual identification as a Tribe, historical and continual habitation on land identified as historically Tribal, a functioning government and constitution, and a membership roll based on criteria determined by the secretary of the interior. All of these rules rely heavily on confirmation by individuals and groups outside the petitioning Tribe. Because of these complications, many Native people are not enrolled in a federally recognized Tribe; as well, many Native American Tribes are not federally recognized. The criterion of enrollment in a federally recognized Tribe thus both works to potentially reduce the number of Native people whom the federal government recognizes as such and simultaneously reifies an externally authenticated racialized identity as "Native" for those who do access federal services such as IHS, thereby discursively marking them as "others" in the (fictive) collective ethnicity.

On reservations, many Native people access health services based on Tribally defined standards, which may include informal community recognition, but Native people who live off reservation may have difficulty accessing IHS or Tribally contracted services, partially due to federal and Tribal enrollment regulations and partially due to a dearth of urban facilities, as well as the often isolated geographic location of many Tribal centers where the majority of IHS facilities are located. Formally, the legal right to access health care through IHS, whether in reservation communities such as Pine Ridge or in urban communities, remains based on an exclusive formulation of what it means to be "Indian," a formulation that is largely derived from the long and convoluted legal relationship between Native nations and the federal government, and the validity of this claim to Indian identity is subject to the authority of various parties and complicated by multiple federal interventions and varied Tribal requirements.

Not only the political construction of race but also the political economy of class organizes Native peoples' access to IHS care. Because Native people are statistically the poorest in the United States, IHS is often the only way they can access medical care. Approximately 60 percent of Native Americans carry private insurance that can be used at both IHS and non-IHS facilities, but many of these people live off reservation in communities that are underserved by IHS, and thus may rely on other avenues for medical care out of necessity if not out of choice. Under the current IHS funding structure, Native people must apply for and utilize Medicaid/Medicare if they are eligible before they can access IHS services, which were originally intended to be available regardless of income. Several of my informants described their frustration with this process, which must be repeated each time they visit IHS facilities regardless of their previous eligibility; Michelle, an enrolled member of the Oglala Lakota Nation, described a recent visit to an off-reservation clinic contracted to provide services by exclaiming, "There I was, fillin' out those forms *again*! I don't need Medicare, I just need to see the doctor!"

In this way, Native people seeking health care from IHS are not only specifically raced (as quantifiably and verifiably Native American), but also classed (as eligible for or ineligible for Medicaid/Medicare). Health care thereby becomes a public negotiation between the individual, the health-care facility, the Tribal nation, and the State. Successfully negotiating this health-care transaction requires the performance of a certain kind of Indian-ness, wherein blood and economics intersect to impose a form of marginalized inclusion in institutionalized health care. Criteria based on this Indian-ness must be met in order to receive IHS services, whether those criteria derive from Tribal requirements, community standards, federal requirements, or IHS rules; a Native person must prove that she is Native, and in some cases, that she is Native enough, or even the right kind of Native; this then becomes conflated with economic class before she can receive care. Her race, class, and citizenship statuses are thereby rendered questionable, and her access to health care relies on her ability to provide the "right" answer. If she is able to do so, she can access care through IHS, but this inclusion into care is rendered potentially less valuable by the economic marginalization of health care for all Native Americans. Native women are still further marginalized in this system by gender and sexuality, as discussed in Chapters 7, 8, and 9.

IHS and Reproductive Health Care on Pine Ridge Reservation

Pine Ridge Reservation is located in the Aberdeen Area of IHS, which serves eighteen Tribes in North Dakota, South Dakota, Nebraska, and Iowa. In 2010 Senator Byron Dorgan, chair of the Senate Committee on Indian Affairs, described the Aberdeen Area as in a "chronic state of crisis" and in need of urgent reform. Among other concerns, his report identified substantially reduced health-care services due to lack of qualified providers and funds;

missing or stolen pharmaceutical narcotics; substantial financial mismanagement; emergency department deficiencies; and active care providers with expired, revoked, or suspended State licenses (Dorgan 2010). Or as my informant Tracey put it much more succinctly, "IHS is just a mess."

The work of IHS on Pine Ridge Reservation clearly encompasses many challenges. One of these is the inadequacy of its facilities; it is widely acknowledged by IHS that their facilities are too few and that many of them are outdated (Trujillo 1996). These deficiencies are due in large part to inadequate funding, although changing relationships with Tribal nations and the evolution of health care in the United States, as well as local IHS and Tribal mismanagement of funds, may also contribute. Pine Ridge has a total of five health facilities, including a hospital, two health centers that are partially managed by the Tribe, and three health stations that offer limited services. The Tribe operates a mobile school-based clinic, which tests adolescents for sexually transmitted infections and offers other limited services in partnership with IHS, and a mobile women's health unit travels throughout the Aberdeen Area offering mammograms, cervical cancer screenings, and other limited services. With the exception of the hospital, all health facilities on the reservation have limited and sometimes irregular hours. Additionally, pharmacy hours on Pine Ridge are limited, and clinic pharmacies are not adequately staffed.

As is the case with other rural health-care systems, there can be a considerable distance between a health-care facility and a community or individual place of residence. The Aberdeen Area of IHS defines reasonable access as a two- to three-hour drive (Aberdeen Area Health Services Master Plan 2003), but given the paucity of resources on the reservation, these distances may be prohibitive for many women who do not drive, do not have regular access to transportation, or must share transportation with family members. For example, Tracey, a twenty-seven-year-old mother of two, described having to share her car with her boyfriend, who would leave with it for days at a time whenever they fought. Nancy also shares one car with family members, at least two of whom require regular transportation for work. This, of course, is not only an inconvenience for Native patients on the reservation; it can be actively detrimental to their health. I spoke with several people who had waited over two hours for a pharmacist at one of the clinics before being told that there would be no pharmacy services until later that day. One of these was an elder waiting for blood pressure medication. Her grandson had driven her to the clinic and waited with her, losing half a day at work; they chose to remain waiting at the clinic because she needed her prescription that day, rather than try to return another day. The grandson was angry at the loss of his workday, but his grandmother expressed patience tinged with resignation, shrugging, "What can you do?" Her acceptance of both the inconvenience and her grandson's lost wages indicate the relative frequency of such occurrences.

The Midwifery Opportunity

IHS has been employing midwives since 1969, and Native women seeking reproductive care on Pine Ridge will most likely find a physician's assistant or a midwife as their provider on the reservation. In fact, Native Americans are more likely than any other ethnic group to receive their care from a midwife, and five times more likely than white non-Hispanic women (Parker 1994); there simply are not enough obstetricians employed by IHS, and none on Pine Ridge. Alternatively, women on Pine Ridge may seek other forms of care off the reservation, utilizing contract health services (which can be difficult to access due to costs, Tribal regulations, and transportation challenges), relying solely on Medicaid to obtain services completely outside of the IHS system, using private insurance if they have it, or paying for services out of pocket. Although the low number of obstetricians working for IHS is probably related to the lower costs associated with midwifery care and the difficulty in recruiting and retaining obstetricians and gynecologists to work long hours in often isolated areas, it has served to create a fairly unique ideological and practical space in terms of reproductive health care. The midwifery model of care is increasingly recognized as patient-friendly and is promoted by feminist scholars and health activists as one that encourages patient agency and minimal intervention except when necessary (Cragin 2004; Hatem et al. 2008; Rothman 1982; Wagner 2008).

Unfortunately, this opportunity has not been taken up in any meaningful way on Pine Ridge Reservation. Despite the potential empowerment to be found, informants generally expressed strong resistance to midwifery care. Twelve of the sixteen women informants who are not themselves health-care professionals or activists expressed a distrust of midwives' training and a preference for an obstetrician/gynecologist (see Chapter 7). Sarah, a fifty-six-year-old Sicangu Lakota who was born on Rosebud Reservation but has lived on Pine Ridge for forty years, told me, "They [IHS] use midwives who aren't even done with their training. That woman over in Oelrichs lost her baby a couple years ago because the midwife didn't know what she was doing. Guess the IHS can't afford the doctors." On the other hand, I heard anecdotally from several community members on Pine Ridge and elsewhere, including the First Annual Maternal and Child Health Conference in March 2009, that midwives offer a valuable and well-respected service to Native women. Unsurprisingly, informants with a professional or activist health-care background (three of whom are midwives) were strongly supportive of the midwifery model, largely for its flexibility and its potential to empower patients.

A great deal of the controversy over midwifery on Pine Ridge stems from a lack of understanding of the extent of training midwives undergo; they are widely perceived by informants and community members as less capable than obstetricians. Tracey explained that she actually stopped using IHS because "they would only let me see a midwife." When I asked her if she thought midwives and obstetricians were different, her response was, "Well, yeah, I mean, doctors are more trained and stuff. They know what they're doing better." She added, "I just always wanted a doctor, 'cuz that's the person who will be delivering my baby. I'd rather have them there. My doctor . . . like, she explained what she was there for, and gave me a book and—you know? . . . I really liked that. I don't know, I just felt more comfortable, I guess." Nancy explained that she "just always thought a doctor was more accurate. I mean, midwives can do your birth control or whatever—that's what a midwife always meant to me." Nancy asked if I would ever want a midwife and I explained that I had chosen a midwife to support me in the births of my children and provide my ongoing reproductive health care. She was surprised by this and asked why. I explained that there is a different philosophy of care between midwives and obstetricians and asked if anyone had explained this difference to her. No one had; in fact, none of my informants who were not health-care professionals or activists were aware of a difference in care philosophies between midwifery and obstetrics. My informants were also largely unaware of the extensive medical training certified midwives undergo. The perception that obstetricians are better trained may stem in part from the fact that many women are sent to obstetricians in Rapid City for their births, as explained by Betty, a midwife who worked briefly with IHS, and several other informants. Midwives are perceived as "second rate" according to Donna, the only providers IHS can afford. My informants' preference for the status of credentials attached to obstetrics may also reflect the work of physicians and their professional associations in the nineteenth and twentieth centuries to discredit midwifery and establish obstetrics as the dominant care model (see Wertz and Wertz 1989; see also Chapter 4).

The lack of information about midwifery clearly has a direct effect on not only my informants' understanding of the health care available to them but also their willingness to engage with that health care, contributing to their general unease with midwives and preference for "more trained" doctors who are harder to access on the reservation. Racial identification may also contribute to the lack of acceptance of midwives on Pine Ridge. Although IHS does not provide detailed statistics on the racial background of its midwifery corps, it seems likely a high number are white; in 2008 93 percent of certified nurse-midwives were white; 1.1 percent were Native American (Schuiling, Sipe, and Fullerton 2010). Given Cooper-Patrick et al.'s (1999) finding that patients in race-concordant relationships with their physicians rated their satisfaction as higher than those in interracial physician-patient relationships, and given the fourth-world context of health-care interactions described in Chapters 9 and 10, it also seems likely that non-Native midwives might not be as well received in Native communities as Native midwives.

In fact, Betty, a non-Native midwife who worked for IHS on Pine Ridge, observed that for non-Natives on the reservation, "there is always a feeling of being the outsider," no matter how many friends and family one makes. Although I only lived on the reservation for sixteen months, I can attest to an ambiguous insider/outsider status that was at times emotionally challenging. I was always invited to public occasions such as memorials and pow-wows as well as—increasingly as my time on the reservation extended and I expressed interest—to prayer ceremonies and family gatherings. There were also, however, moments from which I was deliberately excluded—for example, when a conversation suddenly passed from English to Lakota, a language in which I am not fluent. For me, these challenges were mitigated by the knowledge that I was, in fact, a temporary visitor. Currently, although I visit friends and family on the reservation regularly, I am frequently aware of an outsider status in all but the most intimate of my relationships. Again, my discomfort is tempered by the knowledge that I am a visitor, not a resident, and I can (and do) return to a more emotionally comfortable space when I return to my home, where I can be, once again, the raced, classed, and cultural "norm," no longer the raced, classed, and cultural "other." For those non-Natives who seek to build a long-term career on the reservation, it may be more difficult to manage the discomfort that comes from this ambiguous emotional location.

According to Katherine, a Chickasha midwife who works in the Oklahoma Area, midwives seem to experience greater acceptance in other Native communities. This may be related to their institutional location within IHS; for example, the current chief clinical consultant for midwifery in IHS is a certified nurse midwife from the Diné nation who works in the Navajo Area. Her location within the institutional hierarchy of IHS may offer a certain level of professional status in her role as a midwife, while her Native identity may further legitimate her presence as a health-care provider. The Navajo Area of IHS also regularly employs ob/gyns, thus rendering midwives somewhat more optional than they are on Pine Ridge; greater choice of care providers may also lead to greater acceptance of the options available.

There are currently no Native midwives employed by IHS on Pine Ridge Reservation, although there may be a number of Native lay midwives; due to the ambiguous nature of lay-midwifery (lay midwives are not formally medically trained, but gain their knowledge from other midwives and from experience), a more accurate understanding of lay midwifery on the reservation is difficult to determine. The only midwife currently employed by IHS on Pine Ridge is not Native, but is well known by all of my informants, and well respected. Sarah explained, "Well, the people know who you are and they know they can count on you to be there. Amy has been here forever, and we all know we can trust her." Amy has worked as an IHS midwife on Pine Ridge for over twenty years.

It may be not only the length of time one spends on the reservation but also the level of involvement in local events that builds trust between Native women and their care providers; Amy is known to attend community events regularly, to greet people by relationship, and to inquire about family members' well-being. My own experiences living on Pine Ridge also reflect the importance of commitment in terms of both time and involvement: the first year I was there, relationships were often imbued with a cautious hesitancy. When I returned for the second school year, students and colleagues alike warmed to me considerably, as my return signaled my commitment. Similarly, when I began to attend different ceremonies as well as public events, community members began to call me by relationship rather than name—*takoja* (grandchild) or auntie—signifying their increasing acceptance of me. Time as well as effort are both necessary to build trusting relationships. However, the high rate of turnover in IHS signals a lack of commitment and inhibits the growth of this trust, which can be challenging to create and sustain regardless of personal commitment.

Although many of the challenges facing IHS may not be reasonably within its purview, the State's role in actively providing or withholding myriad resources necessary for the adequate provision of health care on Pine Ridge, from funding to personnel (and including, for example, access to potable water and adequate housing, as discussed in Chapter 2), reveals the double discourse at work in its relationships with Native nations. When contextualized within the history of formal Native-US relations, the social consequences of settler colonialism (including but not limited to poverty and high rates of violence) reflect the intersections of political and cultural economies marked by inconsistencies and fractures, and demonstrate the State's overall ambivalence toward the Native people within its borders. In Chapters 7, 8, and 9, I consider the ways in which these complexities further influence Native American women's reproductive health care.

Part III

Consequences of the Double Discourse

Native Women's Experiences
with the Indian Health Service

7

Resistance and Accommodation

Negotiating Prenatal Care and Childbirth

As shown in Chapter 4, close examination of the historical development of reproductive health care reveals the longue durée of ruling relations that organize all women's reproductive health-care experiences, though in different ways. Not only health-care modalities, but even knowledge about the body reflect the influence of these ruling relations. Because IHS is located squarely in the State's ruling apparatuses and relies on an evidence-based model of care that further reflects the strong hand of these ruling relations, it provides a fulcrum through which State goals may be imposed on Native communities, but through which Native people can also exert influence. Health care thereby becomes a primary site of negotiation between assimilative tactics and assertions of indigeneity, both physically and epistemologically.

When asked what reproductive health care means or includes, most of my informants mentioned prenatal care first. According to its 2006–2011 Strategic Vision, its website, and various other literatures, IHS has prioritized prenatal care, and my informants' ready ability to name it as a form of reproductive care may be a result of the extensive efforts of IHS to encourage prenatal care on Pine Ridge and elsewhere in Indian Country. However, when I asked about childbirth, my questions seemed to elicit some confusion at first; as Michelle explained, "Well, you just don't really think about it. I mean, you think about it, like it's going to hurt or you hope everything goes okay, but you don't really think about more than that." In contrast to ongoing public campaigns urging early, regular prenatal care, there appears to be no public discussion of childbirth. This paradox is also found in the macrocosm of mainstream society, where childbirth is largely understood to be a medical event best handled by professionals and thus rarely debated, even as regular, medical prenatal care as an essential aspect of healthy pregnancy is not fully integrated, available, or utilized, although a visible public health campaign encourages women's participation. Certainly the mainstream medical practice of regularly scheduled repetitive prenatal care is neither adequately integrated in, nor adequately taken up by, many Native communities. The reasons for this are numerous and range from lack of access to lack of acquiescence. Similarly, childbirth experiences can become a locus of accommodation, resistance, and control of the pregnant and birthing body, producing complex subjective experiences for my informants and other Native women. These experiences are further influenced by the isolated location of IHS facilities and its chronic underfunding, which lead to limited options either within or outside of the immediate IHS or Tribal system.

Prenatal Care on the Rez

Reliable data on prenatal care access and utilization among Native Americans is difficult to obtain due to several factors. The consistently low response rate of Native Americans to the Pregnancy Risk Assessment Monitoring System (PRAMS), for example, is possibly due to high mobility rates, lower education, and lack of telephone access. In addition, lack of consistent data collection by IHS and incidents of race misreporting in non-IHS facilities contribute to the difficulty. However, IHS confirms a disparity, noting that between 1999 and 2001 only 67.3 percent of Native women began prenatal care in the first trimester as opposed to 83.2 percent for all US races combined. In the Aberdeen Area, the rate was 65.2 percent (IHS 2008). According to the CDC, in 2008 only 55.8 percent of Native women received prenatal care in the first trimester, and 12.4 percent of Native women did not receive prenatal care at all, or did not receive it until the third semester (CDC 2012b).

Prenatal care is thus an urgent matter for IHS, particularly in the Aberdeen Area where pregnant women exhibit high rates of risk behavior during pregnancy. Alcohol consumption among pregnant Native women is higher in the Aberdeen Area than any other IHS area outside of Alaska and more than four times the US all-races rate, and cigarette smoking is approximately three times as high. The Aberdeen Area also has a 49 percent gestational diabetes rate (the US all-races rate is 29.3 percent) (IHS 2008). All of these risk behaviors as well as delayed or limited prenatal care have been linked to infant mortality, which is 28 percent higher among Native Americans and Alaska Natives than all US races combined, despite IHS's ongoing efforts (IHS 2008). According to the CDC, Native Americans had an infant mortality rate of 8.7 (per one thousand live births) in 2008; the all-US races rate was 6.7, and the non-Hispanic white rate was 5.6 (CDC 2009). (It is important to note the racial disparities masked by a "US all races" rate, however. For example, in 2005 African Americans continued to have the highest national rate of infant mortality at 13.63. Cubans in the United States had the lowest infant mortality rate in the country at 4.42; see MacDorman and Mathews 2008.) Within IHS, the Aberdeen Area has the highest rate of neonatal mortality (6.6 per 1,000 live births), and the second highest rate of post-neonatal mortality (6.8 per 1,000 live births) (IHS 2008). Although IHS claims a total infant mortality rate of 6.6 throughout the Aberdeen Area, this rate masks differences among reservation communities; the Aberdeen Area serves eighteen reservations across four states. As well, there is a wide disparity between IHS's officially reported rate of 6.6 for 2002–2003 (ibid) and findings from a recent study of infant mortality in the Aberdeen Area between 1998 and 2002 that revealed the rate to be 12.5: 74 percent higher than the all-races rate, 40 percent higher than the overall IHS rate, and almost double IHS's published claim for the Aberdeen Area (Eaglestaff, Klug, and Bird 2006). The infant mortality rate for Native Americans in South Dakota, where Pine Ridge is located, was 11.6 in 2005, compared to 6.1 among whites (South Dakota Department of Health 2008).

IHS statistics specific to Pine Ridge Reservation are not available, but several sources indicate that the infant mortality rate is approximately three times the national average (see, e.g., Huska 2007; Iyasu et al. 2002; McGreal 2010). In 2005, the national infant mortality rate was 6.86 (MacDorman and Mathews 2008) and the rate in South Dakota was 7.05 (South Dakota Department of Health 2008). Infant mortality in Shannon County, which constitutes approximately two-thirds of the reservation and has a 95 percent Native population, was 13.55, and in Bennett County (which is partially located on Pine Ridge and has a 58 percent Native population) it was 24.69—almost four times the national rate (South Dakota Department of Health 2008).

The link between prenatal care and infant health in the mainstream medical literature organizes IHS policy through the development of ongoing efforts to encourage Native women to access medical prenatal care through IHS and other medical providers (for example, through public education campaigns and the adoption of a model of care known as Centering Pregnancy; see below). At the same time, not all IHS or Tribally run health facilities provide prenatal care. Although most will facilitate referrals to contracted providers, this means the client must be eligible for Contract Health Services, normally restricted to enrolled members of local Tribal nations (see Chapter 6).

Sharing Stories about Prenatal Care

Among the twenty-two Native female informants in this study, there were thirty-six live births. All of my informants except for Donna sought medical prenatal care during each of their pregnancies, although only seven pregnancies received medical prenatal care before the end of the first trimester. Donna did not seek medical prenatal care for her only pregnancy in 1975 because she "didn't trust the doctors . . . and I didn't need to see any doctors, 'cuz I was fine and I had my mom and my cousins to help me." Donna's pregnancy occurred only two years after the American Indian Movement occupied the site of the 1890 Wounded Knee Massacre on Pine Ridge and the same year as a violent altercation on the reservation between AIM activists and the FBI. As described by numerous scholars, activists, and many of my informants, these years on Pine Ridge were marked by regular violence and intense distrust of the government and its agents, including IHS (see, e.g., Brown et al. 1974; Crow Dog 1991; Matthiessen 1991; Means 1996; Smith and Warrior 1997). At the same time, the involvement of AIM and other Native rights groups on Pine Ridge and elsewhere signaled a resurgence of Native pride and nationalism. Donna's avoidance of IHS reflects the general mistrust of Native people on the reservation at the time. Her reliance on support from her family and community (her reference to "cousins" is not a reference to blood relatives, but rather the women in her extended family community) also reflects the revitalization of tradition-oriented practices among many Native communities during those years.

Talia, a twenty-two-year-old Lakota-Dakota mother of two, didn't experience any complications during her previous pregnancies; at the time of our interview, she was in the middle of the second trimester of her third pregnancy after having confirmed she was pregnant with an IHS midwife two weeks earlier. I asked if she would get prenatal care and she responded, "of course!" then joked about the fact that she was already "starting it late." When I asked her why she had sought prenatal care for her first pregnancy, she laughed and responded, "Well, I don't know! You're supposed to, right?" She explained further, "I don't know, I wanted to have all the tests and everything, make sure the baby was okay. And it was fun to get the ultrasounds. I don't know, I just—you're just supposed to! And I wanted to know the doctor who was gonna deliver my baby. In the end it was a different doctor, though, 'cuz I went up to Rapid" (Rapid City, approximately ninety miles from the center of the reservation).

Talia's response describes a pregnancy experience thirty-five years after Donna's, and illustrates a profound shift in the relationship between IHS and Lakota women on the reservation as well as broader shifts in mainstream understandings of the role of medicine in women's reproductive lives. She does not question the importance of prenatal care, although she is starting it late, and she does not question who will support her in delivering her baby, assuming it will be a doctor, although it was a different one than she had hoped. Because she does not question these things, she does not seek alternatives (for example, the use of a midwife or more community-oriented prenatal practices), or perhaps she understands that they are not in fact readily available to her. She has adopted mainstream reproductive health care in ways that Donna actively resisted. It is tempting to wonder about the role of age in this and ask if Talia is simply too young to question hegemonic practices, but Donna was only a year older than Talia when she gave birth in 1975; similarly, they both have high school degrees but no college education. It therefore seems possible that their very different experiences might result from increasing acceptance of IHS on Pine Ridge in the intervening decades, an acceptance that has diminished support for lay medical practices and care provided by community members but strengthened IHS's ability to provide health care. For Donna, the American Indian Movement and the general civil rights activism of the 1970s disrupted hegemonic understandings of the role of the State on the reservation and in Indian Country generally; for Talia, that disruption has been smoothed over and perhaps forgotten or even rejected as she seeks the medicalized experience offered by IHS.

Tracey, who was pregnant with her third child at the time of our second interview (approximately a year after our first interview and her previous pregnancy), explained that although she accessed "pretty regular" prenatal care during her first pregnancy, she had not sought prenatal care until the end of her second pregnancy because she "already went through it. Besides, it's just a pain to go and sit in the office all that time, you know, they always make you wait. But I did go get an ultrasound, and a—what do you call it? Oh, a chart and stuff. Just in case. But then I never went back until like a month before I was due." I asked if she had had any complications, and she replied, "No, it was fine. I mean, I had my mom and stuff, and like I said, I already been through it once. Oh, but I did get that—what's it? Like, your legs feel all funny? But not until the end, and everything was fine. No diabetes or anything." She intended to seek out prenatal care for her current pregnancy, but explained she was "gonna find an obstetrician and not go to IHS." I asked her why she would not go to IHS, and she responded, "I dunno—I just don't want a midwife. I mean, they're fine for your contraception an' stuff, but I want an OB for my baby."

Like Talia, Tracey expressed a strong preference for the status and presumed better training of an obstetrician. However, unlike Talia, Tracey is less invested in regularly scheduled prenatal care (perhaps because she has not experienced any complications during her previous pregnancies or birth experiences, although this was also the case for Talia), and relied on family members and her own previous experience to guide her. In some ways, then, Tracey's experiences land in between Donna's and Talia's; she resisted the medical authority of IHS during her second pregnancy and instead invested that authority in her own experiences and those of the women around her; still, she intended to eventually seek medical prenatal care for her current pregnancy as well as seeking a medical professional to oversee the birth of her child, for which she "wants an OB." While Donna perhaps represents the "before" of IHS's current prenatal care campaigns in her outright rejection of IHS, doctors, and hospitals, and Talia represents the "after" with her understanding that "you're just supposed to" get medicalized prenatal care and her desire for "all the tests," Tracey represents the negotiating subject, at least to a degree, as she insists on using medical care when and how she decides it is best, as opposed to strictly following ACOG guidelines.

Centering Prenatal Care

Over the last several years, IHS has been seeking to build a group model of prenatal care known as Centering Pregnancy in which women of similar gestational age meet several times during pregnancy and the early postpartum period. Professionals within IHS as well as community members recognize the potential of this model, which is used on several reservations, to encourage the development of culturally appropriate methods of regular prenatal care (Allee 2008), and it was featured in several sessions of the First Annual Maternal and Child Health (MCH) Conference in 2009 as well as the Second International Meeting on Indigenous Women's Health in 2011.

Centering Pregnancy offers several advantages to IHS: it can be utilized in a culturally appropriate manner because it is largely directed by Native participants, although it also allows private time with a midwife or doctor; it incurs no additional cost, and in fact may reduce costs; and it may serve to further invest Native women in their own pregnancy and postpartum health as they develop community networks through the group. This last advantage is particularly important given the high rates of risk behavior during pregnancy in Indian Country. For example, group members might support pregnant women who are trying to quit smoking, or share transportation to group meetings (which are also attended by a midwife or physician). Importantly, the Centering Pregnancy model of care promotes a synthesis of both evidence-based medical care and tradition-oriented knowledge sharing around the reproductive body. On the Diné Reservation, this model of prenatal care has been received with great success, despite initial concerns that tradition-oriented Diné women might find it intrusive. It has also recently been taken up and well received on Akwesasne Reservation in New York, due in part to the efforts of Mohawk midwife Katsi Cook. The Centering Pregnancy model has not yet been instituted on Pine Ridge, and none of my informants had utilized it for their own care.

Native Women's Childbirth Experiences

Previous research on childbirth has tended to focus on economically privileged and/or white women, particularly in urban centers (see, e.g., Leavitt 1986; Nelson 1986; Oakley 1980; Wertz and Wertz 1989). Although some studies have included the experiences of women who do not inhabit these social categories (see, e.g., Lazarus 1994; Martin 1989; Nelson 1983), very little work has been done that offers a sustained intersectional analysis of childbirth for women of color and/or economically disadvantaged women. Even less consideration has been given to the subjective birthing experiences of Native women.

Although scholars have largely neglected a sustained analysis of Native American women's subjective birth experiences, Native women themselves have begun to tell these stories with increasing frequency over the last several decades. Few Native women have written explicitly and at length about the experience of childbirth itself, although individual First Nations women such as Leanne Simpson (2006) and Kim Anderson (2006) have written about their personal politicization as a result of the births of their children, and Mary Crow Dog (1991) describes her first birth experience (which occurred during the 1973 siege at Wounded Knee on Pine Ridge reservation) as a deliberately political act. As well, several Native women have written poetry or essays specifically about their birth experiences (see, e.g., Harjo 1990, 1997; Tapahonso 1987), and several, like Mary Crow Dog (1991), have included the experience of childbirth as part of a larger narrative (see, e.g., Alvord and Van Pelt 1999).

There is currently no research examining the subjective experiences of Native women giving birth on Pine Ridge Reservation, where the only childbirth facility available is Pine Ridge Hospital. This may be due in part to the lack of a permanent obstetrician and the limited midwifery services on the reservation, which requires many women to travel to Rapid City for their births. Of the thirty-six live births I cited above, only eight occurred at Pine Ridge; fourteen occurred at Rapid City Regional Hospital, and fourteen elsewhere (including other IHS facilities as well as non-IHS facilities). Thirty-four of the thirty-six were hospital births. Of the two that occurred out of hospital, one was a planned home birth and one informant gave birth in the car on the way to the hospital. Micah lived approximately ninety minutes from Rapid City Regional Hospital at the time and had no phone or car; she had to walk to a neighbor's house to use their phone and wait for transportation. Her son crowned as her husband pulled into the hospital parking lot, and she told me, "By the time he threw it into park, I was already holdin' him."

When I asked informants who had given birth at Pine Ridge Hospital to describe their experiences, Nancy replied, "Oh, you know. You've done it . . . it was hard. It really hurt. Lyle [her boyfriend] was there, and he was really freaked out," she added, laughing. "An' my mom." I asked her how long the birth had taken and she replied, "Oh, I think about sixteen hours. I kinda lost track of time." I asked if there had been any interventions during labor and she was unsure what I meant, so I prompted: was she given pain relief? How did she handle the pain? Did she have a fetal heart monitor or an IV? "Yeah, I had an IV . . . and I walked a lot, me and Lyle and my mom, up and down the hall. They wouldn't give me any pain medication, I was really pissed, but my mom said I could do it. Then I got in the shower for a while, and then it was time to push!" I asked if, looking back at the experience, she would change anything, and she replied,

> Oh, I dunno. I mean, it was really hard. But I guess it was good that I did it without all the medications and stuff. At one point I was really scared they were gonna wanna do a cesarean, and then they were talking about sending me up to Rapid . . . I didn't wanna go, I just wanted to stay there. My mom said, "No way she's going to Rapid, she'll give birth in the ambulance!" [laughs] I dunno what I would change . . . maybe all those people checkin' me all the time, you know how that is, but they were pretty nice.

Like most women who give birth at Pine Ridge, Nancy labored and delivered with a midwife and nurses, stayed in the same room through labor and delivery, and her newborn stayed with her rather than being taken to a nursery (an increasingly common practice in many hospitals, including IHS facilities).

Sarah, who also gave birth at Pine Ridge Hospital, was much more expressive than Nancy about the pain, laughing while she told me, "Oh, we did it all natural back then . . . no drugs at all! Shit, it hurt like hell!" Her labor lasted about twenty-four hours, and she told me, "At the end, I knew if I didn't push they were gonna wanna cut me open and do a cesarean, so I pushed *hard*!" Sarah gave birth to her only child in the early 1980s and was attended by an obstetrician. She recalled, "I didn't like him, but that may have just been 'cuz I was so mad about the whole thing. All that pain and everything. Oh, I was just cussin' him out!" Overall, she described the experience of birth as "really incredible. But I didn't want to do it again!" When I asked why not, she replied laughing, "It hurt too much! Besides, I was all set once I had Mark." Sarah's mother also attended her childbirth, but Mark's father was "nowhere to be found."

Donna chose to give birth at home and explained, "I didn't need a hospital. We didn't trust the hospitals, either." I asked her who had helped her, and she replied, "Well, my mom was there, and my *unci*" (elders are often referred to by relationship; *unci* is Lakota for "grandmother," but this does not necessarily indicate a genetic relationship). Although Donna avoided interaction with formal medical providers during her pregnancy and her childbirth, her daughter, like Talia, has given birth to all of her children in a hospital, although none was on Pine Ridge and only one of her daughter's three birth experiences was in an IHS facility. When I asked Donna how she felt about the differences between her own and her daughter's birth experiences, she shrugged and replied,

She's gotta make her own decisions, just like I did. Besides, I was with her the whole time, just like my mom was with me. And I think . . . I don't know, but maybe it's not as bad as it used to be with the IHS. I guess I kinda wish she hadn't gone to IHS, but it's harder now to find women who can help you with that. You know, back in my day we still had some midwives, and there were all these other women around who had been through it, but now all the midwives work for IHS anyway. And they're white, which isn't totally a bad thing, I mean if they're here to help, then fine, but it's not like they know all the traditional ways.

Thirty-five years after the birth of her child, Donna continued to express a preference for midwives over obstetricians, and perhaps particularly for Native midwives, who might better "know all the traditional ways." Throughout our interview Donna was very clear in her dislike and distrust of IHS, but in thinking about her daughter's decision to give birth in hospitals, one of which was an IHS facility, she begrudgingly wonders if things have gotten better with IHS and makes note of how it might be more difficult now to find support to give birth outside of the hospital. Times have changed. Her daughter, like Talia, made choices that are different from Donna's because her daughter, like Talia, grew up in a world where IHS and the settler State that directs it have become more integrated in the communities on Pine Ridge than they were in the midst of the Native revolutions that occurred throughout Indian Country in the 1960s and 1970s. Similarly to the experiences described by Kim Anderson (2006), Mary Crow Dog (1991), and Leanne Simpson (2006), Donna's own experience birthing her daughter can be understood as a political assertion of identity: as a young Lakota woman in the midst of a political and cultural resurgence on Pine Ridge, Donna sought and obtained a birth experience that she describes as "traditional," without the interventions of State-directed health care. This emphasis on a sense of traditional identity remains important enough to her decades later that she regrets the potential loss and displacement of tradition-oriented birth knowledge via the introduction of predominantly white midwives.

When I asked other informants if they had ever considered giving birth at home, virtually all of those without medical training told me they would never choose to do so. Tracey explained, "The hospital's just safe, y'know? I mean, what if something goes wrong?" Nancy was shocked at the idea of choosing to give birth outside of a hospital, asking, "Why would you do that? Did you do that?" I responded that I had given birth to my children in a Birth Center, which is similar to a hospital in some respects but uses a midwifery model of care with minimal medical interventions. She responded, "You mean you didn't have any drugs or anything? Oh, I would never do that. I wanted the drugs."

In fact, several of my respondents cited pain management as a top priority in their birth experiences. Pain management (such as the use of epidurals as well as meditation techniques or Lamaze breathing techniques) can certainly be understood as a form of agency in childbirth, as women may use it to retain some control over the experience, although none of my informants who cited pain as a primary concern in childbirth spoke about managing it in order to exert control or agency; for them, pain was simply something to be avoided. However, despite their desire for pain relief, at Pine Ridge Hospital where Nancy and several others gave birth, epidurals are not available. Betty shared that other pain management might be available (for example, through an IV drip), but explained that epidurals are not available at Pine Ridge Hospital because of the cost.

When I asked informants if any had used tradition-oriented birth practices during their births, Donna laughed and replied, "Well, yeah, the whole thing was traditional. I mean, we weren't in a tipi, but everything else was." She described burning sage and sweetgrass in the room where she gave birth and the practice of having a woman elder (her *unci*) wipe the mucus from her newborn's mouth. (I was told during my own pregnancy on the reservation that I should choose an elder to do this, and that that woman would be like a role model to my child; I was advised to choose carefully a woman I would want my child to be like.) She also said it was important to have water, not only for drinking and cooling off, but also because "*mni* [water] is a powerful relative." Aboriginal midwife Katsi Cook has spoken similarly of water, explaining that "the mother's milk and the water and our blood is all the same water. It puts you in that state of relationship" (Wessman and Harvey 2000). One other informant said that she had burned sage, a common cleansing practice, at Pine Ridge Hospital, and Emma told me that at the birth of her second child her sister came and sang "woman" songs for her during labor. The informants who gave birth at Rapid City Regional said they had not used anything "traditional." It hadn't occurred to Anne at the time, and Michelle didn't think the hospital would allow it and so didn't ask.

Two informants who are professional midwives (one Native, one white) spoke about the use of traditional medicines during childbirth. Betty told me that on Pine Ridge, many women want to burn sage in the labor and delivery room and that IHS allows this, although the hospital administration must be informed first due to possible fire hazard. Charlene, a Native midwife who trains other Native midwives and doulas (birth assistants), explained that IHS has been increasingly flexible about allowing tradition-oriented practices, telling me, "They're really getting much better, but still they don't do it enough." IHS's efforts were also confirmed in several sessions of the First Annual MCH Conference. One speaker, a midwife from the Navajo Area, explained that many women, especially grandmothers, want to bring in "tea" (peyote tea) when a woman comes to the hospital in labor. Ingesting peyote is not allowed during labor and delivery at IHS facilities, as the effects on the baby are unknown. She tells the women, "Grandmother, your granddaughter is so strong and her baby is so strong that she doesn't need that tea right now." She suggests that the grandmother wet her hands with the tea and rub the birthing woman's belly with it. When I later asked Charlene about this, she explained, "It's important to have what you need [during labor], and if they need the tea, they should at least have it in the room, even if they don't drink it."

Michelle's assumption that IHS wouldn't allow her to burn sage in the hospital room, like the lack of knowledge about midwifery, indicates that better informing Native women of their options during pregnancy and childbirth might lead to a fuller engagement and a more satisfying experience. Although IHS formally requires informed consent for all procedures, Native women generally do not seem well informed about the range of possibilities available to them, or the advantages and disadvantages of these possibilities. The cultural competence of the Navajo Area midwife who finds a way to allow peyote tea to be a part of the birthing process without disrupting IHS medical practice illustrates the ways in which Native women, their families, and their communities can be better served during pregnancy and childbirth. This type of cultural competence creates a sense of safety and confidence for Native women and empowers them in their health-care experiences, as discussed further in Chapter 10.

Choice and Childbirth

The question of choice and agency in childbirth has been thoroughly examined by feminist scholars (see, e.g., Davis-Floyd 2004; Jordan 1992; Kornelsen 2005; Martin 1989; Rothman 1982). For Native women, as for many women in the United States and elsewhere, agency in childbirth is circumscribed by a number of factors including their own health needs, the resources available to them, and the hegemonic framing of childbirth as a medical event. For example, although many of my informants felt they had had satisfying birth experiences, supported by the family members and partners of their choice, Nancy and Sarah both described feeling worried that they would be forced into a cesarean section if they did not give birth quickly enough. Emily Martin (1989) and Marsden Wagner (2008) examine similar feelings and experiences among laboring women, both white women and women of color. Native women, however, are the least likely in the country to have a cesarean section, with rates as low as 7 percent in some IHS areas (Leeman and Leeman 2003), compared to over 30 percent for the US population as a whole (CDC 2011b; Menacker and Hamilton 2010). Many factors contribute to this differential rate, including IHS's reliance on midwives (who do not perform cesarean surgeries) and the cost of cesarean sections, which require the expertise of an anesthesiologist as well as an obstetrician. Regardless, the fear is still present for Native women, as it is for many women in labor (Martin 1989; Wagner 2008).

Also similarly to many other women, Native women's agency in childbirth is limited by the kind of care available. This is a particularly acute issue for Native women in reservation communities, whose reliance on IHS services and facilities limits their choices of provider and location, and also, at times, even the timing of their birth. In response to my questions about birth outside of the hospital, Emma, a fifty-seven-year-old Lakota woman from Cheyenne River Reservation, told me, "Women do it all the time around here! [laughing] You can't get to the damn hospital!" Women living on the Cheyenne River Reservation, a Lakota reservation north of Pine Ridge, are severely limited in the reproductive care they can receive. There is only one small medical facility on Cheyenne River and no hospital, which means there is no birthing facility at all on the reservation. Women must travel at least ninety miles to reach the nearest IHS-contracted hospital, St, Mary's, for prenatal care during their pregnancies as well as for labor and delivery. St. Mary's is a Catholic hospital, and as such further limits the care that all women can receive there, as it will not provide contraception of any sort, including emergency contraception or tubal ligation.

In late 2009, the American Civil Liberties Union of South Dakota filed a request under the Freedom of Information Act with IHS seeking to learn why plans to build a hospital on the reservation, approved in 2002, had not progressed despite recent additional funding from the American Recovery and Reinvestment Act of 2009. In pursuing information about the need for a birthing facility on Cheyenne River, the ACLU learned that many women had been coerced into inducing labor early at St. Mary's. These inductions often occurred without prior notice, and thus women were unable to have family present or to plan for an extended stay away from home. According to the ACLU suit, "these women fear that if they refuse to be induced, IHS, which they rely upon for health care, will refuse to subsidize the cost of labor and delivery." Further, "these women also report that they do not receive any counseling regarding the risks and benefits of inducing labor and delivery and forgoing spontaneous labor and delivery" (ACLU 2010, 5).

The inherently coercive nature of these fears and lack of information directly violates Native women's right to health and the conditions for health, and belies the federal government's unique responsibility for the health of Native people. Moreover, by failing to provide an adequate medical facility on Cheyenne River Reservation but rather contracting with a facility that is both a considerable distance away and restricted in the care it can provide, the federal government through IHS not only fails to adequately provide for Native women's reproductive health, but in fact actively produces structures that violate the rights of women who live on the reservation. At the beginning of 2014, IHS had not yet responded to the suit filed by the ACLU in late 2009 seeking information about the delayed construction of the medical facility on the reservation, or the suit filed in late 2010 seeking information about coercive induction.

Emma pointed out that women on Cheyenne River are aware of the risk of induction at St. Mary's, "but we've got nowhere else to go. I mean, that place is far enough!" I asked her if she thought prenatal care was impacted by the lack of a birthing facility on the reservation and she replied, "Well, I think you can get prenatal here on the rez, but a lot of women wanna go for their care where their doctor is, so yeah, a lot of 'em probably don't get enough prenatal care, either." Like Pine Ridge, Cheyenne River has a high rate of poverty, and transportation may provide an additional challenge when women have to travel for care.

As this chapter reveals, pregnancy and childbirth are important locations from which to consider the ruling relations that organize Native women's reproductive health-care experiences. For example, although prenatal care is a priority for IHS, it is clear that Native women are not accessing and utilizing prenatal care at the same rates as other women in the United States. The reasons for this are complex and derive not only from the care provided by IHS but also from other factors, such as isolation from care facilities, lack of transportation, lack of consistency of care produced by inadequate and changing medical staff, and Native women's own decisions. Childbirth presents an additional set of concerns for Native women who may not be able to access facilities either on or off their reservation without fear of coercive practices that will directly affect their experiences.

The agency and choice I was able to exercise for the births of my two children stand in almost direct opposition to the experiences of my Native relatives. I chose not to have an obstetrician, though they were easily available to me, and was guided through both of my pregnancies by the midwives of my choice. I was able to access prenatal care regularly and with comparative ease, and I avoided medical interventions I didn't want to engage by choosing to give birth in a birth center, where these interventions are not practiced. The control and agency I was able to exercise were structurally supported by the choices available to me in providers and location, and this allowed me to feel fully engaged in the process of birth without worrying about unwanted interventions or removal to another location.

I am acutely aware now, as I was when I first left the reservation to give birth to my son in Connecticut, that my opportunity to experience pregnancy and birth this way was profoundly dependent on the result of accumulated advantages afforded me through my race and class statuses, among others. As this research reveals, these advantages have been integral in the production of very different experiences for me than the experiences of my relatives on Pine Ridge and elsewhere in Indian Country. Not all women who share my social and political privileges or other advantages similar to mine share pregnancy and birth experiences similar to mine—or perhaps even want to—for a variety of reasons. These reasons do not necessarily, although they may, affect women's agency or otherwise shape their subjective experiences of pregnancy and childbirth. However, although pregnancy and birth experiences themselves may share many similarities within and across social, economic, and political statuses, the ruling relations that bring women to these experiences are not identical. The unique and particular restrictions navigated by Native women emerge from the race, class, gender, sex, and citizenship statuses that direct them to IHS, and reflect the broader double discourse that informs their relationships with the settler State that provides their health care. The consequences of this double discourse affect their access to prenatal care and a range of choices in childbirth, regardless of their individual decisions. These consequences also affect their access to safety and justice as well their ability to avoid unwanted pregnancies, as discussed in the following chapters.

8

One in Three

Violence against
Native Women

When I taught at a high school on Pine Ridge Reservation, one of my students, a junior, became pregnant. Amelia was a good student and a star cheerleader; the reaction from teachers and her cheerleading coaches was one of dismay and disappointment, punctuated by comments such as "What were you thinking?" and "Why would you let this happen?" Other teachers at the school would simply shake their heads or opine, "happens all the time" (and in fact, it does; see Chapter 9). Just before I left the reservation to give birth to my own first child in Connecticut, Amelia came to my apartment for a goodbye visit. In her seventh month of pregnancy, she had a visible bruise on her cheek. I asked her what had happened and although she was initially evasive, she eventually revealed that her boyfriend—the father of her unborn child—had smacked her during a fight. It wasn't until that moment that I realized her pregnancy may have been the result of rape.

According to a report by Amnesty International (2007), Native American women are over two and a half times more likely than other US women to be sexually assaulted; more than one in three will be raped in her lifetime. All of my informants on Pine Ridge think this estimate is too low. Even Amnesty International has said this number might be too conservative, and other studies indicate higher numbers when other forms of violence against Native women are included; using the National Violence against Women Survey,

Patricia Tjaden and Nancy Thoennes (2000) found that almost 65 percent of Native women surveyed reported experiencing rape or physical violence. Lawrence Greenfield and Steven Smith (1999) found the average rate of rape and sexual assault among Native Americans to be approximately 3.5 times higher than the all-races rate of approximately one in five.

Despite the urgency, the issue of violence against Native women remains understudied, although in recent years there has been increasing scholarly interest as well as some increased response from the federal government (including increased funding from the Obama administration for medical training in IHS to improve care for survivors). While Amnesty International's report focused on legal responses to sexual violence, other scholars have looked more closely at both the prevalence of violence against Native women and the links between violence and socioeconomic factors. For example, Lorraine Malcoe, Bonnie Duran, and Juliann Montgomery (2004) found 58.7 percent of respondents in a Tribally operated clinic in Oklahoma experienced physical or sexual violence from an intimate partner during their lifetime, and that low socioeconomic status was strongly associated with violence. In an earlier study, David Fairchild, Molly Fairchild, and Shirley Stoner (1998) also found a correlation between low socioeconomic status and domestic violence in a Diné community in Arizona. Both of these studies concluded that rates of violence in Native communities were disproportionately high. Additionally, these and other studies (see, e.g., Bachman et al. 2008) reveal the interconnected nature of forms of violence; rarely does sexual violence occur without other forms of physical and verbal violence, for example.

Interpersonal violence was not a key question in my original study; in fact I had, with perhaps great cowardice, hoped to avoid it. Although I do antiviolence work in my activist and academic lives, I am not a trained counselor. I am, however, fully aware of the high rates of violence against Native women, and I feared the emotional consequences for my informants if I delved into this area too deeply. I did not feel prepared to keep them emotionally safe in such a conversation, nor did I have adequate information on local resources (because, in fact, there are very few of these). Nonetheless, violence came up as a topic over and over.

The first time was in an interview with Sam, a forty-nine-year-old Lakota man who was born in Oakland, California, but moved to Pine Ridge during high school. When I asked him what he thought were the biggest areas of need in terms of health care for Native women I expected him to identify prenatal care or perhaps adolescent pregnancies, but his first response was, "Well, we gotta take care of all these rapes. Our women are getting hurt all the time." Sam's insistence on making visible the epidemic of violence against Native women was repeated in almost every interview I conducted. In fact, several of my informants who are professional health-care providers or advocates insisted that it be included in the overall study. Charlene, a Native midwife and reproductive health activist, argued vehemently that to neglect violence against Native women weakened my overall focus on reproductive justice, asserting that "there is no justice if women are afraid all the time." She is right, of course; sexual health, including sexual safety, is a major component of the reproductive justice framework. Sexual violence has direct effects on reproductive health, including risks of unintended pregnancies and sexually transmitted infections as well as physical and emotional injury. Violence against women also produces other consequences for women's reproductive freedoms, however, particularly as a link to other forms of structural violence such as poverty and racism. Additionally, as Native antiviolence activists and scholars assert, Native women's physical safety is directly linked to conquest, assimilation, and eradication, as their reproductive bodies provide the settler State with the means of population control and their physical violation enacts a symbolic violation of the Tribal community, as discussed below.

For Native American women, safety, including freedom from physical and sexual assault, is inextricably entwined with health care due to their reliance on IHS. The complex of regulations and resources deriving from the federal government organizes Native women's access to treatment and justice after assault, and may in fact be a potential factor in allowing the general lack of consequences for perpetrators, thereby tacitly permitting if not actually encouraging violence against Native women. Therefore, although violence against Native women was not an intended direction of research for me, I include this chapter in response to the urging of my informants and relatives. The need to do this, and the insistence of so many of my informants that it be done, calls into question the focus on issues of contraception and abortion access in mainstream discourses of reproductive health care; reproductive justice, and our conversations about it, must expand to consider a far wider array of issues.

The Native Body as Political Pollution

The shocking prevalence of violence against Native women reflects deeply held social ideas about gender and sexuality as well as unarticulated political anxieties about indigeneity. As Theo Goldberg (2002) argues, the racially configured other is viewed by the State as a pollution that threatens security, cultural normativity, and the availability of resources by challenging the national narrative of unity and collectivity. Native Americans present a unique threat to the nation-building project of the United States due both to their continued occupation of land within US political borders and their claims to sovereignty—indeed, to existence. Therefore, as the Cherokee scholar and activist Andrea Smith explains, Native people must disappear from the national narrative; "in fact, they must *always* be disappearing, in order to allow non-indigenous peoples rightful claim over this land" (2006, 68, italics original). As the settler State seeks to create a new narrative of belonging with its own carefully designed and managed collective at the center, the hegemonic citizen (white, able-bodied, heterosexual, cisgender) displaces Native people to become the new indigenous of the land.

This displacement is both made possible by and continually reproduces the ideological construction of Native bodies as "others" in a process Smith describes as "the metaphorical transformation of Native bodies into a pollution of which the colonial body must constantly purify itself" (2005, 9). Thus marked as a source of pollution to the national body, Native bodies are stripped of value and become violable. At the same time, Native bodies provide the necessary "other," the "not us" within the (fictive) collective of the national body. The settler State thereby enacts an unending performance of genocide: Native people are always in the process of disappearing but never quite gone completely, for if the violable bodies disappeared completely and the pollution were permanently removed, then how would the settler State determine its ideological boundaries? How would the collective body be defined without a challenge against which to define—and defend—itself?

The history of the settler State's efforts to "disappear" Native peoples is rife with particularly gendered violence. Smith (2005) argues that sexual violence is a tool by which whole communities become marked as "rapeable," and that this tool has been wielded against Native peoples since the beginning of the contact period between Natives and Europeans (see also Stannard 1992). Although sexual violence as a tool of conquest has been wielded against both Native men and Native women, it has landed with unique force on the bodies of Native women. Paula Gunn Allen (1986) argues that the ideological subjugation of Native women was particularly necessary in order to accomplish the cultural domination of Native people, as Native women's statuses in different Native communities often challenged the imposition of settler colonialism, and in particular patriarchal imperialism (see also Anderson 2000; Guerrero 2003; Hart and Lowther 2008; Maracle 1996). The physical domination and assault of Native women's bodies both produced and justified subjugation by attacking not only their bodies but also their social statuses within their communities. Rendered physically and ideologically violable by Europeans and European Americans, Native women thus become the symbol of European Americans' dominance over Native communities (Agtuca 2007; Mankiller and Wallis 1993; Smith 2005; Stannard 1992). Used in this way, the bodies of Native women represent the political bodies of their people; their violability and disappearance produce and reflect the disappearance of Native people from the US political body.

Sarah Deer, a Muscogee antiviolence activist and legal scholar, explains that "it is often difficult for [Native American women who have survived rape] to separate the more immediate experience of their assault from the larger experience that their people have experienced through forced removal, displacement, and destruction" (2005, 455). Or, as Donna put it when the question of violence came up in our interview, "They just keep on raping us. The land, our children, the schools. You just keep on raping us." I don't believe Donna thought I had physically attacked any Native people; but my whiteness situates me within the dominant culture, and for Donna, the dominant culture is a rapist culture; my whiteness marks me as part of the "you" that continues to rape Native people, physically and ideologically. The violent erasure of Native people from the mythology of the nation's new world order is reinforced through and reproduced by the physical violence against Native communities and particularly against Native women, and Native women know it.

Additionally, the nature of violent acts against Native women can be particularly vicious. For example, during the course of my research I was told of a woman who was tortured and mutilated after she was repeatedly raped and before she was left to die in a ditch on Pine Ridge Reservation. Unfortunately, I often hear stories similar to this from the reservation. Ronet Bachman (cited in Deer 2005) notes that there is evidence to suggest that sexual violence against Native women involves a higher level of additional violence than usual; whereas rape is always an act of violence and 30 percent of women in the general US population report additional injuries, 50 percent of Native American and Alaska Native women report additional injuries. Andrea Smith (2005) cites numerous historic and contemporary examples of the sexual assault, torture, and mutilation of Native women (see also Stannard 1992) and situates these within a project of colonization that allowed and allows for the continuing violation of Native women's bodies in order to disappear Native people. She argues that sexual mutilation of Native women has its roots in European American conquest of North America, and is inextricably tied to the racialization of Native Americans, which produces their violability as an "other" who pollutes the national body. This is reflected in the fact that approximately 57 percent of the men who sexually assault or rape Native women are white, a particularly startling statistic given that the majority of sexual assaults and rapes in the United States are intraracial (Bachman et al. 2008).* It is important to note, however, that Native women also experience high rates of violence from other Native people, including family members (Amnesty International 2007; Gardner 2007; LaPointe 2008).

* Amnesty International's estimate that approximately 86 percent of those who attack Native women are non-Native men is widely cited, as is Steven Perry's (2004) finding. However, Perry's finding included both male and female victims; given my focus here on women's experiences, I rely on Ronet Bachman's 2008 finding of 57 percent, which excludes male survivors (according to Bachman et al. (2008), 10 percent of Native women's attackers are Black; 33 percent are American Indian/Alaska Native or Asian American).

There are many reasons for the high rate of violence against Native women: economic depression and rural isolation from resources; lack of law enforcement resources; and a jurisdictional maze that renders conviction of perpetrators extremely challenging certainly contribute (Amnesty International 2007; Dimitrova-Grajzl, Grajzl, and Guse 2013). Several Native activists also point to the history of colonization that has nearly destroyed traditional family and community structures, as well as distorted traditional gender roles; weakened if not outright eliminated traditional spiritual practices and resources; and destroyed traditional economies and linguistic structures (Anderson 2000; Artichoker and Mousseau 2006; Wahab and Olson 2004). Certainly the violences of the boarding school experience are implicated, as numerous scholars assert (Giago 2006a; Noriega 1992; Smith 2005). Rather than explore possible causes, this chapter specifically considers the linked roles of the State (particularly Congress) and IHS in addressing the intersections of violence and reproductive health care. Safety, justice, and wellness are three distinct issues, each seemingly belonging to three distinct areas of regulation and practice. A close examination of the matrix of domination that organizes Native women's experiences of violence reveals, however, that these seemingly disparate areas are closely related, and their absence in Native women's lives is mutually reinforcing.

The Indian Health Service and Sexual Assault Care

Since the release of Amnesty International's 2007 report *Maze of Injustice: The Failure to Protect Indigenous Women from Sexual Violence in the USA,* and also following criticism from the US Commission on Civil Rights (2003) and due largely to the efforts of Native activists such as Cecilia Fire Thunder, Sarah Deer, and Andrea Smith, there has been a growing focus on violence against women throughout the IHS system. In 2009 the IHS Maternal and Child Health website had a dedicated linked area to issues of violence against women; this included a fact sheet as well as a short video of parents talking to their adolescent children about dating violence. There was also a long list of links for care providers on clinical issues, a section devoted to community action, which included a public service announcement, a link to a relevant document library housed by the University of New Mexico, links for patient education and provider education, a link to a list of policies and procedures, and several other links as well. In fact, this was perhaps the most extensive area of the MCH website before it was removed; in 2014, there is no dedicated web space for maternal and child health on the IHS site, and this information is no longer as easily accessed.

National data indicate that women are at greatest risk of intimate partner violence during their reproductive years (Tjaden and Thoennes 1997), and regular screenings for domestic violence are strongly encouraged by the CDC in its *Healthy People 2020* objectives, as it was in *Healthy People 2010*, and by both the American Medical Association and the American College of Obstetricians and Gynecologists. Betty described IHS's initiative to screen regularly for domestic violence during pregnancy, explaining that it should occur every trimester. However, such screenings rely on Native women regularly accessing prenatal care, and need to be conducted in culturally sensitive ways.

Several informants shared their experiences of being screened for domestic violence on several occasions during prenatal check-ups. Nancy found this intrusive and racist, exclaiming, "I mean, would they keep asking a white woman all those questions? Would they keep asking you?" I told her I had never been asked about violence in any medical check-up. She conceded that "it's better that they ask than that they don't, I guess. Still—y'know?" Her frustration at what she perceived to be racist assumptions (that a young, pregnant Native woman must be involved in a violent relationship) was somewhat mollified when I shared with her some of the statistics around violence against Native women. She told me, "I know it's bad and all, but I just never experienced anything like that. I have friends who did, though."

Unfortunately, despite expressed commitment to detecting and preventing sexual assault through the use of screenings and public education, IHS's engagement with the issue of violence against women has not yet produced substantial improvement in the quality of care it offers to survivors. According to Amnesty International, many IHS facilities do not have clear protocols for treating survivors of sexual assault and do not consistently provide sexual assault forensic examinations. These findings have been confirmed by the US Commission on Civil Rights (2003, 2004) as well as NAWHERC, the Native American Women's Health Education Resource Center (2005). NAWHERC found in a 2005 study that 30 percent of responding IHS facilities did not have a clear protocol in place for the treatment of sexual assault survivors or the collection of forensic evidence. Of the facilities that did have a protocol in place, only 56 percent reported that it was posted and accessible to staff members.

Appropriate medical care includes not only treatment for injuries and psychological counseling but also treatment for sexually transmitted infections and access to emergency contraception. Yet according to NAWHERC (2005), 44 percent of the IHS facilities surveyed lacked personnel trained to provide emergency care to survivors of sexual violence. There was simply no one employed at these facilities who was professionally trained to provide care for these women, in communities that experience the highest sexual assault rates in the country. There are no data publicly available on how many IHS facilities do have adequately trained sexual assault providers, but Amnesty International (2007) indicates that it is fewer than 10 percent. This lack of care was confirmed by Betty, who told me that during the two years she worked on Pine Ridge, there was no one on staff at Pine Ridge Hospital who was trained to conduct a forensic examination (commonly known as a "rape kit"). She further explained that when sexual assault survivors come to the Pine Ridge Emergency Room, they may be turned away completely "because no one wants to mess up any evidence." This was still the case in early 2011 when I asked Jaydeen, an antiviolence activist originally from Pine Ridge who now lives in nearby Rapid City, about sexual assault care on the reservation. This lack of care directly violates the National Protocol for Sexual Assault Medical Examinations issue by the Department of Justice (Department of Justice 2013). Federal funding initiatives since 2009 have allowed for greater sexual assault training for IHS personnel, and in early 2012 trainings were scheduled for the Aberdeen Area (where Pine Ridge Reservation is located) as well as several other areas.

In areas where IHS does not provide emergency services for sexual assault survivors, women may need to travel up to 150 miles round trip to reach a facility where a forensic examination can be performed and appropriate medical care provided. Additionally, many IHS facilities are closed over the weekend or only offer services during the daytime. Given the dearth of care available in IHS facilities, Native women may need to be transferred to an unfamiliar facility, possibly without family or friends who may have otherwise been available; further, this transfer requires transportation, which is not provided by IHS; as well, care received in non-IHS facilities may not be culturally appropriate. Amnesty International (2007) reports that if a Native woman seeks care at a non-IHS facility (even if sent there by IHS) she may be charged by that facility for her examination. IHS does have a reimbursement policy for contract health services, but survivors may not be aware of it (Amnesty International 2007; see also NAWHERC 2005; US Commission on Civil Rights 2003) and in some cases, IHS has failed or refused to pay for forensic examinations at outside facilities (Amnesty International 2007).

For decades an additional complication to providing care on Pine Ridge derived from the criminalization of alcohol on the reservation; Pine Ridge was a dry reservation where possession of alcohol was illegal. According to Betty, women seeking care for a sexual assault who went to the emergency room of Pine Ridge Hospital might first be tested for their blood-alcohol level. If alcohol was detected, they might be subject to arrest. Betty and Jaydeen both felt this possibility inhibited women from seeking care. At the very least, as Jaydeen explained, "It's insulting. Whether or not a woman is drinking should never affect whether or not she can get care for sexual assault." In August 2013, Tribal members voted to lift the ban on alcohol sale and possession on Pine Ridge, in a profoundly controversial public referendum (the final vote count was 1,843 in favor of legalization and 1,678 opposed; the number of votes cast represents a small minority of eligible voters); whether or not this will impact women's willingness to seek medical care if alcohol is involved in a sexual assault remains to be seen.

The consequences of this obstructed care for Native women are many; for example, Native women who wish to press charges against their assailant may have trouble doing so or be actively discouraged from doing so due to inadequate forensic evidence or complete lack of it. Both NAWHERC (2005) and Amnesty International (2007) cite this obstacle as contributing to the number of unreported cases, as Native women understand the challenge of conviction when physical evidence is lacking. More important, women simply cannot access the care they need after being sexually traumatized, and/or cannot access this care without fear of possible arrest.

The Links between Care, Safety, and Justice: Federal Indian Policy

Providing safe and adequate care for Native survivors of assault is further complicated by the convoluted legal systems that have arisen around Native sovereignty and Tribal jurisdiction. Much of this convolution is due to Public Law 280, passed by Congress in 1953, which directly hampers Tribal jurisdiction and privileges regional state jurisdiction over criminal acts committed on reservation lands. In sixteen states and for 23 percent of the reservation-based Tribal population, PL 280 imposes regional state privilege in the prosecution of all violent crimes committed on Tribal land and restricts or prohibits Tribal jurisdiction, particularly against non-Native perpetrators. In essence, this means that Tribal police and courts in states where PL 280 is active have virtually no power over non-Native criminals, even if those perpetrators reside on Tribal land or are married to Tribal citizens, an interpretation upheld by the US Supreme Court in *Duro v. Reina* in 1990. This has intersecting race, sex, gender, and citizenship consequences for Native women, reflecting a uniquely legislated vulnerability to their racialized/"othered" identities that reproduces the historical use of sexual violence as a tool of conquest, as a disproportionate percentage of their attackers are non-Native. It also undermines the sovereignty of Tribal nations by restricting their jurisdictional authority.

Public Law 280 is widely understood as part of the federal government's broader agenda to reduce its responsibility to Native nations and reflects the ideological construction of Native people as a dangerous pollution to the general national body that needs to be controlled and managed by the dominant culture. Tribal law expert Carole Goldberg explains that at the time of PL 280's passage, "reservations were described as places of rampant crime and disorder. Public Law 280 was supposed to provide the solution to this problem of 'lawlessness' by empowering state . . . courts to do what the tribal and federal systems supposedly could not" (1996–1997, 1408). The Senate report containing the justification for PL 280 never acknowledged some of the central problems of Tribal law enforcement, including the passage of previous legislation impacting Tribal jurisdiction (such as the Major Crimes Act of 1885, which placed several crimes under federal jurisdiction if committed by a Native American against a Native American) or the federal government's continued reluctance to invest resources in reservation law enforcement.

At the same time that passage of PL 280 reflected prevalent ideas about reservation lands as lawless and in need of containment as well as the State's efforts to parse out its financial obligations to regional states, it was also predicated on the idea that Native people had reached a stage of social development that enabled further assimilation. For example, in discussions of the law one senator noted that Indians had "reached a state of acculturation and development" that would allow for a smooth transition into mainstream society (quoted in Twetten 2000). All three goals—to reduce federal responsibility, to contain potential pollution of the general population, and to further assimilate Native people into the collective ethnicity of the United States—culminated in the passage of PL 280.

Although ostensibly intended to enhance safety for Native people by relocating criminal jurisdiction to better equipped and staffed regional state systems, PL 280 in fact resulted in the institutional neglect of criminal prosecution against non-Natives who commit violent crimes against Native people by increasing reliance on these distant judicial systems. According to the US Government Accountability Office (GAO) (2010), between 2005 and 2009 US attorneys declined to prosecute 52 percent of violent crimes that occurred in Indian Country; 67 percent of these were sexual abuse cases (South Dakota, where Pine Ridge Reservation is located, was the top district requesting federal investigation). The GAO found that 42 percent of declinations were based on weak or insufficient evidence, directly related to the lack of care provided by IHS (GAO 2010).

A direct consequence of this lack of formal justice is the rise of vigilante justice in Native communities; as Carole Goldberg argues: "Public Law 280 has itself become the source of lawlessness on reservations. . . . jurisdictional vacuums or gaps have been created, often precipitating the use of self-help remedies that border on or erupt into violence . . . [and] where state law enforcement does intervene, gross abuses of authority are not uncommon" (1997, 12). This conclusion was confirmed recently by Valentina Dimitrova-Grajzl et al. (2012), who found in a study of counties where PL 280 is active that it directly contributed to an increase in crime by Native as well as non-Native offenders.

One informant for my study, a twenty-one-year-old Lakota woman and a survivor of assault, asserted that "these white guys, they just come onto the rez and do whatever they want. Nobody cares. There ain't nothin' you can do about it." A second informant, twenty-three years old, described being stalked by her former boyfriend, who had also threatened members of her family. When I asked if she had reported this to the police, she responded, "The Tribal police can't do anything—he's not from Pine Ridge. Besides, it happens all the time. It's no big deal out here." These women had both heard of PL 280 but when I asked, neither could explain or describe it; one said only, "Yeah, that's that law thing with the police, right?" However, knowing the legal history of Tribal jurisdiction is clearly not necessary to understand the effects of that history on daily life. This informant understands that a "law thing" that was passed a long time ago—long before her parents were born—continues to impact her access to justice today.

In July of 2010 President Obama signed the Tribal Law and Order Act (TLOA) into law. TLOA is intended to address some of the issues created by PL 280, particularly around jurisdiction and funding and training for Tribal police, and to improve communications between Tribal, regional state, and federal authorities, enhance research capabilities, and improve the delivery of victim services. According to the US Departments of Justice and the Interior, major foci (developed in consultation with Tribal leaders) also include developing alternatives to incarceration and culturally appropriate programming for juvenile offenders (Department of Justice 2011). Following passage of TLOA, in 2011 the Office for Victims of Crime provided funding to three Tribal governments and organizations to improve their capacity to address the needs and rights of sexual assault survivors. In 2012, the Department of Justice, in partnership with Tribal leaders and IHS, began to train Sexual Assault Response Teams, beginning with reservation communities in Montana.

The TLOA is potentially a strong tool for both justice and safety in Indian Country; ultimately, Native women are likely to see improved policing and investigations as well as improved care. However, TLOA is also an interesting legislative site to consider the ongoing struggle over sovereignty and its meanings in the relationship between the settler State and the Tribal nations within its borders. For example, TLOA empowers federal roles in Indian Country by authorizing the deputizing of special US attorneys, enhancing Drug Enforcement Agency powers, and granting concurrent jurisdiction to federal courts over public lands. The strengthened presence of the State on Tribal land will hopefully improve safety, but it also potentially further confuses rather than clarifies accountability and responsibility for investigations and prosecution. Most important, despite its stated goal to combat violence against Native women, the bill fails to recognize Tribal authority to prosecute rape and other serious felonies and continues to restrict Tribal jurisdiction. The welfare and safety of Native women are inextricably linked to the ability of Tribal authorities to address the violence perpetrated against them, yet rather than enhance the powers of Tribal systems to do so TLOA further strengthens the role of the settler State in Indian Country and reproduces the paternalism that marked the passage of PL 280 in 1953.

The Discourse of Violence in the Twenty-first Century: Race, Gender, Sexuality, and the State

Although a positive step forward in many ways, TLOA reveals the State's ongoing racialization of Native people, which is always already gendered and sexed. For example, prevention measures in TLOA are focused primarily on Native men, who commit fewer than 33 percent of violent crimes against Native women; the non-Native men who commit over 67 percent of rapes and sexual assaults against Native women remain largely unaddressed in prevention efforts. The racial dichotomy embedded in this legislative framework potentially relies on and reproduces common stereotypes of Native men as savage, uncivilized, and dangerous, and Native women as victims ("squaws" or drudges) of Native men and Native society in general. At the same time, the actual violence of non-Native (and predominantly white) men is made invisibile, relying on and reproducing ideas of white men as civilized saviors. Ironically, through TLOA, Native women (the presumed victims of Native men) are placed under the protection of these civilized white men through the racial, patriarchal State.

The racialization, gendering, and sexualization of struggles over sovereignty and safety also informed debates surrounding the 2013 Violence Against Women Act (VAWA). VAWA has historically included the safety and care of Native women survivors, and included specific provisions for Native women since 2005 due in part to the work of then-senator Joe Biden, one of the key architects of the original bill in 1994. However, its renewal in 2012 proved to be politically contentious as the Senate approved, among other changes, increased authorities to Tribal courts to prosecute domestic violence cases against non-Native perpetrators if they occur on Tribal land, an expansion of Tribal jurisdiction from the restrictions imposed by PL 280 which is in line with need and with the intentions of TLOA. Throughout 2012 and into 2013 the House of Representatives attempted to reduce these revisions.

Unlike many previous pieces of Indian legislation such as PL 280 and termination policy, the reasoning behind efforts to block VAWA's revisions was not financial austerity; their excision from the act would not affect financial obligations to Tribal nations at all. The response of the Republican-dominated House of Representatives to the proposed changes to VAWA—in essence, cutting them—relied on the argument that such Tribal powers are unconstitutional. Although the new provisions mandate equal protection under the law for non-Tribal citizens and do not affect state or federal jurisdiction, the justification for removing them rested on resistance to the potential growth of Tribal powers—in other words, Tribal sovereignty. The argument that increasing Tribal jurisdiction is unconstitutional reveals the State's discomfort with the expansion of Tribal sovereignty, even when that sovereignty is limited to crimes perpetrated against Native people, on Tribal land.

The prospect of enhanced Tribal jurisdiction over non-Natives produced and relied on racializing discourses in multiple ways. For example, Senator Chuck Grassley of Iowa told voters at a town hall meeting in early 2013 that "under the laws of our land, you got to have a jury that is a reflection of society as a whole, and on an Indian reservation, it's going to be made up of Indians, right? So the non-Indian doesn't get a fair trial" (quoted in Keyes 2013). Actually, the Sixth Amendment requires juries to be drawn from the "state and district wherein the crime shall have been committed," not "society as a whole." More important, the implication that Tribal courts and Native American jurors are incapable of fair and legal assessment is reminiscent of the debates that shaped PL 280's passage, when reservation communities were discursively framed as lawless and Tribal authorities as incapable, not undermined or under-resourced. Worse, such discourse deflects the white supremacist ideologies that underpin concerns over enhanced Tribal sovereignty by claiming that it is Native people who will act out of prejudicial bias and ignoring the history of State neglect of even investigating allegations against white perpetrators of violence in Indian Country. Grassley's comments revealed the framing of VAWA as a battle for supremacy between Tribal sovereignty and the US Constitution for what it really was: a fight to maintain the settler State's dominance over its (fictive) collective ethnicity. Native women's sexed and raced bodies merely provided the mechanism through which this dominance can be maintained. Their bodies, their health, and certainly reproductive justice for their communities do not merely fall victim to the State's double discourse in its relationship with Tribal nations; they provide the very means through which this double discourse is enacted.

It is important to note that changes in the 2012 version of VAWA also included enhanced protections for LGBT individuals by requiring recipients of federal grants to demonstrate non-discrimination. These provisions met with attack from predominantly Republican legislators as well. Improved services for immigrant women, particularly undocumented immigrants, were also staunchly opposed. Opposition to temporary visas for undocumented immigrants who are the victims of domestic abuse reflected not only the broad-based denial of immigrant rights as these intersect with gender, but also further brought to light the State's discomfort with challenges to its (fictive) collective ethnicity. Multiple sexual and citizenship statuses, which threatened the heteronormative, white supremacist collective ethnicity sought by elite members of State apparatuses, were thereby rendered vulnerable in the debates surrounding VAWA.

The ultimate passage of VAWA in early 2013 despite opposition rooted in heterosexist, racist, and misogynist settler ideologies is a clear victory for feminists and other antiviolence advocates, but VAWA itself is not without its problems, particularly for Native people. For example, Tribes will continue to have narrow sentencing ability (up to three years) and new provisions are strongly focused on domestic and dating violence, potentially neglecting other forms of violence. In addition, and similarly to TLOA, VAWA relies on a criminal justice approach that potentially imposes a strong State presence rather than encouraging the underlying social change needed to address violence in all its forms. As well, the focus in TLOA on violence perpetrated by Native men fails to adequately acknowledge and address violence by non-Native men. Conversely, the lack of consistent and accurate data on violence against women on reservations (which TLOA is intended, in part, to address) and the heavy reliance in VAWA on a narrative of non-Native violence against Native women potentially silences survivors of intraracial violence who may already experience shame, victim blaming, and pressure to remain silent from family members and others.

Taken together, VAWA, TLOA, and the negligence of IHS produce a complicated mix of material and discursive violence against Native women's raced, sexed, and classed bodies. The complex double discourse of care and neglect, control and resistance that organizes this violence reveals the discomfort of the State with indigeneity as it seeks to build and maintain its (fictive) collective ethnicity, but also reveals the resistance of Native people to State control as they continue to seek and build sovereignty and safety through a variety of channels. The prevalence of sexual violence against Native women cannot be excised from the larger social fabric produced by federal Indian policy, as Native peoples' legal relationships with the US government continues to shape in intersecting ways Native women's abilities to live healthy lives, including access to health care and freedom from violence. The role of the State in organizing access to care, safety, and justice is deeply reflective and reproductive of colonialist structures of domination, assimilation, and removal. At the same time, sexual violence against Native women must also be understood as it links to restricted access to contraception, high rates of unintended and adolescent pregnancy, and restricted access to abortion counseling and services, all of which are also organized to some extent by federal Indian policy and the role of the State through IHS. Together, these structures produce profound experiences of reproductive injustice through the mechanism of State-organized and delivered health care.

9

Genocidal Consequences

Contraception, Sterilization,
and Abortion in the Fourth-
World Context

The organization of reproductive health care, even outside of IHS, is often shaped by ideologies of race, class, gender, and citizenship status. However, the IHS system is particularly vulnerable to the shifting political and social intersections of gender, race, class, sexuality, and citizenship because of its reliance on multiple points of authority, including Congress and the president, regional states, and Tribal governments as well as social edicts from religion, tradition-oriented cultural practices and beliefs (which themselves are often influenced by patriarchal colonization), and local and national public opinion. The links between access to contraception, unintended pregnancies (including but not limited to those experienced by adolescents), and abortion services provide a glimpse into the multiple ways in which reproductive health care for Native women is organized in intersecting ways by institutional forces and political and social ideologies. This organization also reveals the double discourse that shapes the settler State's efforts to manage the threat to homogeneity presented by Native women's reproductive bodies.

Contraception and Unintended and Adolescent Pregnancy

As evidenced by conservative responses to the contraception mandate in the 2010 Patient Protection and Affordable Care Act (as evidenced, indeed, by the fact that a legal mandate to cover contraception costs even needs to exist), women's sexual and reproductive freedoms remain controversial in the twenty-first-century. Our national reluctance to make contraception available and affordable affects all women, regardless of race, sexuality, class, and citizenship, but, as with so many aspects of reproductive justice, it is poor women who are most deeply affected by restricted access, as economically privileged women (who are predominantly also racially privileged by whiteness) may have greater access to resources. Adolescent women experience even greater restrictions on the resources to explore and control their reproductive bodies, particularly their fertility.

According to the American College of Obstetricians and Gynecologists Committee on Adolescent Health care, each year approximately 750,000 adolescents (under twenty years of age) become pregnant in the United States (ACOG 2007). Roughly 82 percent of these pregnancies are unintended. Native American adolescents are almost twice as likely as young women of all US races combined to become mothers during adolescence: 41 percent as opposed to 21 percent (IHS 2002–2004). In 2000, one-fifth of all births to Native women were to women twenty or younger; the national rate was one in nine (Ventura, Matthews, and Hamilton 2001). It is again important to note here the racial differences masked by "all US races combined"; according to the Kaiser Foundation (2008) Hispanic adolescents have the highest pregnancy rate at 32 percent, followed by African Americans at 24 percent, and Native Americans at 21 percent. The significantly lower adolescent pregnancy rates of white and Asian/Pacific Islander adolescents bring the overall US all-races rate down.

The issue of adolescent pregnancy generally is fraught with assumptions about the role of sexuality, sex education, and sexuality socialization. These assumptions, in turn, are deeply influenced by religious beliefs and race, class, and gender ideologies as well as conceptualizations of citizenship, sexuality, and adulthood. Sociologist Kristin Luker (1984) argues that mainstream American opinion often understands adolescent pregnancy as the result of promiscuity, failure to properly take contraceptives, and an inability to control sexual urges (all faults focused on the individual and neglectful of broader social contexts). Additionally, adolescent pregnancy is frequently framed in the economic terms of its cost to society (Ward 1995), thus further potentially vilifying the pregnant adolescent. Several of my informants became pregnant as adolescents, and each of these pregnancies was, in fact, unintended; however, although adolescent pregnancy is most often unintended, it is important to note that not all adolescents who become pregnant do so accidentally; nor, of course, are unintended pregnancies limited to adolescents.

Overall, there is a dearth of research on Native American adolescents and sexuality, including pregnancy; nonetheless, it is clear that explanations for the high unintended pregnancy rate among Native adolescents are complex and in many ways similar to the causes among all adolescents. For example, Ann Garwick et al. (2008) note that socioeconomic disadvantage has been linked to high rates of adolescent pregnancy, and Brent Miller and Kristen Moore (1990) identified frequency of contraceptive use and effectiveness of contraceptive methods as factors related to adolescent pregnancy. Elizabeth Saewyc et al. (1998) found similar factors among Native American youth who self-identified as heterosexual, gay/lesbian/bisexual, and "unsure." Velma Murry and James Ponzetti (1997) identified similar factors in their study; they also found that educational aspiration and religious commitments tend to delay early onset of sexual activity, which is linked to adolescent pregnancy.

Many factors related to adolescent pregnancy are not reasonably the responsibility of IHS. However, in a recent multicountry study of adolescent pregnancy, Ann Blanc et al. (2009) found that adolescents' success in avoiding pregnancy often depends on having access to contraceptive information, methods, and services, a finding that has been confirmed by the Guttmacher Institute (2009) and the Kaiser Foundation (2008). Ann Garwick et al. (2007) argue that inadequate access to health care may contribute to high rates of adolescent pregnancy for Native Americans and other adolescents of color (see also Center for Reproductive Law and Policy 1998; Davis 2003; Guttmacher Institute 2009). Contraception and health care are the responsibility of IHS. Adolescent pregnancy is a particularly urgent matter on Pine Ridge Reservation: Shannon County (which composes approximately two-thirds of the reservation and has a 95 percent Native population), has an adolescent pregnancy rate of 87.5 percent (South Dakota Department of Health 2008), far higher than the average for all US races combined and more than double the rate for Native Americans overall. Given the reliance of Native women on IHS for reproductive health services, it is important to understand the links between national and local ideas of gender, sexuality, and pregnancy and the ways in which these ideas inform IHS's institutional provision of contraceptive care.

Although sexually transmitted infections (including, increasingly, HIV/AIDS) are a growing area of concentration for IHS and the use of condoms is encouraged for sexually active adolescents (for example, through educational sessions and school clinics), pregnancy prevention receives far less attention in the IHS literature. In mid-July 2009, the IHS Maternal and Child Health website contained a link for family planning which led to several academic articles and included a section on adolescent rights with a frequently asked questions link. The website also offered links to at least two academic articles specific to adolescent pregnancy prevention in the general population. None of my informants who are not health care professionals had visited this site, nor did they know of any peers who had. The Maternal and Child Health section of IHS's website itself is no longer available. Hard copy literature available at IHS clinics contained little to no mention of contraception as a form of pregnancy prevention, nor does the IHS Strategic Vision 2006–2011, although the prevention of sexually transmitted infections is encouraged through abstinence, condom use, and testing.

One possible explanation for the near invisibility of pregnancy prevention in IHS literature may be efforts on the part of IHS and its employees to be sensitive to perceived cultural norms; Sally Davis and Mary Harris (1982), Stephen Kunitz and M. Tsianco (1981), and Charles Slemenda (1978) have all noted in studies on Native adolescent sexuality that community and family norms as well as religious beliefs negatively affect Native adolescents' use of contraception. (It is important to note that the most recent of these studies was almost twenty years ago; the oldest was conducted over thirty years ago. However, Murry and Ponzetti found similar factors in 1997.) As well, M. Liberty, D. Hughey, and R. Scaglion (1976) noted in their study on fertility among rural and urban Omaha that personal preference for many children may be a cultural survival strategy in response to historic and ongoing genocide. Similarly, Mary Crow Dog (an activist with the American Indian Movement throughout the early 1970s) explains that in AIM's philosophy, "birth control went against our beliefs. We felt that there were not enough Indians left to suit us. The more future warriors we brought into the world, the better" (1991, 133). This echoes the pronatalist stance of other civil rights movements of the 1960s and 1970s, in which women's reproductive bodies were centralized in nationalist rhetoric as a means of resisting racist population control policies (see, e.g., Nelson 2003; Ross 1992). Both Crow Dog's story and Liberty et al.'s study are from the mid-1970s, just after the height of American Indian Movement activism. It is unclear whether AIM's pronatalist stance had a direct impact on the respondents in my study or whether these findings would still be valid today or could be generalized to Indian Country broadly. Nonetheless, although a community may embrace population growth for a variety of reasons, a reliance on pronatalist community desires to determine contraception access may work against an individual woman's desire and right to control her own fertility.

There is some evidence of strong community and family support for pregnant adolescents in reservation communities. A recent study of culture and sexual risk-taking among adolescents on a Northern Plains reservation found that teen pregnancy was viewed as a problem, particularly by younger adolescents, but traditionally high cultural value placed on children strengthened family support (Kauffman et al. 2007). A study by Dalla Rochelle and Wendy Gamble (2001) found similar responses on the Diné reservation. Sixteen of my twenty-two female Native informants experienced an unintended pregnancy at some point in their lives (eight of these women experienced unintended pregnancies in their teen years). They all described feeling supported by their families. Tracey explained, "Well, my mom wasn't too happy . . . but she came around." When I lived on Pine Ridge, several female students in the school where I worked became pregnant during the school year. While these pregnancies were often greeted with some disappointment by adults in the community, the young women were never shunned in any way, and in fact, the births of their children were most often celebrated by family and community members. I was invited to several of these celebrations, and was always moved by the plethora of handmade star quilts, beaded baby moccasins, and even cradleboards (all labor-intensive gifts) that were interspersed with the diaper bags, crib sheets, and baby clothes.

As discussed in Chapter 6, access to reproductive health care is limited for Native women on Pine Ridge due to, among other factors, limited funding and staffing and their isolated locations. Yet it is not only access to facilities and providers that may be limited but also access to and knowledge of treatment options. Some Native activists assert that the full range of contraceptive options is not available through IHS and attribute the lack of options directly to physician preference (NAWHERC 2003; see also Arons 2007). This certainly seems to be true in terms of emergency contraception (EC). There is ongoing debate among IHS providers over the distribution of EC through IHS personnel and facilities (see Pittman 2006), echoing the national debate around Plan B (approved by the FDA in 1999) and Preven (approved by the FDA in 1998), which are often erroneously framed in popular discourse as abortifacents. The Public Health Service chief pharmacy consultant has encouraged all IHS sites to develop policies that allow pharmacists to refuse to dispense items based on personal ethics and still make medications, including patient choice of contraception, available to patients (Pittman 2006). However, at IHS sites with only one pharmacist or limited pharmacy hours, the expectation that a patient can access a prescription at another site or at another time may not be viable. The cost to IHS is also a factor in the availability of emergency contraception; in response to the Food and Drug Administration's 2005 decision to approve over-the-counter distribution of Plan B to women eighteen and older, the IHS chief ob/gyn clinical consultant expressed concern that this would limit its availability to Native clients due to higher costs for IHS pharmacies (Fifer 2006). According to a study conducted by NAWHERC (2003), emergency contraception was not universally available at that time through all IHS facilities (see also Smith 2005), and it is certainly not available through all contracted facilities.

On Pine Ridge Reservation at this time, Plan B, which is better tolerated than Preven (with a lower incidence of side effects), is available for women who have been raped; Plan B is not available for women seeking emergency contraception who have not experienced a sexual assault, but the less well tolerated Preven is. Although the availability of EC is organized by both IHS funding as well as, potentially, pharmacists' (and possibly prescribing physicians') personal ethics, this differential access to care simultaneously reflects and produces an ideology of punishment for sexual activity wherein the female Native body is disciplined for its sexuality. Either sexual assault provides an adequate punishment (and better tolerated treatment is therefore provided), or punishment is enacted through restricted therapeutic options following coitus.

In contrast to emergency contraception, condoms are comparatively easily accessed on Pine Ridge, both for free at school clinics and sex education sessions and for purchase in local convenience stores. This may be due in part to IHS's emphasis on the prevention of sexually transmitted infections. Condoms are also more affordable for IHS to obtain and distribute than prescription contraceptives, and in fact can be fairly easily obtained outside of the IHS system for those with access to other resources. However, condoms require the participation of male partners in ways that other contraceptives may not, and thus potentially reduce Native women's personal agency in their sexual relationships. This is particularly relevant given the high rates of sexual violence in Native communities. As Jaydeen, a fifty-seven-year-old Lakota antiviolence activist, pointed out, "women don't always get a chance to say 'let's put a condom on'"; women in abusive relationships may not have the opportunity to use or even discuss barrier methods of contraception, and in fact, numerous studies indicate that control over contraception is a distinguishing behavior of abusers (see Boyer and Fine 1992; Moore, Frohwirth, and Miller 2010; Wingood and DiClemente 1997). Women may prefer non-barrier forms of contraception for other reasons, as well. For example, Tracey described condoms as "gross," and Talia laughed as she said pointedly, "Well, they're kind of a pain, right?"

Oral contraceptives might seem to empower women's sexual agency in the sense that women themselves are fully responsible for them. However, monthly cycle birth control pills, while available through IHS, are dispensed only one month at a time on Pine Ridge Reservation. This necessitates a repeat visit to the pharmacy every month, an obstacle for many women. Limited pharmacy hours further inhibit women's ability to access oral contraceptives and further narrow their options. Given these challenges, contraceptive sterilization and long-term contraceptives may become viable alternatives, but as discussed below, these, too, are complicated by IHS and the hand of the settler State.

Sterilization Racism

The history of coerced sterilizations throughout Indian Country during the twentieth century emerges from a matrix of population control and eugenics that targeted women of color, poor women, and women deemed medically unfit (Reilly 1991; Roberts 1997; Stubblefield 2007), and is considered by many Native people to be part of a continuing State-sponsored agenda of genocide (Johansen 2001; Langston 2003; Lawrence 2000; Ralston-Lewis 2005; Smith 1995). The website of IHS neither confirms nor denies this history. In response to the question of involuntary sterilizations in its frequently asked questions section, in 2009 the IHS website provided links to several resources that "discuss evidence that refutes that hypothesis" (IHS/MCH 2010); one of these links led to an undergraduate term paper. None of the links offered support for the "hypothesis" that Native women were involuntarily sterilized in the 1960s and 1970s. All of these links have since been removed.

However, the occurrence of coercive sterilizations in IHS and its contracted facilities has been increasingly documented since the late 1990s (Johansen 2001; Langston 2003; Lawrence 2000; Ralston-Lewis 2005; A. Smith 1995, 2002, and 2006; see also Torpy 2000). Many Native activists argue that the number of Native women coercively sterilized during the 1960s and 1970s is in fact much higher than previously estimated. Dr. Connie Pinkerton-Uri, who conducted research into coercive sterilization of Native women in the 1970s, estimated that up to 25 percent of Native women of childbearing age were sterilized in some IHS areas. Women of All Red Nations contends that sterilization rates were as high as 80 percent on some reservations (Ralston-Lewis 2005). Between 1968 and 1982, approximately 42 percent of Native women of childbearing age were sterilized, as compared to 15 percent of white women (Ralston-Lewis 2005), although it is unknown how many of these may have been coerced. Due largely to poor record keeping by IHS as well as the potential shame and loss felt by coercively sterilized women, it is unlikely exact numbers will ever be ascertained.

Rates of surgical sterilization among Native women continue to be high in the twenty-first century; in 2004 33.9 percent of Native women were using tubal ligation as a form of contraception (Volscho 2010). The rate for non-Hispanic white women was 18.7 percent. Even controlling for variables such as socioeconomic class, the odds of pursuing tubal ligation as a form of contraception are 123 percent greater for Native women than for white women (ibid.). Although surgical sterilization can be understood as located on a continuum of contraceptive methods, NAWHERC (2008) asserts that many Native women turn to tubal ligation due to a lack of other options or to the limited nature of those options within IHS. This was confirmed by Betty, a former midwife with IHS, who explained in our interview that many women come into IHS seeking tubal ligation because it's "the easiest way to avoid getting pregnant again."

Betty further asserted that women seeking tubal ligation receive counseling by IHS physicians regarding the permanence of the procedure. Additionally, the federal government imposes a thirty-day waiting period for all tubal ligation requests within IHS, a standard protocol that developed following the rise in sterilizations by IHS and the Public Health Service during the 1960s and 1970s. Although a waiting period is particularly important given the history of sterilizations without fully informed consent as well as the current disproportionately high rate of contraceptive sterilization in Indian Country, without concurrently providing better access to less permanent options, a thirty-day waiting period may impose additional hardships on Native women.

Although rates of permanent sterilization remain high among Native women, the use of long-term chemical contraceptives in Native communities has risen since the mid-1980s. Depo-Provera in particular has become increasingly commonly used in IHS facilities, despite adverse side effects and the potential for abuse. Depo-Provera works by inhibiting ovulation for up to three months. Once injected, it cannot be removed from the body, and once the drug is discontinued, the average time to ovulation is just under six months. It is, therefore, a temporary sterilization for eight to nine months at a time, although it is offered as a three-month contraceptive. Additionally, Ralston-Lewis (2005) and Andrea Smith (2002) both assert that many, possibly most, Native women are not fully informed of side effects, which may include depression, osteoporosis, sterility, cervical cancer, and headaches.

Margaret, a thirty-five-year-old mother of four from Pine Ridge, is currently single, so when I asked if she was using a form of contraception she laughed and replied, "Yeah, what do you call it? Abstinence!" She told me she would probably use condoms if she became sexually active now, because "you can't be too careful, right? It's not like it used to be." She relied on Depo-Provera when she was younger because she "didn't want to get pregnant again, y'know? You just go for that one shot, and then you're good for a while, what is it, three months? But I had to get off it, because my moon [menstrual period] would still come, but at weird times, and I never knew when it was coming. And besides, I started getting these wicked headaches, so I didn't go on it no more after that." Although Margaret appreciated the convenience of Depo-Provera, she was unprepared for the side effects and the impact they would have on her daily life. She recalled being told by her health care provider that she might cramp and spot blood for a few weeks after the initial shot, but she was not informed that she would continue to bleed irregularly for months or that she would get migraines.

One of the greatest problems presented by Depo-Provera is the side effect of heavy and irregular bleeding. Native women who are menstruating cannot attend many tradition-oriented ceremonies and in some cultures, neither can their husbands. Additionally, they may not be able to prepare or serve food to others. In many cultures they may be asked to refrain from visiting certain people, such as the sick or the elderly, particularly if those people are in a prayer state or seeking spiritual help. On Pine Ridge, traditional Lakota practices prohibit menstruating women from active involvement in or even attendance at many events; at times, this may affect not only the woman herself, but the ceremony as well. Virtually all of my informants were aware of these proscriptions, and several expressed concern about the impact irregular bleeding might have on their spiritual practices.

Additionally, "set it and forget it" methods of birth control such as Depo-Provera and intrauterine devices, although often touted as convenient for women, nonetheless impact women's agency around their fertility, as these methods require physician insertion and removal. This is particularly salient for Native women, given the high turnover rate in IHS and the lack of regular gynecological care in some areas. As well, there is tremendous potential for medical coercion with these methods, as noted by numerous feminist scholars (see, e.g., Bunkle 1993; Roberts 1997; Scully 2002; A. Smith 2002). According to Marie Ralston-Lewis (2005), Depo-Provera was being used by IHS physicians to manage menstruation in Native women with cognitive disabilities for close to two decades before it was approved as a contraception by the FDA in 1992 (see also A. Smith 2002). Despite the potential for abuse, as with surgical sterilizations, long-term contraceptives may present an authentic choice for Native women who are fully informed of possible risks and side effects. NAWHERC has been working with IHS since 1993 to develop stronger, regular protocols for the prescription, distribution, and monitoring of these contraceptives.

It is not clear from my research how fully adolescents and other women utilize the contraceptive resources available to them on Pine Ridge, but the high adolescent pregnancy rate would seem to indicate that pregnancy prevention methods, whether they rely on contraception or abstinence, are underutilized. It does seem likely from this research as well as previous studies that numerous factors—dissatisfaction with care providers, with the methods themselves, lack of access, and physician preference—play a role in the high adolescent pregnancy rate in Indian Country and on Pine Ridge Reservation. Equally important may be the influence of pronatalist community attitudes, cultural preference for children, and constructions of motherhood that work outside of mainstream ideals of adulthood. Nonetheless, the need for improved access to contraception, and perhaps particularly emergency contraception, becomes particularly salient when understood as linked to sexual violence against Native women on Pine Ridge and across Indian Country. It becomes even more imperative given that for Native women, safely terminating an unwanted pregnancy is extremely challenging.

Access to Abortion Counseling and Services

In the United States there are in essence three sovereigns: the federal government, regional state governments, and Tribal governments or their non-Native equivalent, municipal governments. In the case of Native women's access to abortion counseling and services, all three of these exert some measure of control over women's reproductive freedoms, with IHS centered in the matrix of regulations, funding, and policy.

Legal restrictions on abortion access for Native women of limited income are enacted through the Hyde Amendment, just as they are for all women who rely on state and/or federally funded health care such as Medicaid. The Hyde Amendment forbids the use of federal funding for abortion procedures and counseling. Many scholars have noted the intersections of race, class, and gender in the Hyde Amendment (see, e.g., Boonstra 2008; Cohen 2008; Roberts 1997; Silliman et al. 2004). As Cecilia Fire Thunder, the first Tribally-elected woman president of the Oglala Lakota nation of Pine Ridge and a reproductive rights advocate, argues, "Women of color and poor women have always known that regardless of what happens, women with money will have access to abortion. Women with money will have access to contraception. No matter which way you cut it, it's always on the backs of poor women" (quoted in Aguilar 2006).

Individual states can and have chosen to provide Medicaid funds for abortion under a slightly broader spectrum of reasons than those outlined in the Hyde Amendment (including cases where either the physical or mental health of the woman is threatened by the pregnancy). Therefore women relying on Medicaid may in fact have a slightly greater opportunity to access abortion services in these individual states than in others. Native women who rely on IHS for their care have not even this limited flexibility. Because IHS is directly funded at the federal level, Native women across the United States can access abortion through IHS only under the three circumstances allowed in the most recent (1997) modification of the Hyde Amendment: rape, incest, and endangerment of the mother's life.

In 2008 Republican Representative David Vitter of Louisiana sought to further curtail Native women's access to abortion services and counseling through the Vitter Amendment, attached by the Senate to the Indian Health Care Improvement Act (IHCIA). The proposed amendment sought to impose further restrictions on Native women's access to abortion counseling and services based on the federal funding of IHS. It was widely critiqued by feminist and Native activists (including several of my informants) for its redundancy, as the Hyde Amendment has been effectively limiting access to abortion services for Native women since 1976. However, there were important differences between the two.

Although the Hyde Amendment disproportionately impacts women of color (Arons and Agenor 2010), the exclusions it imposes are framed as economic. The reliance of Native women on IHS for their health care enforces an additional set of restrictions based specifically on the very racialized identities Native women are required to produce in order to access health care through IHS. As Charon Asetoyer, director of the Native American Women's Health Education Resource Center, noted of the Vitter Amendment, "It's a very racist amendment . . . it puts another layer of restrictions on the only race of people whose health care is governed by the federal government. All women are subject to the Hyde Amendment, so why would they put another set of conditions on us?" (quoted in Lillis 2008). Additionally, while the Hyde Amendment must be renewed by Congress every year, often after significant debate (although it has never failed to renew), the Vitter Amendment sought to render funding restrictions to IHS permanent. Also, although both amendments make allowances for survivors of incest and rape, the Vitter Amendment limited these allowances to minors, thus further restricting access to abortion counseling and services for women over the age of eighteen. The Vitter Amendment was also more expansive than the Hyde Amendment in that it applied not only to the direct use of federal funds, but also limited how individual Tribal nations could use IHS funds to support the purchase of private health insurance or contract for abortion related services, thereby impinging not only on Native women's reproductive rights, but also on Tribal nations' sovereignty rights as outlined in the 1978 Indian Self-Determination and Education Assistance Act.

Nonetheless, health activists interviewed for this study were adamant that passage of the IHCIA, which provides budgetary and programmatic directions for IHS, took precedence over fighting the restrictions imposed by the Vitter Amendment. In the political discourse that framed the Vitter Amendment's initial attachment to the IHCIA, both pro-life and pro-choice activists described it as an effort to slow down passage of the IHCIA, and thus stall financial provision for Native health care. My informant Charlene explained, "The needs of Indian Country are too important to slow [passage of the IHCIA] down over Vitter." Jaydeen, whose antiviolence work occurs at both the community and national levels, asserted that it (Vitter) "was a stalling tactic, and y'know what? It worked" (debate over the Vitter Amendment was partially responsible for obstructing passage of the IHCIA in Congress during the fall 2008 legislative session).

The Vitter Amendment was ultimately excluded from the final version of the IHCIA, which passed as Article X of the Patient Protection and Affordable Care Act in 2010. However, the previous approval of the Vitter Amendment by the Senate demonstrates the willingness of State apparatuses to violate Native women's reproductive freedom for political and economic

purposes, and further reveals a strong ideological reliance on racial constructions in order to do so. The willingness of Native health activists and organizations to similarly sacrifice Native women's reproductive freedom to ensure
that the health needs of all Native people could be better addressed, while
politically expedient, equally demonstrates a willingness to perceive the needs
of Native women as separate from the needs of Native communities. Their
reproductive health care can thereby be understood as marginalized at both
the federal and Tribal levels.

Although the Vitter Amendment did not become law, IHS remains
restricted by the Hyde Amendment. However, a study by NAWHERC in
2002 revealed that 85 percent of IHS service units surveyed did not offer abortion services and counseling at the full range allowable under Hyde, and 62
percent did not provide abortion services at all; IHS, therefore, fails to provide adequate abortion counseling and services to Native women even within
the limits allowed by law. The restrictions thus imposed through IHS's failure
further inhibit Native women's reproductive freedom.

Native women on Pine Ridge are still further restricted by regional state
politics. Currently, abortion in South Dakota is severely restricted legally.
In July of 2008, a law went into effect mandating that South Dakota physicians tell all women seeking an abortion that they are "terminating the life of
a whole separate, unique living human being" (Lazzarini 2008). All physicians
performing abortions for any reason were required to use this exact language.
The law also requires a woman to certify in writing that she fully understands
the implications of her chosen medical treatment, including that she "is will-
ingly putting [herself] at higher risk of suicide and depression" and that "in
choosing to end the life of her child she is terminating an "'existing relationship' that is protected by the US Constitution" (ibid.). A 2011 challenge to the
law brought by the American Civil Liberties Union and Planned Parenthood
resulted in a temporary block of portions of the law, although its ultimate fate
remains undecided.

Previously to that, in March of 2006 the South Dakota state legislature
passed its most restrictive abortion legislation to date, prohibiting almost
all abortions, including for rape and incest survivors. Although this law
was overturned by voters the following November, its impacts in Indian
Country—and particularly Pine Ridge Reservation—continue to reverberate. This is due largely to the response of the then-president of the Oglala
Sioux Nation, Cecilia Fire Thunder. A former nurse as well as the founder
and former director of *Cangleska*, the only domestic violence shelter on
the reservation (closed since summer of 2009), Fire Thunder immediately
framed South Dakota's 2006 abortion law as a feminist issue, a race issue,
and a threat to Native sovereignty. She explained, "I got really angry about
a bunch of white guys making decisions about my body" (quoted in Briggs

2006) and further, that "it is now a question of sovereignty" (quoted in Giago 2006b). "An Indian reservation is a sovereign nation, and we're going to take it as far as we can to exercise our sovereignty. . . . As Indian women, we fight many battles. This is just another battle we have to fight" (quoted in WorldNet Weekly 2006). Her response to the ban was to offer her own land on the reservation as a site for a women's wellness clinic that would include abortion counseling and services. On reservation land, the clinic would be exempt from state control; on Fire Thunder's privately owned land, it would be exempt from Tribal control.

Reservation residents were divided in their response to Fire Thunder's proposal, and tensions ran high for several months afterward. Many Lakota people reject abortion because they feel it is not traditional and is thus, perhaps, a form of assimilation or even genocide in ways similar to those argued by pronatalist civil rights groups (see Nelson 2003). Others, including many deeply tradition-oriented people I have spoken to, argue that Lakota women have always retained control over their bodies, and therefore their exercise of abortion rights, while individuals may or may not agree with it morally, is, in fact, a modern expression of traditional rights.

This divided response to the South Dakota abortion ban may have contributed to Fire Thunder's impeachment from the presidency later that year (Briggs 2006). In fact, the Tribal council followed Fire Thunder's impeachment with further abortion restrictions, criminalizing the very acts of seeking an abortion or helping someone seek an abortion (Briggs 2006; Keeler 2006). When I asked Nancy in 2009 if she thought this ban was impacting Native women's ability to access abortion services or counseling, she replied, "I don't think too many people even know about it. Besides, I don't even think you can get an abortion around here, anyway." Pine Ridge is not the only reservation to impose a ban on abortion; the Turtle Mountain Band of Chippewa in North Dakota and several others have enacted similar bans.

Knowing this contentious history and acutely aware of my limited insider status as well as my presentation as a white feminist (who might be perceived as pushing a pro-choice agenda, one with potentially racialized undertones), my interview questions did not focus heavily on abortion. It did emerge as a theme, however, mentioned by nine informants, three of whom are Native health activists and one of whom is a Native midwife. One informant told me she had had an abortion as a teenager, but declined further comment. Tracey told me, "I didn't even think about abortion [with her first pregnancy, unplanned and in her teen years]. Well, maybe I did. But I wouldn't've gotten one." I asked her why not, and she replied, "Well, my mom is really against 'em, y'know? It's not really traditional." I asked if she knew anyone who had ever gotten an abortion and she replied, "Oh, sure. I think girls get 'em. But I don't know where. Anyways, I wouldn't've gotten one."

Asetoyer asserts that despite the difficulties, "Native women have abortions . . . and anyone who tells you differently is out of touch with their community" (quoted in Lillis 2008). According to the South Dakota Department of Health, in 2000 10.6 percent of abortions were sought by Native women (cited in NAWHERC 2002). Just under 9 percent of the state's residents are Native (US Census Bureau 2000), indicating a relatively high incidence of abortion among Native women. Yet none of the abortions were performed through IHS; virtually all were performed outside of IHS's own or contracted facilities.

According to NAWHERC (2003) and two of the Native health activists with whom I spoke, many of the Native women who seek abortion services outside of IHS do so later in their pregnancies, due to many reasons including shame, lack of information, and lack of funds. Seeking abortion services or counseling outside of IHS requires Native women to step outside of the health care system that has been legally guaranteed them through their unique relationship with the federal government, and with which they may have the most familiarity and readiest access. Stepping outside of this institutional relationship also requires the resources to negotiate socioeconomic structures that restrict Native women's access to private funding.

Thus for Native women, access to abortion services becomes not a private decision between a woman and her doctor (as intended in *Roe v. Wade*) but rather a very public negotiation between a Native woman, her Tribal council, the regional state in which she lives, and the federal government. Similarly to women's subjective experiences of childbirth, the material effects of this reproductive health care for Native women may or may not differ from other women's, particularly women in marginalized communities. However, the ruling relations that organize Native women's access to care based on the intersections of race, class, gender, sexuality, and citizenship produce unique structures of health care for Native women.

The logic of simultaneously restricting access to contraception and abortion may seem at first glance to be pronatalist, particularly when lack of contraception access through IHS potentially contributes to high fertility rates, which may ultimately be welcomed in Native communities. However, as Walters and Simoni assert, "Any discussion of the health of Native women must begin with a consideration of their 'fourth world' context, a context unique to colonized peoples in which a minority indigenous population exists in a nation wherein institutionalized power and privilege are held by a colonizing, subordinating majority" (2002, 52). Contextualizing these health care restrictions within the violent historic and current relationships between Native nations and the settler State clarifies the logic that organizes Native women's health care: because Native women are left with few options in their reproductive lives, the restrictions they must navigate often lead to permanent solutions. As Andrea Smith argues, when contraceptive options are limited "abortion policies then become another strategy to coerce Native women to pursue sterilization . . . to avoid the trauma of unwanted pregnancy" (2002, 139). Rather than pronatalist, this is a potentially genocidal enactment of population control in which women "choose" sterilization because their other options are so severely limited.

Native women's curtailed access to abortion services must be understood as these occur simultaneously with inadequate contraceptive services, high rates of adolescent and unintended pregnancy, and high rates of sexual violence: all four of these areas forcefully organize the reproductive experiences of Native women; all four of these areas remain egregiously mismanaged by the federal legal system and by IHS, which is itself constrained by its reliance on various points of authority within the federal government as well as Tribal governments; and all four of these areas reveal the intersecting influences and consequences of race, class, gender, sexuality, and citizenship ideologies at work in Native women's health care. Understood still more broadly as linked to a eugenicist formulation of Indian identity such as that reflected in blood quantum requirements for tribal enrollment, these restrictions coalesce to impose a convoluted system of interlocking marginalizations on Native people's health care. The confluence of these multiple oppressions land with profound force on the bodies of Native women as ideologies of race, class, gender, sexuality, and citizenship intersect with the political and cultural economies of the settler State to organize the experiences of Native women seeking reproductive health care.

The lack of access to adequate care engendered by Native women's uniquely produced social, political, and economic locations thus perpetuates and reproduces social inequalities already at work in the production of Indian-ness on which IHS care relies. Gendered ideologies of sex and sexuality further restrict access to the full range of reproductive care for Native women whose racialized and classed Indian identity grants them access to IHS, but whose gendered and sexed identities are marginalized. The resulting double discourse of care that emerges from IHS enacts a continuing project of disappearing Native people in the settler State's drive toward assimilation by marking them as separate from the national body when they are identified as "Native," but subsuming them under a mainstream medical model that fails to adequately consider social contexts, let alone long-standing treaty rights and legal precedent. This understanding of Native people as "both, and" as well as "neither, nor" enables the institutional neglect of Native women's care and safety; further, the legal and institutional limitations on their reproductive freedoms, framed in economic terms, reflect the ongoing social production of racializing discourses that effectively brand Native people as "other" and discursively justify their removal from the national body. These entwined political and cultural economies produce profound reproductive oppressions for Native women and potentially genocidal consequences for their communities.

Part IV

**Reproductive Justice
for Native Women**

10

Community Knowledge, Community Capital, and Cultural Safety

As this study reveals, the organization of certain resources contributes to Native women's health disparities and even their behavior in seeking health care. Lack of ready transportation and financial resources, for example, combine with the evidence-based paradigms that organize mainstream medical care and the political economy that determines IHS's inadequate staffing and outdated facilities to produce particular subjective experiences that, I argue, are marked by expressions of restriction, acquiescence, negotiation, and resistance. However, focusing on the ruling relations—the structures that shape these experiences—tells only a partial story. Although the technologies of settler colonialism organize Native peoples' lives to differing degrees, Native people themselves, of course, are not without agency. It is important to consider more closely not only the macro-level processes initiated by State apparatuses and the institutional-level interpretation and enactment of these by IHS but also what resources exist on the local level and how IHS facilitates or interferes with these.

As discussed in Chapter 2, communities are complex and multifaceted, and community capital must be understood as uniquely produced and experienced. In the case of Pine Ridge Reservation, I argue that community capital is inextricably tied to an historical and enduring sense of Lakota identity; just as the settler State seeks to create and maintain a collective ethnicity, so too do Lakota people seek to maintain an identity that is ultimately theirs to define, regardless, despite, and against State interference. This shared sense of Lakota identity produces and contributes to community capital by providing foundational guidelines for personal and interpersonal behavior through traditionally celebrated values of wisdom, bravery, fortitude, and generosity. Here, I consider two additional and intersecting forms of community capital: the role of knowledge and the role of tradition-oriented practices. Knowledge and knowledge production are integral to indigenous identity in the settler State, where assimilation and disappearance are cultural and epistemological as much as they are physical. In the context of this study, how knowledge about reproductive health care and the reproductive body is produced and understood on Pine Ridge Reservation intersects with how health care is provided and experienced through historical processes as well as evidence-based medicine. Because all of my informants identified as tradition-oriented to some degree, I also consider the function of tradition-oriented practices in knowledge production, identity formation, and in health care. Although tradition-oriented healing modalities are in evidence on Pine Ridge, the assimilative tactics of the State have had a profound impact on the availability and practice of indigenous knowledge for the Lakota as well as other Native people, and have engendered particular processes of erasure or adaptation of tradition-oriented knowledge practices. At the same time, evidence-based health care as it is institutionally practiced by IHS may not adequately address the health needs produced by the unique fourth-world context in which many Native people live. The resulting gaps in knowledge and resources for Native women potentially contribute to the ongoing health disparities they experience.

As discussed in Chapters 5 and 6, IHS serves as a fulcrum between the State and Native communities; it is organized by State apparatuses, but ostensibly exists to meet the needs of Native people. It has failed to meet these needs adequately, though its failure is neither simple nor complete. A sustained consideration of the role of knowledge in shaping practice brings to light not only areas in need of improvement but also existing strengths and potential partnerships that might support a reproductive justice agenda. I conclude this chapter by considering an epistemic shift which might help IHS better identify and meet the needs of Native communities as these emerge from the fourth-world context of indigeneity within the settler State.

Knowledge

Knowledge is a cultural artifact, learned and transmitted through social processes enacted within and across sociocultural networks. These may be formal, as they are in educational settings, or informal, as among peer groups or through intergenerational storytelling or even gossip. Just as cultures are never static or monolithic, neither is knowledge; what is known is constituted in part by the knower, by the processes and contexts of learning, by the statuses accorded certain kinds of knowledge and certain knowers, and many other factors. The role of knowledge, indeed, the very question of what gets to count as knowledge in Native women's health care, can be understood as an important form of capital which has been differently utilized by the State and by Native communities.

The historic and ongoing assimilative tactics of the State organize cultural identity through a form of epistemic violence that denigrates tradition-oriented practices and imbues Western practices with a superior value. For example, the late nineteenth and early twentieth centuries saw the legislative criminalization of tradition-oriented spiritual practices such as the Sundance ceremony, at the same time that churches and boarding schools, structurally and financially supported by the State, sought to impose non-indigenous religions, Victorian gender roles, and even heteropatriarchal family forms. All of these were linked in some way to the provision of health care and other resources. Broad assimilative tactics thereby produced ideological and material space for the insertion of biomedical practices in place of indigenous ways of promoting wellness and treating diseases.

At the same time, Native people themselves resist this erasure of their indigeneity and assert their identities through continually evolving forms of knowledge-sharing. One example of the ways in which knowledge preservation and dissemination, even as it evolves, becomes a strategy of resistance and empowerment is the proliferation of star quilts among the Lakota and other Plains Indians. When young Lakota girls were brought to the boarding schools, quilting was one of the domestic skills they were taught. When offered their choice of quilt patterns, Lakota girls embraced the star pattern as reflective of their origins in the heavens (Albers and Medicine 1983). Patricia Albers and Beatrice Medicine (1983) also suggest that star quilts are descended from the ceremonial buffalo hides bearing the morning star design, and that women's adaptation of this traditional design to a new medium has been essential in its preservation. Thus young Lakota girls were able to use the very skills taught by teachers attempting to assimilate them into the dominant culture as a subversive form of resistance against that assimilation, and a way of knowledge preservation. Today star quilts serve many purposes—social, ceremonial, decorative, commercial, and spiritual—and have become a common, though labor-intensive, gift on Pine Ridge, thus circulating histories of spirituality and histories of resistance that preserve and claim a distinct identity apart from the (fictive) collective ethnicity.

Although biomedical practice through IHS has become the dominant health-care paradigm, tradition-oriented practices are still in use and in evolution on Pine Ridge and elsewhere in Indian Country, and almost all of my informants value these practices and engage in them regularly. This does not necessitate a complete rejection of evidenced-based medicine; many of the same informants who attend *inipi* ceremony on Sunday night can be found at IHS on Monday morning. Similarly, Douglas Novins et al. (2004) found in their study that identification with Native culture is strongly correlated with the use of traditional healing, but combined use of both biomedicine and traditional healing modalities is common. As Sam explained to me, "We've been adapting to you guys ever since Lewis and Clark."

Women's Knowledge: Exclusions, Inclusions, and Evolutions

On Pine Ridge Reservation these processes of assimilation, resistance, accommodation, and adaptation result in a patchwork of knowledge, misinformation, and lack of information, which potentially leaves women, and perhaps particularly young women, without adequate understanding of their health needs and the multiple resources that may be available to them, both within and outside of the formal IHS system. Women's knowledge of reproductive health, health needs, and health care varies widely across the sample in my study, due partly to the different occupational roles of my informants. Seven of my informants—six Native health-care providers or activists, and one non-Native midwife who worked for IHS both on Pine Ridge and elsewhere—have professional training in and extensive experience working on Native health issues that differentiate the quality of their knowledge about mainstream medical practice from informants who have not engaged in similar educational, professional, or activist activities.

Of those informants who do not have these educational and professional experiences, almost half needed prompting to describe reproductive health care generally. Prenatal care, which has been an important area of focus for IHS, was the first aspect of "women's care" that came to mind for all of these informants except Sam, who first mentioned violence to me. Despite rising rates of cervical cancer and HIV infection, high rates of unintended pregnancy, and egregiously high rates of infant mortality in Indian Country, these informants exhibited a limited sense of the health-care needs unique to women, particularly sexually active women. Without further study it is impossible to compare this to the general population on Pine Ridge; it may be that my informants are generally less well informed than members of the general population, or approximately the same. Based only on anecdotal evidence, it seems unlikely that these informants were substantially better informed than their peers in the general population.

With prompting, informants readily identified other aspects of reproductive health care, most notably testing for sexually transmitted infections, breastfeeding, and contraception. All of these with the exception of contraception have been growing areas of focus for IHS, and the ability of my informants to identify them may indicate some success on the part of IHS in informing the communities on Pine Ridge and elsewhere of these issues. It also raises the question of how my informants come to understand the very meaning of "reproductive health care." Similarly to the ways in which reproductive rights have dominated late twentieth-century discourses around women's reproductive health (for example, by centralizing the political battle over abortion) to the partial exclusion of reproductive justice, the impact of IHS's focus on certain areas of reproductive health care may in actuality shape what Native people and others consider to *be* reproductive healthcare needs, potentially to the exclusion of other needs such as sexual safety. The prevalence of IHS in public discourses around Native health care, and the dominance of evidence-based, biomedical knowledge in the organization of IHS's care modalities, may thus produce certain ways of knowing and preclude others.

My respondents' seeming lack of immediate knowledge about women's diverse reproductive needs was explained in part by three informants. When I asked Rosemary, a Lakota grandmother of eleven, how women learn about reproductive health care, she told me:

> There is still a sense of embarrassment involved with seeking care for your woman-parts. Although it's getting better, young women still don't talk about these things openly here, they're afraid other people will talk about them and think they're sleeping around. Plus, there's a great deal of modesty among more traditional people, and you don't talk about this stuff very much. Plus, I think there's always that feeling of "it can't happen to me."

This fear of being talked about was mentioned by two other informants, as well. Tracey explained, "I kinda don't like goin' to IHS 'cuz, you know, a lot of people might know you. And you don't know if they're—if they even go by the rights to privacy law. It's just . . . like they know your whole family, y'know? Like, my auntie works at Native Women's Health." (Native Women's Health is a contract health facility located in Rapid City, approximately ninety minutes from the reservation's center. It provides a wide range of reproductive health services as well as several other health services, such as diabetes treatment.) Talia told me, "I know people who work there [at the clinic]. I don't know what they're saying and all, who they're talkin' to. I mean, I know they're not supposed to talk about it and all, but you know how people are." I do indeed understand the role of gossip in the small towns on the reservation; my own pregnancy was the source of it for several months, and in fact on one of my research trips to the reservation (nine years later), I was still referred to as "that woman who got pregnant over there at the school that time." It is rare to have a conversation on the reservation that is not marked with news of what others are "up to." While being the subject of conversation can be uncomfortable, gossip can also become a form of social capital within and between the different communities on the reservation, by facilitating the sharing of information, creating and strengthening networks, and potentially serving as a sanction against perceived misbehavior. Given this last, it is certainly possible that a concern for privacy inhibits women's abilities to seek information from professional care providers or even lay healers in the community, where many people are related and regularly share news.

When the women in my sample did seek care from professionals, they were often further challenged by the use of medical language in the care setting, which they did not always easily understand. Tracey expressed anger at the radiologist who performed her ultrasound at a contract health facility, describing him as "very rude . . . he even insulted me 'cuz I asked what orbits were, 'cuz I never took anatomy before and he goes, 'oh, you never took anatomy before?'" (Tracey explained that "orbits" is the technical term used to describe the eyes of the in-utero fetus. I have had a total of three ultrasounds, all performed at mainstream health facilities [one in Rapid City, South Dakota, and two in Waterbury, Connecticut], and no one ever referred to "orbits.") Two other informants spoke of similar incidents at IHS facilities on Pine Ridge, in which technical terms were used without adequate explanation, and they felt their care provider looked down on them for their lack of understanding. Susan Fifer (1996) found similar responses in a study of client perceptions of IHS providers; patients in her study stated that providers showed superior attitudes and used confusing terminology. In her study as in mine, this left patients feeling dismissed, uncomfortable, and angry.

Nancy explained that she had been using oral contraceptives for several years and then stopped because she found out about potential risks involved from a friend. "But that midwife—she never told me anything like that, all those years I went and got that pill from her," she explained. I asked if the pharmacist who filled her prescription ever explained anything to her and she replied, "No. Well, I mean, they give you this pamphlet that comes with the pills, but I didn't read it." These informational pamphlets are written for laypeople but produced by the pharmaceutical company and can be potentially intimidating. The print is small and crowded, and there are few diagrams or illustrations to clarify the information. When I asked Nancy if she had ever asked the midwife for further information, she replied, "Well no, I guess I just figured she'd tell me." Nancy's assumption and her lack of active pursuit of information may be indicative of conversational behavior on the reservation; adolescents are often hesitant to ask questions of those in authority, and tradition-oriented people in general may consider it rude to pursue conversations beyond what is immediately offered. At the same time, Nancy's reluctance to pursue further information also speaks to Christina's assertions that "people need to take care of themselves" (see Chapter 5); because Nancy never asked, she never heard from the midwife about side effects and potential risks. However, the informed consent required for any drug regimen puts the burden of knowledge sharing on the health-care professional, not the patient.

Christina agreed that women, particularly young women, may lack knowledge about their health needs and explained that there could be many reasons, including "a lot of these young women especially don't check the Internet for that kind of information. And they don't get it from IHS unless they're already there for a check-up. We need to get into the schools, into the communities. We need to talk to the elders about this kind of thing." Rosemary added,

> In the old days, we learned these things from our mothers and grandmothers. The women had this knowledge and passed on the stories, in the songs and in the ceremonies. Colonization broke up all these things, and now we need to rebuild them. We need to use these other ways, too, because that's what our youth is using, but we need to bring back the traditional ways, too, because those are the right ways for us as Lakota people.

The importance of traditional forms of reproductive health knowledge sharing has also been noted by other Native women (see, e.g., Anderson 2000; Asetoyer 2004; Bushnell 2004; Cook 1989, 2009; Tasina Ska Win 2003; Yee 2010), and has served as the focus of much indigenous feminist activism. For example, Mohawk midwife Katsi Cook has worked with Women of All Red Nations, Tewa Women United, and other Native women's organizations to reinvigorate women's traditional knowledge and agency in pregnancy and childbirth through the training of Native midwives and doulas (birth assistants) as well as the promotion of culturally appropriate and safe knowledge sharing amongst indigenous women. Cook is currently the director of Woman Is the First Environment Collaborative, which brings together indigenous women leaders from across North America to share their knowledge about the links between environmental health and the safety and well-being of their communities. Women's reproductive bodies provide the central focus of the collaborative's work, thus asserting an agenda strongly grounded in reproductive justice.

Adolescents and Sex Education

As noted by several of my informants as well as Velma Murry and James Ponzetti (1997) and Ann Garwick et al. (2008), standard forms of sex education are available on at least a limited basis throughout much of Indian Country, including Pine Ridge Reservation, although Lenna Liu et al.'s (1994) study of Navajo and Apache adolescents found that a majority of them had little to no formal sex education in school. Murry and Ponzetti (1997) found that Native American adolescents who received sex education in school were more likely to delay their first pregnancy. This is important in light of the high rate of adolescent pregnancies in Indian Country and the limited knowledge reported by many of my own informants as well as by Sally Davis and Mary Harris (1982) in their study of sexual practices among adolescents of color, including Native American adolescents.

Multiracial Mohawk activist Jessica Yee Danforth argues that sex and sexuality education must engage and support culturally specific initiatives (2008). In 2007 she founded the Native Youth Sexual Health Network, an organization that reaches across multiple political borders to promote sexual health for Native youth in Canada and the United States. The Native Youth Sexual Health Network relies on a deeply ingrained ethic of reproductive justice, operating through community networks that address needs identified by community members. Danforth and the Native Youth Sexual Health Network work on a myriad of fronts from social media to the United Nations Permanent Forum on Indigenous Issues to create youth-specific spaces focused on sexual health, but indigenous principles concerning the conjoined roles and responsibilities of youth and elders are foundational to the network's efforts, and reflect the organization's commitment to traditional forms of knowledge and knowledge sharing.

Suggestions from Native teens on pregnancy prevention in Garwick et al.'s (2008) study include enhancing peer-led programs such as those supported by the Native Youth Sexual Health Network as well as improving school-based programs. When I lived on the reservation, I was able to observe two sex education sessions moderated by Amy, an IHS midwife on Pine Ridge. One of these sessions was just for female students at the high school where I taught, and one was for both females and males. Students were impressively participatory, particularly in the female-only session, and I recall several follow-up conversations with students who had previously been in a women's studies class I taught the semester before and with whom I had developed a close relationship. I was also able to informally observe a sex education session for adolescents directed by Amy eight years later. This session, which focused heavily on sexually transmitted infections and included a graphic PowerPoint presentation, was held over the summer in a local health center, and students were paid for attendance (a common incentive on the reservation due to the high rate of poverty). Although students were not very participatory, many left with the condoms Amy made available.

Several community members on Pine Ridge described Amy's efforts to encourage testing for sexually transmitted infections and make it easily accessible for adolescents. For example, she and her assistant regularly attend pow-wows and school athletic events, where they raffle off various items to students who undergo STI testing at these events (testing is accomplished through a simple urine test, done in the facility's bathroom). Many community members expressed their appreciation for their work, and told me students were enthusiastic about the raffles due to the opportunity to win valuable items such as iPods and gift certificates. Although IHS's restrictions prevented me from interviewing Amy directly, it is my understanding that these items are provided through IHS grant funding.

When I asked Dani, a twenty-six-year-old mother of two from Pine Ridge, how she had learned about childbirth, she replied, "I dunno. I mean, you just sort of hear about it, I guess. And then when you get pregnant you start asking and people tell you what it's like. Like, when I was pregnant with Byron, I started talkin' to my mom and my friends about it and they all told me how much it hurts." I asked if she had had any formal education about reproduction prior to becoming pregnant, and she replied, "Yeah, I guess so, you mean in school? Yeah, maybe in biology. And I remember Melissa [a teacher at Dani's high school] used to have this midwife come into her class to talk to us. And in your class we did some stuff, didn't we?" I was a teacher at Dani's high school during her adolescence, and I can attest to all three aspects of formal education that she mentions. However, the vagueness of her response seems to indicate that these avenues were not sufficient to be recalled specifically less than ten years later, although they may nonetheless have provided a foundational understanding. Dani more readily recalled information she learned more recently from family members and friends.

Yet informal socialization into health care, particularly around sexuality, may also be inadequate at this time; informants were largely in agreement that colonization and the intrusion of Western forms of patriarchy have disrupted more traditional ways of knowing and learning about sexuality (see also Anderson 2000; Artichoker and Mousseau 2006; Danforth 2009; Smith 2005). Neither biomedical knowledge nor Western forms of education have been easily taken up in Native communities as a replacement for earlier forms of knowledge sharing. The near destruction of tradition-oriented ways of learning combined with the general inadequacy of formal education in most reservation communities may leave Lakota women with gaps in their knowledge of their own bodies as well as their health-care needs. Of course, it is not the sole responsibility of IHS to educate its patients on all aspects of reproductive health; nonetheless, as the primary provider of health care for Native women on Pine Ridge, it is incumbent upon IHS to actively foster community education that would enhance their mission. This is particularly salient in patient-provider interactions, where care providers bear the ethical responsibility of ensuring informed consent.

Tradition, Identity, and Wellness

There is wide evidence of a growing commitment to tradition-oriented Lakota practices on Pine Ridge, particularly spiritual practices (see, e.g., Crow Dog 1991; Mohatt and Eagle Elk 2002; Powers 1986; Thunder Valley 2009; Young Bear and Theisz 1996) and Lakota activist Tasina Ska Win asserts that "our medicine people are in constant demand for the entire spectrum of tribulations our people face" (2003, 43). Thunder Valley Community Development, a grassroots nonprofit organization on Pine Ridge, considers spiritual health inextricable from community health and explains that "through these ceremonies people have defeated many types of cancer and have gathered strength to make life-changing decisions to improve their personal health. Young people have also discovered their culture and spirituality, giving them a reason to become more aware of their health . . . a combination of traditional healing, western medicine, and healthy habits can lead to a more holistic way of living" (2009). Although this commitment undoubtedly varies in both intensity and interpretation across the reservation, it may nonetheless offer an additional source of care and support for women seeking reproductive health care. Yet the impact of what medical anthropologist Pamela Erickson (2008) calls the "folk sector," which includes secular and sacred healers who are not a formal part of the medical system, is understudied on Pine Ridge, and understudied in terms of reproductive health particularly.

Further inquiry into the influence of the folk sector on women seeking various forms of reproductive health care may not only bring to light underlying differences in Native women's understanding of health and well-being but also reveal existing cultural structures of health care. One way to consider the potential impact of sacred and lay healers on Pine Ridge might be to better understand the role of tradition-oriented practices in identity formation and community wellness. Although tradition is itself a dynamic concept and my study did not incorporate any formal rubric to measure traditional orientation, I understand it to include aspects of enculturation in Lakota identity such as historically shared values, language, and participation in Lakota ceremonies.

Interviews as well as numerous conversations with community members reveal a strong underlying spiritual foundation to traditional orientation. For example, eighteen informants who described themselves as traditional have all attended numerous prayer ceremonies, half of them from childhood. All of my informants know several *wicasa wakan*s (holy men, or medicine men), and most have gone to ceremonies with different spiritual communities (not all on Pine Ridge), although most consider one spiritual community (led by one particular *wicasa wakan*) to be their *tiospaye* (family community). I knew eight of my fourteen Lakota informants before beginning this research, and four of them were able to—and kind enough to—guide me in the organization of my son's naming ceremony, which occurred at the end of a Sundance ceremony held on the reservation. Eight of my informants described children and babies as "sacred" without prompting, and five spoke of mothers and motherhood as sacred. Sixteen of my twenty-five informants have attended *yuwipi*, a Lakota healing ceremony, to pray for themselves and/or family members and friends. All of these informants expressed deep conviction that the prayers offered in these ceremonies provided healing. Sarah told me, "I wasn't sick when I went, but you know, I just felt better anyway when I left!" She laughed, "I just feel good after Ceremony." I frequently hear such comments during the meal that often follows ceremonies.

Four of my informants had participated in traditional Lakota womanhood ceremonies (*isnati lowancapi*) during their adolescence. Several years ago I was invited to support one of these young women in this ceremony. This included two weeks of working together with her, several other young women in preparation, and several women elders. We met daily at the local high school, and among other activities, we beaded (or at least, they beaded and patiently tried to teach me), made prayer skirts to wear in attendance at *wiwanyang wacipi* (Sundance ceremony), and shared stories about womanhood and motherhood. We also told rather off-color jokes about men and sex. This time provided an opportunity for all of us to share wisdom and ask questions informally, and for several of the young women in preparation, it enhanced their sense of being *Lakota winyan*, women of the Lakota. Similarly, during my pregnancy on the reservation I was told that typically a welcoming ceremony for the baby is held during pregnancy, soon after the fetus's first movements are felt by the woman. At the welcoming ceremony friends planned for my son, gifts were given as might happen at any baby shower, but sage was also burned and my son's relatives offered prayers for him and me. One relative told me it was important for me to remember these things so I could bring my child into the world "in a good way" and so that he would know he is Lakota. These lessons enhanced my own feelings of agency during my pregnancy, and also served to include both me and my unborn child in the community. This sense of belonging offers a potentially powerful way to enhance Native women's reproductive health care, as evidenced by the growing success of the Centering Pregnancy model of prenatal care in reservation communities.

As Nancy Krieger (1999) and Karina Walters and Jane Simoni (2002) assert, identity processes and self-expression can serve to mitigate health stressors. Mark Zimmerman et al. (1996) report similar findings in their study of Native American adolescents and alcohol use, arguing that enculturation in indigenous practices and beliefs may strengthen resilience and minimize the effects of social stressors. Similarly, in a study on historical grief among the Lakota, Maria Yellow Horse Brave Heart noted that "the integration of traditional spirituality and culture enhance protective factors against the development or exacerbation of PTSD [post-traumatic stress disorder]" (1999, 15–16). Kenneth Pargament (1999) and Neal Krause (1999), using empirical measures to determine the relationship between religiosity/spirituality and health and well-being, found strong correlations between the strength of religious or spiritual affiliation and participation and ability to navigate stressors brought on by socioeconomic status, racism, and trauma, among other phenomena encountered throughout the life-course.

These forms of community capital vary across Indian Country, but they undoubtedly exist; on Pine Ridge Reservation they center around a strong historical and enduring sense of Lakota identity (see, e.g., Brown et al. 1974; Crow Dog 1991; Mohatt and Eagle Elk 2000; St. Pierre and Long Soldier 1995; Young Bear and Theisz 1994). The work of tradition-oriented and other community leaders on Pine Ridge Reservation and elsewhere in Indian Country—women like Katsi Cook and Jessica Yee Danforth and organizations such as Woman Is the First Environment Collaborative and Thunder Valley Community Development—reflect the resources available within Native communities and the commitment of Native people to address the needs they and their communities identify.

Cultural Safety: Bringing Evidence-Based Medicine into the Fourth-World Context

Cultural competence in health care is generally understood to include "the ability of systems to provide care to patients with diverse values, beliefs and behaviors, including tailoring delivery to meet patients' social, cultural, and linguistic needs" (Betancourt et al. 2002, 2). Former director of IHS Charles Grim describes cultural competence as "being able to understand, appreciate, and utilize culturally appropriate strategies in the delivery of health care . . . cultural competence acknowledges and incorporates at all levels the importance of culture, the assessment of cross-cultural relations, vigilance toward the dynamics that result from cultural differences . . . and adaptation of services to meet culturally unique needs" (2007). Institutionally, IHS understands that cultural competence must include but reach beyond linguistic barriers and respecting diverse values and beliefs. Grim's reference to "the dynamics that result from cultural differences" and the need to "incorporate at all levels the importance of culture" indicate a broader conceptualization of cultural competence than may be common. Yet the very concept of cultural competence in health care seems grounded in a particular understanding of culture as it is expressed through difference: different language needs, different beliefs and values. But different from whom? Similarly to critiques of "color-blindness" made by race scholars (see, e.g., Brown et al. 2003; Hernandez 1998; Lawrence 1995), the discourses that shape cultural competence may in fact work to keep whiteness, or europeaneity, as an invisible norm even as they espouse respect for "differences."

IHS literature emphasizes IHS's ongoing commitment to cultural competence, and several sessions at the First Annual Conference on Maternal and Child Health focused on cultural competency. However, although IHS seems sincerely committed to the practice of cultural competence, it does not seem to have made deliberate and sustained efforts to encourage its development throughout its twelve areas. For example, while sitting in a café across the street from Pine Ridge Hospital during one research trip, I overheard a conversation between two IHS employees in which one complained about the preponderance of illnesses in his patients, exclaiming, "Don't these people know how to eat healthy?" His disregard for the potential challenge of finding healthy, affordable food on the reservation revealed his ignorance about the community he serves. It certainly did not indicate adequate training in cultural competency. Betty, who previously worked for IHS on Pine Ridge, explained that cultural competence did not develop through any formal channels, but rather through work and social situations. As my unintentional eavesdropping confirms, this may not be adequate.

Not only must cultural competence be taken up in deliberate and sustained ways, it must also go beyond consideration of "difference" to address many aspects of culture, including the culture of adolescence, which can include adherence to perceived cultural norms or concern with public visibility; community cultures, which may include reluctance or inability to read and understand medical information or ask for further clarification; local availability of resources such as regular transportation and fresh food; and, specifically for IHS, understanding institutional racism and the consequences of colonization in Native communities. Additionally, on Pine Ridge as in many other Native communities, historical grief and high rates of depression become normalized in everyday behavior and can be exhibited through addictions, violence, and even death; the impact of historical trauma must be better understood if its associated health behaviors are to be adequately addressed. This becomes particularly urgent when one considers that suicide is the number-one cause of death for Native Americans between the ages of ten and thirty-four; in fact, Native Americans have the highest suicide rate of any ethnicity in the United States (CDC 2012b). All of these factors are "cultural" in the sense that they become regularly practiced local behaviors. It is therefore not enough to address "diverse beliefs and values" and "linguistic needs," although these are essential. Cultural competence must be localized, but it must also take into consideration broad social and historical structures that help to produce the local.

These needs require an acute and well-developed understanding of the fourth-world context of life for many Native people, particularly in reservation communities. As noted by Walters and Simoni, failure to account for the factors that result from and shape the fourth-world context of Native women's lives "can lead to pathologized perceptions of Natives, reinforce power inequities, and perpetuate paternalism and dependency in regard to health care" (2002, 522). Considering Native women's health needs from a reproductive justice perspective which necessarily incorporates sustained examination of their fourth-world context as well as local factors that may impact health and wellness requires a systemic move from a paradigm of cultural competence to one of cultural safety.

Originally developed by indigenous Maori nurses in New Zealand, cultural safety incorporates analysis of structural inequalities and limited life opportunities, including unequal access to health care, and specifically includes consideration of power inequities, individual and institutional discrimination, and the dynamics of health-care relations in a postcolonial context. The health of indigenous peoples in settler societies—indeed, of anyone—cannot simply be abstracted from social contexts, which are forged within the dominant power relations of a society. This recognition forces biomedical health care to more fully consider the social world, outside of a model predicated on evidence-based medicine and individual lifestyle decisions; cultural safety necessarily considers the historical effects of settler colonialism and requires that the power dynamics inherent in health-care interactions be made visible.

The Indian Health Service has expressed its institutional commitment to working with Tribal leaders through listening sessions, consultation summits, and workgroups. However, the exclusion of traditional Lakota practices from the evidence-based model that informs IHS practice on Pine Ridge, and indeed, shapes the very structure of IHS and perhaps even Native peoples' understanding of what reproductive health care entails, inhibits its abilities to understand Tribal leadership beyond the formal levels of governance, thereby potentially excluding grassroots leaders and community practices. For example, currently on Pine Ridge there does not seem to be a formal partnership between the *wicasa wakan* or tradition-oriented communities generally and IHS in terms of reproductive health care. Yet many community members, including elders and spiritual leaders on the reservation, have expressed concern to me about the health of the Lakota people, and particularly relevant to this research, high rates of teen pregnancy, infant mortality, and violence against women and children. Many of my informants advocate for a synthesis of biomedical knowledge and tradition-oriented ways of healing, for example, seeking health care from IHS as well as attending ceremonies, or by bringing traditional practices such as the burning of sage or the use of peyote tea into the hospital birthing room. Stronger partnerships between IHS and community leaders from the folk sector on Pine Ridge might provide Native women on the reservation with a broader, more culturally safe foundation for reproductive health care that utilizes both evidence-based medicine and traditional knowledge.

A greater sense of cultural safety might also empower women to assert greater agency in their own care and in seeking the knowledge they need for this care. At the same time, a broader integration of cultural safety in health care might empower IHS care providers in their relationships with their clients. Most important, a full incorporation of cultural safety into the very structure of IHS would have the potential to radically alter the mainstream paradigm of health and health-care delivery that dominates Native women's health and health-care interactions, yet fails to meet their needs.

11

Conclusions

Native Women in the Center

As this study reveals, the ruling relations that organize reproductive health care for Native women emerge from multiple locations and reflect the intersections of race, class, gender, sex, and citizenship ideologies in the settler State. The stories that drove my research bring to light how these ideologies combine with State interests to impose a complex organizing force on the experiences of Native women seeking reproductive health care and reveal the links between Native women's embodied experiences of reproductive health care and the multiple locations from which these experiences are organized.

For example, the role of Congress and the executive branch in determining the funding and organizational directions of health care for Native people reflects the double discourse embedded in the settler State's ongoing drive toward homogeneity. However, this drive is tempered by multiple influences, including the nature of pluralist governance, shifting notions of sovereignty and dependence, national and regional state economic structures, and the perseverance of Tribal nations. The State, in this sense governed by the rules of democracy, is further influenced by social constructions of race, class, gender, sexuality, and nation. In turn, the State modifies and reproduces these constructions and assumptions through legislation and policy directives such as funding restrictions and eligibility criteria, which directly influence IHS's reproductive health-care programming.

The provision of health care to Native women is further organized by the State apparatuses found in the Department of Health and Human Services, such as the Centers for Disease Control, the National Institutes of Health, and the Public Health Service. The evidence-based model upon which these agencies rely is deeply ingrained in IHS practice, and the research and policy initiatives they espouse influence the priorities which IHS sets for funding as well as its programmatic initiatives. The boundaries thus imposed by the institutional foundation of health care for Native people complicates resistance to, or even modification of, mainstream medical practices and potentially inhibits both IHS's ability to incorporate indigenous community health practices and its ability to adopt culturally competent and safe delivery of care.

Within IHS, the funding and program structures that derive from Congress, the executive branch, and its collegial agencies within the Department of Health and Human Services are further fractured by the needs of almost six hundred individual Tribal nations. On Pine Ridge this fragmentation is still further reflected in the diversion of funds to emergency care, diabetes care, cardiovascular health, and, specifically within reproductive health care, prenatal care. Although these areas absolutely require the attention and focus of IHS care providers and administrators, the consequences for Native women appear to include neglect of the broad range of reproductive health care, including limited access to contraception, abortion services and counseling, and competent, safe care after sexual assault. In these ways, the embodied experiences of Native women are shaped to fit into a complex, poorly articulated biomedical model of care that simply does not have the resources to address their needs adequately.

Lack of resources, however, is not the only reason for the inadequate service to Native women. Equally important is the lack of cultural safety. IHS's commitment to cultural competence appears sincere; it is mentioned several times in their literature as a primary objective, and was discussed in several sessions at the First Annual Maternal and Child Health Conference by care providers, community health representatives, and administrators, including the former directors of IHS. Additionally, as discussed in this book, IHS has made allowances for traditional practices in the birthing room, both on Pine Ridge and elsewhere, and has worked to meet the needs of sexually active adolescents through culturally appropriate means such as raffle prizes for STI testing. The work of Native health advocates both within and outside of IHS to achieve certain goals such as improved care for survivors of sexual violence, training of Native midwives and doulas, and resistance to abortion restrictions cannot be overstated, and reflects both IHS's commitment to providing health care to Native people (a commitment that is particularly striking given the constraints of budget shortfalls and bureaucratic complexities) and the strong commitment of Native health advocates to the well-being of their communities.

However, this commitment has not translated into adequate, culturally safe care for women on Pine Ridge. Part of the reason for this may lie, again, in the limited resources available to IHS and in the funding structure of the Pine

Ridge service unit, as well as potential mismanagement by IHS administrators and care providers. Part of the reason for this undoubtedly lies with racist and misogynist federal and regional state policies and IHS practices. At least part of the reason lies also with a long history of colonization, which has resulted in the dire health conditions and limited sovereignty of Native nations. A shift from cultural competence, with its emphasis on "diverse values, beliefs, and behaviors" (Betancourt et al. 2002, 2) (already inadequately addressed, as revealed by Betty's lack of training), to a more systemically holistic cultural safety approach might better enable care providers to adequately address the complex community norms found on a reservation with a high number of adolescent pregnancies, a high rate of poverty, high rates of sexual violence, and a profound sense of historical trauma. Additionally, a focus on cultural safety might open a space for IHS to build both formal and informal partnerships with community leaders at the grassroots level, particularly spiritual leaders. A sustained consideration of the fourth-world context in which Native communities continue to survive, and in which Native women seek reproductive health care, is an essential aspect of developing this cultural safety.

The cartography of State organization that emerges from this research brings to light some of the complexity of Native women's reproductive lives and illustrates the restrictive nature of State control over reproductive health care for a population that is simultaneously and multiply gendered, sexed, classed, racialized, and nationalized in a quasi-postcolonial system. However, this research offers only a glimpse of the embodied experiences of Native women on Pine Ridge Reservation; future research must follow the emergent themes from this study to further explicate these experiences and give voice to Native women as they speak from diverse locations. For example, because this research focused on IHS services in reservation communities, Native women living in urban communities were largely neglected. This reflects the institutional structure of IHS, which focuses primarily on reservation centers, and the broader literature around Native people's health care, which has not adequately addressed the health care of Native people living off the reservation. Given that many Native families live in nonreservation communities and often change residences to find employment, be closer to family and community, and for a variety of other reasons, it is important to consider health-care services in off-reservation areas.

More specific to the research conducted in this project, future inquiry should consider in greater detail the links between culturally safe care and IHS structures, including the application of a Centering Pregnancy approach to prenatal care on Pine Ridge and the development of partnerships with community members. There are several organizations on the reservation that seek to support Native well-being, such as "1, 2, 3 . . . Hi, Baby!" (a nonprofit organization on Pine Ridge that supports pregnant women in obtaining prenatal care) and Thunder Valley Community Development (a community-run nonprofit organization on the reservation that centralizes tradition-oriented approaches to sustainable community development). Future research should include consideration of the roles and impact of these organizations. Community health representatives offer another resource to Native women that requires further consideration.

Not surprisingly, few of my informants expressed a thorough understanding of the implications of the cartography revealed through this study. However, it is not necessary to fully understand the history of IHS, its structural location within the Department of Health and Human Services, or its specific policy directives and programmatic initiatives in order to expect adequate and competent care; after all, many of us are unaware of the ruling relations that produce our social experiences. This lack of awareness should not translate into a lack of dignity or rights. Nonetheless, a greater understanding of certain key aspects of IHS might help Native women advocate for themselves and each other. For example, although individualistic perspectives in which the responsibility for care lies with Native women themselves were expressed by several informants, most informants in this study expressed anger and resentment at the quality of care they and other Native women receive through IHS and alternately blamed IHS and the federal government for their treatment. They are not wrong to do this; despite whatever individual responsibility Native women themselves hold for their health, responsibility for Native health care does, indeed, also lie with IHS and the federal government, as outlined in Chapters 5 and 6. A clearer understanding of the far-reaching structure of responsibility for Native health care might lead to more effective communication between IHS and Native women, and potentially mitigate the emotional challenges of seeking—and providing—medicalized reproductive health care on Pine Ridge. In this way, Native women's agency in their embodied experiences of health and wellness might be enhanced.

Native women may choose to delay or forgo entrance into the IHS system in order to avoid long wait times, because they feel unwelcome or unsafe in some way, and/or because they simply do not trust they will be adequately treated medically. They may also be inhibited from accessing adequate care by geographic isolation, inadequate facilities or personnel, and bureaucratic complications. Ultimately, however, it seems that women on Pine Ridge will enter the IHS system at different times and for different reasons, whether they continue their care with the Pine Ridge service unit or seek to change providers within or outside of the IHS system. Emergent themes around Native women's sense of agency and satisfaction with their reproductive health care experiences indicate that further inquiry into these areas may yield a richer understanding of their needs.

The themes that emerge from this research also provide the opportunity to understand better the roles of elite institutions in coordinating and shaping reproductive in/justice in the lives of all women by revealing the links between Native women's embodied experiences of reproductive health care and the multiple locations from which these experiences are organized. Future research should seek to further understand the numerous and interactive linkages between the macro-level State elite parties that organize Native women's reproductive health care and the micro-level embodied experiences of Native women themselves, particularly as these are mediated at the institutional level by IHS. However, given the structural constraints imposed by elite parties, future inquiries must push beyond formal governance structures to consider community structures of health and well-being. For example, consideration of community knowledge and the mechanisms for promoting health outside of the formal IHS system may reveal opportunities to develop culturally safe reproductive health care, including a broader knowledge base for Native women that incorporates both biomedical knowledge and diverse types of community knowledge. This will allow for a more complete (though perhaps still partial) understanding of reproductive health needs in Indian Country, and the strategies needed to meet these needs effectively and respectfully.

The delivery of reproductive health care, however, is only one aspect of the reproductive justice model. The multiple issues necessarily incorporated in a reproductive justice framework require recognition of the interactive nature of social inequalities, including but not limited to unequal distribution of resources and lack of physical and cultural safety. The current mainstream narrative of reproductive health care, which relies on a mythology of individual choice, ignores the complexities of diverse racial/ethnic, economic, cultural, and geographic locations. Relocating Native women in the center of this narrative, rather than at the margins, potentially allows for a meaningful consideration of the intersections of the social and political particularities of women's lives with their reproductive experiences, thereby expanding medical reliance on generalizable evidence as well as limited liberal notions of choice and rights to incorporate reproductive justice as this is conceptualized by Native women themselves. This relocation from margin to center will further enable a deeper understanding of reproductive justice for all women, and particularly for women in marginalized communities, as the patriarchal and racial architecture of nation building that undergirds reproductive health care reveals the State's sought-after collective ethnicity for the fiction it must, in fact, always be.

The stories that prompted this research offer an important opportunity to push beyond mainstream discourses of reproductive health care by centering particular local experiences in a broader analysis. Further centering the voices of Native women in future inquiry is essential if their multiple forms of marginalization—from reproductive health care itself and from the discourses that construct reproductive health care—are to be addressed. Any less than this continues the historic and egregious marginalization of women in all of their diverse locations, and prohibits genuine change. Feminist standpoint theorists urge scholars to consider the social world from the perspective of those who inhabit disadvantaged, rather than elite, categories, arguing that this provides a fuller view of social and political organization; in the case of Native women's reproductive health, the particular and unique perspectives offered by Native women themselves must constitute the guiding force of inquiry in order to more fully understand the embodied consequences of intersecting federal, regional state, and Tribal structures, as well as community resources and social inequalities, in women's health care experiences.

The longue durée of political relations between indigeneity and the State on this continent reflects the epistemological frameworks of the dominant culture in its organization of these relations. Ultimately this epistemology, which enables and reproduces structures of oppression for Native people and for Native women in particular, has proven resistant to change because, although the State is seemingly ambivalent in its relationship with Native nations, its double discourse of control and neglect in fact reflects its underlying drive to dominance. In many ways, the settler State has been successful in its efforts to displace Native people, materially and epistemologically. As discussed previously, Native peoples, whose population numbers have certainly been diminished over the last five centuries, are today among the poorest and the sickest among the nation's citizens. Their land base is constantly under threat by regional and federal State authorities. They are the most likely to drop out of high school, the most likely to commit suicide, the most likely to be unemployed—forms of marginalization that are more than metaphors for invisibility. Native people are perhaps, as Andrea Smith asserts, "always disappearing" (2005).

But they are still here.

As the United States as a nation (as a multitude of Nations) moves forward in the pursuit of better health care for all Americans, Native people must no longer be marginalized as "others," racially and economically. Native women's voices are essential to a meaningful conversation about the multiple healthcare systems at work in the United States. A greater understanding of Native women's experiences must be sought out by scholars, activists, Tribal leaders, and legislators and included in meaningful ways in the creation of change. This study provides only a glimpse into what can be learned through such effort. More stories must be told—and heard. We stand to learn a great deal about health and wellness, about race, class, gender and sexuality, and about nation-building and the reproductive body from these stories.

The truth about stories is that they not only tell us who we are; they can also teach us how to be something different.

Mitakuye Oyasin.

Appendix A

Methods and Methodologies

Institutional Ethnography

Institutional ethnography (IE), originally developed by Dorothy Smith (1987, 1992, 2004) as a means of retaining the subjectivity of women in sociological research, provides a methodological tool to examine the mechanisms by which the local, "everyday/everynight" world of individuals (Smith 1987) is shaped and coordinated extralocally through institutionally organized social relations. The focus of IE is thus the organizational forces that shape individual experiences, which reveal the linkages between personal experiences and structural processes. As Smith explains, IE seeks "to know more about how things work . . . how things happen to us as they do" (1990, 34). One of the hallmarks of IE is the constant location of the situated knower in the center of the analysis (or map); the experiences of this expert knower (in the case of this study, Native women seeking reproductive health care, particularly on Pine Ridge Reservation) provide the entry-level data for the larger explication of ruling relations that organize particular experiences. In this way, IE can be understood as a form of cartography; according to Smith (1999), the map that develops as the researcher follows multiple lines of inquiry reveals the social relations that coordinate our lives beyond a specific moment, location, or individual.

The data that result from IE, therefore, are not necessarily intended to be generalizable or transferable to other contexts; rather, they are intended to provide a specific explication of the social organization of a situated knower's experiences. In the case of this study, the specific experiences of Native women on Pine Ridge Reservation cannot be simply transferred to another reservation or Native community. However, my findings do provide insights into the roles of the State in organizing and providing reproductive health care, particularly to women in marginalized communities. This research thereby provides an opportunity to better understand the roles of the State in coordinating and shaping the daily lives of those who are raced, classed, gendered, and sexed in particular ways. As well, I hope that this research potentially expands prevailing discourses about reproductive health care to incorporate broader intersectional analyses of women's reproductive bodies as these are situated in, and move through, various social locations.

I chose to do an institutional ethnography of the Indian Health Service because I was interested in the organization of reproductive health care for Native women, an interest that was piqued by the stories of friends and relatives on Pine Ridge Reservation and driven by my own feminist sociological imagination. Importantly, this framework allowed me to objectify the institution of IHS, rather than my informants; IHS became the object of my study, while my relatives on the reservation remained as subjects whose experiences guided my inquiry. My informants were the expert knowers whose stories offered me signposts to follow as I sought to explicate the ruling relations that govern their embodied experiences, but it is the governing itself, what Michel Foucault might call biopower, that is most closely examined in this book.

Most institutional ethnographies are conducted through access to the institution under study. This allows for particular kinds of observations, access to texts that the institution relies upon such as forms and manuals, and of course the mainstay of ethnography, interviews. In my case this access was effectively denied. I spent almost a year of graduate school seeking official approval from IHS to conduct interviews with its employees and observations of its facilities before finally being told by an IHS employee, "Oh, they'll never give you permission."

There are many reasons IHS might refuse access to a researcher. For example, IHS is frequently targeted by detractors who may wish to reduce its funding or demand change IHS is not ready or willing to undergo. At times, these demands may be well justified; at other times, they may result from a lack of comprehensive understanding of the challenges inherent in the IHS system and mission. By effectively blocking my research access, IHS may have simply been circling the wagons (to use an ironic metaphor) in order to protect itself from criticism, both warranted and unwarranted.

It is equally possible that IHS personnel themselves do not understand the chain of command for such requests; numerous times I was given incorrect contact information and directed to incorrect personnel for my request. This confusion may also have been due to the high turnover rate in IHS; at one point, the person to whom I had been directed, and from whom I was awaiting word regarding my approval status, simply stopped coming to work. My proposal was never found in her materials. As discussed in Chapter 7, mine is certainly not the only request for access or information that IHS has refused; in a scathing indictment of IHS, the chair of the Senate Committee on Indian Affairs, Senator Byron Dorgan, asserted that IHS policies and directives discourage employees from communicating with Congress, tribal governments, other agencies and groups without permission from either their direct supervisor or staff at the headquarters office (Dorgan 2010, 42). In another instance, as of early 2014 the American Civil Liberties Union of South Dakota has not yet received a full response from IHS to a Freedom of Information suit it brought in late 2009. My lack of access apparently puts me in prestigious company.

In mid-2009, I did receive word from IHS that my request for access could be approved pending several final considerations. One of these was my agreement to allow IHS final approval of the research before any public presentation of it. As I had already granted the Oglala Sioux Tribal Council that final approval, I was unable to comply. I was then informed by IHS that without this change, I would not be granted permission to interview IHS employees. In 2010, I revisited this issue with several people in the IHS administrative offices, but was told the policy would not change, and therefore, due to this blocked access and my own unwillingness to transfer final authority to what is, essentially, a government agency with which I found some fault, I was unable to interview IHS employees for this research. I discuss how I addressed this problem below.

One of the most important consequences of my decision not to give IHS final approval and my resulting lack of access to IHS personnel is that IHS itself has had no opportunity to review this work or comment on it. I say this to be fair: publicly available data on IHS, including vital statistics information for their Native constituencies, are hard to find (and in many cases do not exist). Interviews with IHS personnel might have been able to add to my understanding of their processes in ways I could not glean from public literature. Although I have no doubt my decision to respect the Oglala Lakota Tribal Research Review Board's final authority was the right one, it is important to note that my refusal to meet IHS's requirements locked IHS out of the opportunity to respond to my data or my conclusions, just as their refusal to meet mine locked me out of interviews with their current employees and access to texts not publicly available. This changed the nature of doing an institutional ethnography as I sought ethical ways to gather information without formal access. I cast a wide methodological net to do this, relying particularly on five specific methods: historical research, descriptive policy analysis, document analysis, ethnographic observations, and interviews.

Methods

Historical Analysis

For my historical analysis, I relied largely on scholarly journals of history such as the *Journal of Social History* and peer-reviewed journals from Native studies such as *Wicazo Sa Review* and *American Indian Quarterly*, as well as autobiographical works by Native people such as Severt Young Bear, Mary Crow Dog, Wilma Mankiller, Katsi Cook, and others. The IHS "Gold Book," released by IHS to celebrate its fiftieth anniversary in 2005, and the National Library of Medicine's online resources (including a photo exhibit of the history of Indian health care) were also used to clarify the institutionalization of health care for Native people and the meanings of this institutionalization. I analyzed these texts for the following: 1) dynamic notions of Native American identity, which is essential to accessing care through IHS and reflects a State-organized drive toward assimilation; 2) the intersections of Native sovereignty with federal policies, which affects the programmatic directions of IHS as well as its funding; 3) the bureaucratic development of IHS as a federal agency accountable to numerous, often conflicting, points of authority; and 4) nationalist as well as community-based and subjective meaning construction around Native women's reproductive bodies.

Descriptive Policy Analysis

Policy analysis in this research included specific interrogation of the ways in which federal policies have impacted the development of Native-US relations as well as the development of IHS and the directions taken by IHS in seeking to fulfill its mission. Particular attention was also paid to the ways in which federal policy defines reproductive health care and organizes its delivery. Policy analysis, like the document analysis described below, included ongoing consideration of the discourses that produce knowledge: knowledge about indigeneity, knowledge about reproductive health care and the reproductive body, and conceptualizations of individual and group rights.

Examples of congressional policies include: the Snyder Act of 1921; the Indian Reorganization Act of 1934; House Resolutions 108 and 280 (passed in 1953); the Self-Determination and Education Assistance Act of 1975; and the Indian Health Care Improvement Act of 1976, the proposed amendments to it in 2008 and 2009, and its most recent version as passed in 2010. I also examined the proposed and passed federal budgets of 2009, 2010, and 2011, the 2009 Omnibus Appropriations Act, the 2010 Tribal Law and Order Act, the 2010 Patient Protection and Affordable Care Act, and the endorsement by President Obama of the United Nations Declaration of Indigenous Rights, which affirms, among other rights, Native Americans' right to health.

In addition, I analyzed several reports that have been influential in the development of many of these policies, including the Meriam Report of 1928, the Hoover Commission's Task Force on Indian Policy released in 1949, and the US Commission on Civil Rights reports on the state of Native American health care in 2003 and 2004. I examined several communications, including letters, memoranda of understanding, and hearing transcripts, between the State and Tribal parties such as the Senate Committee on Indian Affairs, IHS, the Centers for Medicare and Medicaid, the Government Accountability Office, the Portland Area Indian Health Board, and the National Indian Health Board. I also reviewed President Nixon's address to Congress in 1970, which specifically urged the repeal of termination and the institution of self-determination for Native nations, thus opening up a political opportunity for increasing development of sovereignty in the creation of Indian policies, including the expansion of health-care policies in Indian Country.

Many of the policies I examined dealt directly or indirectly with health care for Native people and specifically with reproductive health care. However, I also considered federal reproductive health care policies, including the Violence against Women Act of 2013 and the Hyde Amendment as it was originally passed in 1976 as well as the version passed in 2009. I also examined several pieces of reproductive health-care legislation passed on the regional state level, particularly in South Dakota where Pine Ridge Reservation is located. With these I sought to understand not only the legal basis for providing or withholding certain forms of reproductive health care but also the ideological foundations, particularly as these relied on race, class, gender, sexuality, and citizenship.

In addition, I considered several reports released by nongovernmental organizations such as Amnesty International's landmark studies *Maze of Injustice: The Failure to Protect Indigenous Women from Sexual Violence in the USA* (2007), and *Deadly Delivery: The Maternal Health Care Crisis in the USA* (2010); the American Civil Liberties Union report on birthing practices in IHS (ACLU 2010), particularly in South Dakota; and numerous reports on reproductive health care and reproductive rights produced by the Kaiser Family Foundation, the Alan Guttmacher Institute, the American Center for Progress, and the Center for Reproductive Rights.

Document Analysis

I closely examined several key documents produced by IHS to understand the ways in which these texts serve to organize both the delivery and receipt of reproductive health care, including its ideological conceptualization and the linkages between these ideological foundations and the material experiences of Native women as revealed through interviews. Here I paid particular attention to: the IHS pharmaceutical protocol and its drug formulary; the 2008 IHS Director's Initiatives; the IHS Strategic Vision 2006–2011; the IHS *Indian*

Health Service Manual (an online resource for IHS employees, n.d.); the IHS *Annual Report* for 2007 (the most recent available at the time); and the IHS website, particularly its Women's Health page. Through the IHS website I was able to access several texts intended to disseminate information within the IHS community of providers and administrators, including compiled responses from IHS listservs, notes from working sessions, several PowerPoint presentations, and several issues of the *Chief Clinical Consultant's Corner*, a regular newsletter distributed through IHS. Because access to IHS personnel for interviews was denied, I turned to texts written by former and current IHS care providers and administrators, including statements to Congress; publicly available listserv comments, letters, and memoranda; and historical perspectives on IHS found in peer-reviewed journals such as the *Milbank Quarterly* as well as in edited collections. All of these texts were examined for the ways in which reproductive health care is conceptualized and organized throughout IHS, particularly from an institutional perspective. Interestingly, the IHS website has undergone several evolutions since I began looking at it in 2008. One of these changes has been the disappearance of the Maternal and Child Health section; it is entirely gone, and the information it once provided has been either removed or embedded elsewhere on the website. I also examined various documents published by the World Health Organization and the Centers for Disease Control to better understand the broad context of health and healthy conditions.

As the links between Native American health care and human rights law became increasingly apparent, I turned to numerous international human rights instruments such as the Convention on the Elimination of All Forms of Racial Discrimination, the Convention to End Discrimination against Women, and the United Nations Declaration on the Rights of Indigenous Peoples; Tribal nongovernmental organizations such as *Owe Aku* (an indigenous environmental rights organization located primarily on Pine Ridge Reservation); and Tribal governmental organizations such as the Black Hills Sioux Nation Treaty Council. These were analyzed for the ways in which they shape Native-US relations, Native and US understandings of rights and obligations, and Native and US efforts to identify issues of concern and develop appropriate strategies of redress.

Ethnographic and Participant Observations

Prior to the formal phase of this research, I attended the United Nations Permanent Forum on Indigenous Issues annual meetings in New York in 2004 and 2008. The forum's sessions as well as several conversations I had with attendees provided a broader context in which to understand indigenous women's access to health care and the conditions for health globally as a human rights issue for indigenous peoples. In 2009 I participated in a three-day academic medical conference on Indigenous Women's Health, where I was able to observe continuing education around reproductive health care for Native women and learn more about the work processes within IHS, as well as further explore how institutional structures of reproductive health care for Native women are interpreted by professional staff and others affiliated with IHS.

I also had the opportunity to observe a sex education session for adolescents during the summer of 2010. This ninety-minute session focused on the prevalence and prevention of sexually transmitted infections on the reservation. This was a particularly valuable opportunity, as it enabled me to observe and listen even without formal access.

I continue to travel to Pine Ridge regularly, where I am frequently welcomed into kitchens, prayer ceremonies, pow-wows, and other community events. All of these opportunities are at least twofold; they allow me to learn, which has been invaluable to the understanding I developed through this research, but just as important, they allow my relatives on Pine Ridge to learn about me. Numerous community members have offered comments and suggestions on my research, and just about everyone I come into regular contact with is aware of both my goals and my findings, at least to some degree. In fact, they're probably tired of hearing about this research.

Interviews

In the twelve years between my first visit to Pine Ridge Reservation in 1999 and my dissertation defense in 2011, I had countless conversations with Native people about health care, health disparities, and reproductive health. Many of these conversations occurred on the reservation around kitchen tables or campfires, over meals following prayer ceremonies, and even in convenience stores. Many took place off of the reservation in nearby Rapid City or Hill City or Hot Springs, and several occurred over the phone or by e-mail. Several occurred at the United Nations, and others at pow-wows in South Dakota, Connecticut, and Massachusetts. From mid-2009 to late 2010 I conducted thirty-two formal interviews with twenty-three women and two with men, all of which were on or around Pine Ridge Reservation in South Dakota except for three phone interviews and one interview conducted in Connecticut.

My informants ranged in age from nineteen to seventy-two; both of the men are Lakota, fourteen of the women are Lakota, and the others are Diné, Mohawk, Dakota, Chickasha, or describe themselves as Lakota and another Native heritage (for example, one woman is Lakota and Hopi). One woman is white. This white woman (Betty) is a midwife who worked for IHS on Pine Ridge Reservation for approximately two years, but was no longer employed by IHS at the time of our interview. I also interviewed two other midwives (both Native) as well as four women who describe themselves as health-care advocates or activists; three of these work on both the local and national level and one works primarily on Pine Ridge. Twenty of my twenty-five informants have at least a high school education, six of them have completed at least a bachelor's degree (two of them at Oglala Lakota College on Pine Ridge, one of the first Tribally run colleges in the country), three are certified nurse-midwives, one is a former nurse, and one is currently in nursing school.

My sample by no means offers an adequate diversity of experiences. For example, all my informants are parents, and all are typically physically abled. As well, my sample includes a disproportionately high educational level; currently, fewer than 50 percent of Native Americans graduate high school (Faircloth and Tippeconnic 2010), as opposed to 80 percent of my sample. It is also important to note (and I fail to do this adequately in this book) that reproductive justice scholars and activists are increasingly questioning the very idea of "woman" as a biologically centered and heteronormative category; my informants are all cisgender and heterosexual, and therefore in following their experiences I do not give adequate attention to the reproductive health care needs of non-cisgender, non-heterosexual women. Similarly, there is very little Tribal diversity, as my primary interest is in Pine Ridge, which is a Lakota reservation. As well, virtually all of my informants described in various ways a commitment to being Native as a distinct and valued identity. However, not all Native people express similar commitments, and my sample, which relied on snowball sampling beginning with people I knew, missed Native people who do not identify this way. Nonetheless, despite the limitations, my findings reveal structures of regulation and control, as well as moments of agency, resistance, and acquiescence, which bring to light broad concerns over the settler State's drive to regulate the reproductive body.

Interviews were sought through snowball sampling, following a request for introductions from previous informants and other contacts on the reservation. Interviews were semi-structured, following a predetermined set of questions, but allowing for informants to share what they wanted in terms of overarching issues. Formal interviews took place in various locations, including a local café on the reservation, a playground, and informants' homes. One took place over the course of several days; this interview totaled almost seven hours.

Other interviews were shorter, but more awkward. For example, I learned when I first moved to the reservation that tradition-oriented men and women generally avoid looking each other directly in the eye or speaking directly to each other outside of public transactions. I also learned that first names are rarely used; instead, people are referred to by familial relationship or nicknames (I still find myself occasionally slipping into these behaviors in my interactions with non-Native people; students in my classes often think I simply don't know their names, and I'm sure the barista at my local Starbucks thinks I'm shifty, as I never meet his eyes when we exchange pleasantries). The two men who agreed to be interviewed both describe themselves as "traditional," and at times expressed some discomfort at being asked direct questions about reproductive health care through their body language and verbal avoidance, although they were both generous with their time and with their responses.

These men were gracious and knowledgeable, as were all my informants, and I am grateful for their time and their insights.

Indian Country is small, and Pine Ridge Reservation is smaller. Many of my informants are well known on the reservation and elsewhere, and it has proven challenging to maintain their anonymity. In order to do this, I have withheld a great deal of descriptive information about them. Additionally, I was unable to include certain meaningful comments from informants because they would have made the speaker too readily identifiable in the small communities of Pine Ridge and even the broader community of Indian Country, or because informants asked me to remove certain comments they had made or stories they had told. I hope that my efforts to respect their trust but still tell their stories have been adequate.

Data Analysis

Generally speaking, the purpose of IE is to explicate social relations, beyond the boundaries of any one person's experience, or even the collective experience of a group. The broader purpose of IE generally is not to explore individual, subjective experiences in the same ways as conventional ethnography, but rather to identify and trace the points of connection between different institutional activities. Analysis of the data therefore included conventional ethnographic techniques, but also required different methods that speak to the particularities of IE. These included visual mappings of institutional relationships, which allowed for the tracing of ruling relations from Native women themselves to various extralocal points of authority (for example, the US Department of Health and Human Services, in which IHS is located).

Several themes emerged from interviews that alternatively echoed and contradicted perspectives expressed in IHS literature and preliminary research. I followed these emergent themes in further historical and policy analysis. I then pursued specific emergent themes in both follow-up interviews and further discourse and content analysis. I eventually devoted an entire wall in our spare bedroom (spare only because I made my children share a room for a year and a half so I could have work space at home) to visually mapping these themes. The wall was covered with white paper, on which I wrote key players (Congress; the president; IHS; and so on) as well as the names of informants, the titles of key reports and pieces of legislation, relevant quotes from informants and from content analysis, etc. These were then connected by threads (literally): red thread for reproductive health care, yellow for sovereignty issues, green for collective ethnicity/settler colonialism, black for knowledge construction, and so on. I wish I'd taken a picture of that wall—it was quite a tapestry by the time I was done.

Conventional ethnographic techniques such as thematic coding were also used. Emergent categories were then further developed by memo. Further data analysis occurred through examination of text-mediated discourses about reproductive health and health care from selected sources (see above for examples of texts). Documents were analyzed similarly to interviews and observations, following a thematic coding procedure and developing categories that were included in memo writing. This approach required that analysis remain somewhat flexible in response to ongoing data collection, which in turn was guided by continual evaluation and reevaluation of analytic points.

I maintained a separate field journal in which to take notes as soon as possible after interviews and observations. This journal includes notes on the details of each interview such as date and time, how long the interview was, and where it took place. I also wrote about the emotional work of interviews for both myself and my informants; for example, how I felt when meeting a new informant (usually nervous); my personal assessment of how the informant and I attempted to establish or resist rapport with each other; and my own emotional responses to the stories shared with me during interviews are all described in these entries. I also traced the changes to my relationships on the reservation as I assumed this relatively new persona of "researcher," an aspect of my shifting outsider/insider identity that produced responses from community members ranging from distrust and new emotional distances to an eagerness to collaborate in the opportunity to create change, and, frequently, an expressed appreciation for what I, now understood to be a researcher, could bring to my relatives on the reservation. These notes are particularly important to my own growing knowledge of indigenous methodologies, and were often included in coding, categorizing, and memo writing.

Study Limitations

This study is restricted by three main limitations: data available through and about IHS, sampling strategy, and access. Due largely to underfunding, IHS data is neither current nor fully coherent, particularly in such areas as patient usage of IHS facilities and vital statistics. The problems of data collection are widely acknowledged by IHS and others (see, e.g., Faircloth and Tippeconnic 2010; IHS 2006; Kraus 2001; Rhoades, D'Angelo, and Rhoades 2000; US Commission on Civil Rights 2004), and the reasons are varied; for example, I was told by the IHS Aberdeen Area Office in 2009 that they had not employed a statistician since the early 1990s because they could not afford one. Therefore, they rely on individual service units to maintain their own data, which is done inconsistently on the local level. Additionally, many Native people who rely on IHS may also use contracted facilities or private care providers; this interrupts the already limited abilities of IHS to collect and synthesize a cohesive body of data. A further complication arises from race misreporting, which is more common in contracted and private facilities than in IHS facilities, and more common in states with a low Native population (IHS 2002–2003).

The limited data available on health and health care in Indian Country complicate research into health care and demographics. In some instances, data are simply not available at all to answer research questions, or at least not available without specific access. Data that are available may be outdated, or different sources may offer conflicting data. When this occurred during the course of this study, I sought a variety of data sources and carefully considered their validity and credibility. I also sought confirmation and further information from community members and informants.

An additional limitation to this study is the recruitment strategy; because this study utilized a snowball sampling technique that began with preexisting contacts, the diversity of Native women's experiences is not adequately represented. I attempted to address this limitation by seeking introductions to women with diverse social and embodied experiences. I also sought out information about similar, though probably not identical, health and health-care situations in other marginalized, as well as privileged, communities in order to better understand, though perhaps not adequately address, diverse experiences.

As discussed above, IHS itself did not grant me access. I addressed this in three ways. The first was to closely examine materials published by IHS, including both printed literature and the IHS website. Through the website I found a great deal of information about the organizational framework of IHS as well as presentations, memos, and articles written by IHS personnel (many of these are no longer available in early 2014). These were examined not only for information about IHS practices and programs but also for their intended audience, most often other IHS employees. In addition to seeking out extensive literature by IHS about IHS, I also sought interviews with numerous people who have worked with, but not for, IHS, or who had previously worked for IHS; these informants were able to offer me insights into many of the themes that emerged from other interviews and literature reviews.

Finally, my attendance at the First Annual Conference on Maternal and Child Health sponsored by IHS in 2009 provided me with the opportunity to hear from IHS employees and allies at many different levels and many different geographic locations. For example, one plenary session consisted of a panel of two former IHS directors with the current IHS director, all of whom discussed challenges and progress for IHS since its formation in 1955. I did not ask questions during these sessions, given the complications of my presence as a researcher who did not have explicit access to interviews; however, many other attendees asked questions that were extremely helpful. In fact, I found everyone who worked with IHS, including the director of the Maternal Health Division, to be very interested and supportive of my research; however, without exception every employee of IHS made clear to me that they would not answer questions or grant interviews without specific permission from IHS.

Telling Stories

I continue to learn from Native women through our conversations, through sharing meals, prayers, e-mails, and Facebook updates, and through our shared context, always differentially understood and experienced, of gender, motherhood, and relationship. However, this learning is frequently captured in ways that do not map neatly onto sociologically categorized notions of "methods," particularly as these methods encode a sense of epistemological objectivity. Therefore this study incorporated elements of autoethnography, which Stacy Jones (2005) describes as "a balancing act" of reciprocity that can create "charged moments of clarity, connection, and change" (764). My own experiences and knowledge woven in throughout this book are intended to openly acknowledge my shifting positionality in this study, a dynamic amalgamation of changing insider/outsider/mediator statuses that reflects both my previous and ongoing relationships on the reservation and the somewhat awkward insertion into my relationships there of my relatively new status as a researcher.

My transparent presence indicates my reliance on what Sandra Harding (2007) calls "strong objectivity"; by reminding the reader that I have personal as well as professional investments in the communities on Pine Ridge, I hope to allow the reader to engage critically with my methods and my findings. Thus, my presence in this study is a dialogic one, in conversation with informants, texts, and readers alike. As indigenous scholar Shawn Wilson has noted, the researcher's story is a part of the collaborative nature of research in Native communities (2001, 2008; see also Innes 2009). The space of engagement produced by autoethnography thus becomes a space of democratic participation in which collaboration, solidarity, and reciprocity are understood to include multiple sources of knowledge. This includes that knowledge, gained over the previous ten years, which brought me to the formal (university and Tribally approved) phase of this research as well as the disciplinary knowledge which enabled the sociological design of this study, collection and analysis of data, and development of theory.

As the storyteller, I shaped the story you read here; I chose which data you had access to, whose voices you heard and whose you did not, and even how you could hear them. I sought the guidance and input of numerous people in seeking to tell the story in the right way: relatives from Indian Country and from academia, through member-checking and revision, and both formal and informal peer review. But ultimately, the decisions have been mine. Of course these decisions are political; all knowledge is, at some level. All stories teach us something. I hope I have done justice to the stories with which I was entrusted.

Appendix B

A Brief Chronology of Federal Actions Affecting Native Health Care

---

1803 The federal government became involved with Native health care and assigned responsibility for it to the War Department; responsibilities largely focused on containment of contagious diseases.

1819 Federal legislation provided for annual appropriations of $10,000 to religious groups and missionary organizations that provided medical services specifically to Native Americans.

1832 Indian Vaccination Act is passed; this is the first piece of legislation specifically targeting Native American health.

1849 Responsibility for Native health care was transferred from military to civilian control when the Bureau of Indian Affairs was transferred to the Department of the Interior.

1871 The Indian Appropriation Act removed independent status from Native nations for the purpose of treaty negotiations.

1891 Doctors in the Indian Service were required to pass competitive examinations and possess medical degrees, reflecting the growing professionalization of medicine.

1903 Indian schools were instructed to enroll only healthy children due to ongoing concerns with hygiene, overcrowding, and ventilation following a long period of high mortality from infectious diseases.

1921 The Snyder Act was passed, consolidating various previous acts, defining the scope of federal Indian programs, and providing for congressional appropriations of funds to provide health care to Native Americans.

1928 The Merriam Report was published, and condemned the federal management of Indian health care.

1938 Congress authorized the collection of fees for medical (as well as certain other) services from Native people able to pay.

1953 House Concurrent Resolution 108 was passed, beginning the official process of termination. House Concurrent Resolution 280 was passed, removing jurisdiction over criminal acts committed on Indian land from Tribal authorities and placing jurisdiction in the hands of regional states. Six states were originally granted jurisdiction; in the years that followed, ten more states took over jurisdiction.

1955 Responsibility for Native American health care was transferred from the Bureau of Indian Affairs to the United States Public Health Service.

1964 Congress passed the Economic Opportunity Act, providing for several programs dedicated to improving the health, education, and general welfare of the poor.

1965 Congress passed legislation to provide health care for the elderly (Medicare) and the poor (Medicaid).

The first tribally contracted program was inaugurated; it was for community health representatives (CHRs) on Pine Ridge Reservation.

1970 President Richard Nixon called for the end of termination policy and federal support of Tribal self-determination.

1975 The Indian Self-Determination and Education Assistance Act was passed, providing mechanisms for transferring programs traditionally administered by the BIA and IHS to Tribal governments.

1976 The Indian Health Care Improvement Act was passed, formalizing the goal of providing the highest possible health status to Native people.

1977 The White Buffalo Calf Woman Society was founded on the Rosebud Sioux Reservation, the first nonprofit organization dedicated to advocacy on behalf of American Indian women who are victims of violence.

1978 The Indian Religious Freedom Act was passed.

1988 Indian Health Service was granted Agency status within the Department of Health and Human Services.

1992 The Indian Health Care Improvement Act was reauthorized, reaffirmng the government's responsibility and legal obligation to assure the highest possible health status for Natives.

2008 The Indian Health Care Improvement Act failed to pass due in part to ongoing debates over the Vitter Amendment and the financial crisis of fall 2008.

2009 President Barack Obama allocated close to $1 billion for Indian health care and violence prevention and treatment through the 2009 Omnibus Appropriations Act and the proposed FY 2010 federal budget.

2010 Congress passed the Patient Protection and Affordable Care Act, rendering the Indian Health Care Improvement Act permanent as Title X. The Patient Protection and Affordable Care Act continues to be debated and the specific details of its implementation remain unclear.

President Obama signed the Tribal Law and Order Act, intended to reverse some of the damage done to Tribal law enforcement systems through Public Law 280.

President Obama signed the United Nations Declaration on the Rights of Indigenous Peoples. His signature was accompanied by numerous formal reservations, which make specific mention of the lack of a clear definition regarding who is indigenous, and weaken the overall intentions of the declaration. The United States was the last UN member state to sign the declaration, which is not a legally binding document.

2012 The Supreme Court ruled on the Patient Protection and Affordable Care Act, deciding that tax penalties for individuals above a determined income who remain uninsured are constitutional. The effects of this on IHS and in Indian Country remain unclear.

2013 Congress passed the Violence against Women Act, including provisions to strengthen Tribal jurisdictions.

References

Aberdeen Area Health Services Master Plan. 2003. Area Analysis Meeting, PowerPoint presentation. Accessed June 11, 2009. http://www.ihs.gov (page discontinued).

Abramovitz, Mimi. 1996. *Regulating the Lives of Women: Social Welfare Policy from Colonial Times.* Cambridge, MA: South End Press.

ACLU (American Civil Liberties Union). 2010. "Complaint for Injunctive Relief, Civil Action." September 27. Accessed June 1, 2013. http://www.aclu.org/files/assets/2010-9-27-ACLUvIHS-Complaint.pdf.

ACOG (American College of Obstetricians and Gynecologists). 2007. "Strategies for Adolescent Pregnancy Prevention." Washington, DC: American College of Obstetricians and Gynecologists. Accessed June 19, 2009. http://www.acog.org/~/media/Departments/Adolescent%20Health%20Care/StrategiesForAdolescentPregnancyPrevention.pdf.

ACRJ (Asian Communities for Reproductive Justice). 2005. *A New Vision for Advancing Our Movement for Reproductive Rights, Reproductive Health, and Reproductive Justice.* Oakland, CA: Asian Communities for Reproductive Justice.

Agtuca, Jacqueline. 2007. "Beloved Women: Life Givers, Caretakers, Teachers of Future Generations." In *Sharing Our Stories of Survival: Native Women Surviving Violence,* edited by Sarah Deer, Bonnie Clairmont, Carrie A. Martell, and Maureen L. White Eagle, 3–26. Lanham, MD: Alta Mira Press.

Aguilar, Rose. 2006. "The Power of Thunder." AlterNet, April 3. Accessed July 21, 2009. http://www.alternet.org/rights/34314/?page=1.

Albers, Patricia, and Beatrice Medicine. 1983. "The Role of Sioux Women in the Production of Ceremonial Objects: The Case of the Star Quilt." In *The Hidden Half: Studies of Plains Indian Women,* edited by Patricia Albers and Beatrice Medicine, 123–142. Lanham, MD: University Press of America.

Alexander, Greg, and Milton Kotelchuck. 2001. "Assessing the Role and Effectiveness of Prenatal Care: History, Challenges, and Direction for Future Research." *Public Health Reports* 116 (4): 306–315.

Alfred, Taiaiake. 1999. *Peace, Power, Righteousness: An Indigenous Manifesto.* Don Mills, ON: Oxford University Press.

Allee, Lisa. 2008. "Centering Pregnancy: A Model of Prenatal Care." *CCC Corner* 6:9. Accessed July 27, 2009. http://www.ihs.gov/MedicalPrograms/MCH/M/ob.cfm?module=9_08ft#midw (page discontinued).

Allen, Paula Gunn. 1986. *The Sacred Hoop: Recovering the Feminine in American Indian Traditions*. Boston, MA: Beacon Press.

———. 1991. *Grandmothers of the Light: A Medicine Woman's Sourcebook*. Boston, MA: Beacon Press.

Alvord, Lori, and Elizabeth Van Pelt. 1999. *The Scalpel and the Silver Bear: The First Navajo Woman Surgeon Combines Western Medicine and Traditional Healing*. New York: Bantam Books.

American Cancer Society. 2011–2012. *Breast Cancer Facts & Figures 2011–2012*. Atlanta, GA: American Cancer Society.

Amnesty International. 2007. *Maze of Injustice: The Failure to Protect Indigenous Women from Sexual Violence in the USA*. New York: Amnesty International.

———. 2010. Deadly Delivery: The Maternal Healthcare Crisis in the USA. London: Amnesty International.

Anderson, Kim. 2000. *A Recognition of Being: Reconstructing Native Womanhood*. Toronto, ON: Sumach Press.

———. 2006. "New Life Stirring: Mothering, Transformation, and Aboriginal Womanhood." In *Until Our Hearts Are on the Ground: Aboriginal Mothering and Oppression, Resistance, and Rebirth*, edited by Dawn Memee Lavell-Harvard and Jeanette Corbiere Lavell, 13–24. Toronto, ON: Demeter Press.

Arons, Jessica. 2007. "The Failing State of Native American Women's Health: An Interview with Charon Asetoyer." Center for American Progress. Accessed May 15, 2013. www.americanprogress.org/issues/women/news/2007/05/16/2970/the-failing-state-of-native-american-womens-health-interview-with-charon-asetoyer/.

Arons, Jessica, and Madina Agenor. 2010. *Separate and Unequal: The Hyde Amendment and Women of Color*. Washington, DC: Center for American Progress.

Artichoker, Karen, and Martha Mousseau. 2006. *Violence against Native Women Is Not Traditional*. Rapid City, SD: Sacred Circle.

Asetoyer, Charon. 2004. "Biographical Sketch." *Indigenous Woman* 5 (4): 8–9.

Bachman, Ronet, Heather Zaykowski, Rachel Kallmyer, Margarita Poteyeva, and Christina Lanier. 2008. *Violence against American Indian and Alaska Native Women and the Criminal Justice Response: What Is Known*. Unpublished grant report to the US Department of Justice. Available from: www.ncjrs.gov/pdffiles1/nij/grants/223691.pdf.

Beck, Andrew. 2004. "The Flexner Report and the Standardization of American Medical Education." *Journal of the American Medical Association* 291: 2139–2140.

Belluck, Pam. 2009. "New Hopes on Healthcare for American Indians." *New York Times*, December 2, A1 and A26.

Bergman, Abraham, Ralph Forquera, Angela Erdrich, David Grossman, and John Todd. 1999. "A Political History of the Indian Health Service." *Milbank Quarterly* 77 (4): 571–604.

Betancourt, Joseph, Alexander Green, and Emilio Carrillo. 2002. *Cultural Competence in Health Care: Emerging Frameworks and Practical Approaches*. Commonwealth Fund. Accessed April 1, 2012. http://www.commonwealthfund.org/~/media/Files/Publications/Fund%20Report/2002/Oct/Cultural%20Competence%20in%20Health%20Care%20%20Emerging%20Frameworks%20and%20Practical%20Approaches/betancourt_culturalcompetence_576%20pdf.pdf.

Black Hills Treaty Council. 2011. "Black Hills Treaty Council Rejects U.S. Limited Support of U.N. Indigenous Declaration." Accessed March 3, 2011. http://bsnorrell.blogspot.com/2011/01/black-hills-treaty-council-rejects-us.html.

Blanc, Ann, Trevor Croft, Jamie Trevett, and Amy Tsui. 2009. "Patterns and Trends in Adolescents' Contraceptive Use and Discontinuation in Developing Countries and

Comparisons with Adult Women." *International Perspectives on Sexual and Reproductive Health* 35 (2): 63–71.

Bloodsworth-Lugo, Mary. 2007. *In-between Bodies: Sexual Difference, Race, and Sexuality.* Albany: State University of New York Press.

Bobel, Christina. 2001. *The Paradox of Natural Mothering.* Philadelphia, PA: Temple University Press.

Bordieu, Pierre. 1977. *Outline of a Theory of Practice.* New York: Cambridge University Press.

———. 1986. "The Forms of Capital." In *Handbook of Theory and Research for the Sociology of Culture*, edited by John Richardson, 241–258. New York: Greenwood Press.

Boonstra, Heather. 2008. "The Impact of Government Programs on Reproductive Health Disparities: Three Case Studies." *Guttmacher Policy Review* 11 (3): 6–12.Boyer, Debra, and David Fine. 1992. "Sexual Abuse as a Factor in Adolescent Pregnancy and Child Maltreatment." *Family Planning Perspectives* 24 (1): 4–11 and 19.

Brave Heart, Maria Yellow Horse. 1999. "Gender Differences in the Historical Trauma Response among the Lakota." *Journal of Health and Social Policy* 10 (4): 1–21.

Brenneman, George. 2000. "Maternal, Child, and Youth Health." In *American Indian Health: Innovations in Health Care, Promotion, and Policy*, edited by Everett R. Rhoades, 138–150. Baltimore, MD: Johns Hopkins University Press.

Briggs, Kara. 2006. "Pine Ridge Leader Faces Battle over Abortion Ban." *Women's ENews*, June 27. Accessed July 29, 2009. http://www.womensenews.org/article.cfm?aid=2793.

Brophy, William, and Sophie Aberle. 1966. *The Indian: America's Unfinished Business.* Report of the Commission on the Rights, Liberties, and Responsibilities of the American Indians. Norman: University of Oklahoma Press.

Brown, Donald, Henry Dobyns, Jack Frisch, Robert Harmon, John Honigmann, et al. 1974. "Value Themes of the Native American Tribalistic Movement among the South Dakota Sioux." *Current Anthropology* 15 (3): 284–303.

Brown, Michael, Martin Carnoy, Elliott Currie, and Troy Duster. 2003. *Whitewashing Race: The Myth of a Color-Blind Society.* Berkeley: University of California Press.

Brown, Thomas. 2006. "Did the U.S. Army Distribute Smallpox Blankets to Indians? Fabrication and Falsification in Ward Churchill's Genocide Rhetoric." *Plagiary: Cross Disciplinary Studies in Plagiarism, Fabrication, and Falsification* 1 (9): 1–30.

Bruyneel, Kevin. 2007. *The Third Space of Sovereignty: The Post-colonial Politics of U.S. Indigenous Relations.* Minneapolis: University of Minnesota Press.

Bunkle, Phillida. 1993. "Calling the Shots? The International Politics of Depo-Provera." In *The 'Racial' Economy of Science: Toward a Democratic Future*, edited by Sandra Harding, 287–302. Bloomington: Indiana University Press.

Bushnell, Jeanette. 2004. "The Responsibilities and Powers of Reproduction." *Indigenous Woman* 5 (4): 23–34.

Cantu, Lionel. 2009. *The Sexuality of Migration: Border Crossings and Mexican Immigrant Men.* Edited by Nancy Naples and Salvador Vidal-Ortiz. New York: New York University Press.

Cassidy, Tina. 2006. *Birth: The Surprising History of How We Are Born.* New York: Atlantic Monthly Press.

Castle, Elizabeth. 2003. "Keeping One Foot in the Community: Intergenerational Indigenous Women's Activism from the Local to the Global (and Back Again)." *American Indian Quarterly* 27 (3/4): 840–861.

CDC (Centers for Disease Control). 2006. *Preconception Health and Care.* Atlanta, GA. Accessed September 15, 2010. http://www.cdc.gov/ncbddd/preconception/default.htm.

———. 2009. *Eliminate Disparities in Infant Mortality.* Accessed July 25, 2009. http://www.cdc.gov/omhd/AMH/factsheets/infant.htm.

———. 2011a. *Teen Birth Rate Hits Record Low in 2010: CDC Report Also Notes First Decline in Cesarean Rate in Over a Decade.* Accessed January 5, 2012. http://www.cdc.gov/media/releases/2011/p1117_teen_birthrate.html.

———. 2011b. *STDs in Racial and Ethnic Minorities.* Accessed November 15, 2011. http://www.cdc.gov/std/stats10/minorities.htm.

———. 2012a. *Cervical Cancer Rates by Rate and Ethnicity.* Accessed June 12, 2012. http://www.cdc.gov/cancer/cervical/statistics/race.htm.

———. 2012b. *Health, United States 2011: With Special Feature on Socioeconomic Status and Health.* U.S. Department of Health and Human Services, Centers for Disease Control and Prevention National Center for Health Statistics, publication #2012–1232.

Center for Reproductive Law and Policy. 1998. *Exposing Inequity: Failures of Reproductive Health Policy in the United States.* New York: Center for Reproductive Law and Policy.

Chalmers, Iain, Murray Enkin, and Marc Keirse, eds. 1989. *Effective Care in Pregnancy and Childbirth.* Oxford, UK: Oxford University Press.

Champagne, Duane. 2005. "Rethinking Native Relations with Contemporary Nation-States." In *Indigenous Peoples and the Modern State,* edited by Duane Champagne, Karen Jo Torjesen, and Susan Steiner, 3–24. Walnut Creek, CA: Altamira Press.

Churchill, Ward. 2003. *Perversions of Justice: Indigenous Peoples and Angloamerican Law.* San Francisco, CA: City Light Publishers.

Cohen, Susan. 2008. "Abortion and Women of Color: The Bigger Picture." *Guttmacher Policy Review* 11 (3): 2–5.

Connell, Raewyn. 1990. "The State, Gender, and Sexual Politics." *Theory and Society* 19 (5): 507–544.

Cook, Katsi. 1989. "The Women's Dance/Woman's Thread." In *New Voices from the Longhouse,* edited by Joseph Bruchac, 80–90. New York: Greenfield Review Press.

———. 2009. "At the Center, Native Women." *Indian Country Today.* Accessed August 1, 2009. http://indiancountrytodaymedianetwork.com/ictarchives/2009/07/18/cook-at-the-center-native-women-84171.

Cooper-Patrick, Joseph Gallo, Junius Gonzales, Hong Thi Vu, Neil Powe, Christine Nelson, and Daniel Ford. 1999. "Race, Gender, and Partnership in the Patient-Physician Relationship." *Journal of the American Medical Association* 282 (6): 583–589.

Cragin, Leslie. 2004. "The Theoretical Basis for Nurse-Midwifery Practice in the United States: A Critical Analysis of Three Theories." *Journal of Midwifery and Women's Health* 49 (5): 381–389.

Crow Dog, Mary. 1991. *Lakota Woman.* New York: Harper Perennial.

Danforth, DJ. 2009. "'Kill the Indian, Save the Man': A Young Oneida Man's Perspective on Sexuality." *Our Schools, Our Selves* 18 (2): 17–19.

Danforth, Jessica. 2008. "What's Sex Got to Do with It? Everything!" *Our Schools, Our Selves* 17 (3): 51–57.

Davis, Angela. 1983. *Women, Race, and Class.* New York: Vintage Books.

———. 1990. *Women, Culture, and Politics.* New York: Vintage Books.

Davis, Laura. 2003. *Adolescent Sexual Health and the Dynamics of Oppression: A Call for Cultural Competency.* Washington, DC: Advocates for Youth.

Davis, Sally, and Mary Harris. 1982. "Sexual Knowledge, Sexual Interests, and Sources of Sexual Information of Rural and Urban Adolescents from Three Cultures." *Adolescence* 17: 471–492.

Davis-Floyd, Robbie. 2004. *Birth as an American Rite of Passage.* Berkeley: University of California Press.

Deer, Sarah. 2005. "Sovereignty of the Soul: Exploring the Intersection of Rape Law Reform and Federal Indian Law." *Suffolk University Law Review* 38: 455–468.

———. 2010. "Relocation Revisited: Sex Trafficking of Native Women in the United States." *William Mitchell Law Review* 621 (36): 621–683.

Deloria, Vine Jr. 1970. *Custer Died for Your Sins: An Indian Manifesto.* Norman: University of Oklahoma Press.

Deloria, Vine Jr., and Clifford Lytle. 1984. *The Nations Within: The Past and Future of American Indian Sovereignty.* New York: Pantheon.

Denavas-Walt, Carmen, Bernadette Proctor, and Jessica Smith. 2011. *Income, Poverty, and Health Insurance Coverage in the United States: 2010.* U.S. Census Bureau Current Population Reports, P60–239. Washington, DC: U.S. Government Printing Office.

Department of the Interior. 1917. Correspondence of Southern Ute Agent Walter W. West and Southern Ute Agency Physician Lee Curran with the Commissioner of Indian Affairs Regarding 'Baby Week.' Accessed January 5, 2011. http://iweb.tntech.edu/kosburn/Documents/Baby%20Week.htm.

Department of Justice. 2011. *Tribal Law and Order Act (TLOA) Long-Term Plan to Build and Enhance Tribal Justice Systems.* Accessed March 3, 2013. http://www.justice.gov/tribal/docs/tloa-tsp-aug2011.pdf.

———. 2013. *A National Protocol for Sexual Assault Medical Forensic Examinations: Adults/Adolescents.* 2nd ed. U.S. Department of Justice Office on Violence against Women. NCJ 228119. Accessed May 10, 2013. https://www.ncjrs.gov/pdffiles1/ovw/241903.pdf.

Dimitrova-Grajzl, Valentina, Peter Grajzl, and A. Joseph Guse. 2013. "Jurisdiction, Crime, and Development: The Impact of Public Law 280 in Indian Country." Social Science Research Network, June 26. Accessed July 12, 2013. Available at SSRN: http://ssrn.com/abstract=2093681 or http://dx.doi.org/10.2139/ssrn.2093681.

Dorgan, Byron. 2010. "In Critical Condition: the Urgent Need to Reform the Indian Health Service's Aberdeen Area." United States Senate Committee on Indian Affairs. Accessed January 3, 2012. http://www.indian.senate.gov/sites/default/files/upload/files/ChairmansReportInCriticalCondition122810.pdf

Durazo, Ana Clarissa Rojas. 2006. "The Medicalization of Domestic Violence." In *Color of Violence: The Incite! Anthology*, edited by Incite! Women of Color against Violence, 179–190. Cambridge, MA: South End Press.

Eaglestaff, Mary Lynn, Marilyn Klug, and Larry Burd. 2006. "Infant Mortality Reviews in the Aberdeen Area of the Indian Health Service: Strategies and Outcomes." *Public Health Reports* 121(2): 140–148.

Eckholm, Erik. 2009. "Gang Violence Grows on an Indian Reservation." *New York Times*, December 14, A14.

Eddy, David. 2005. "Evidence-Based Medicine: A Unified Approach." *Health Affairs* 24 (1): 9–17.

Ehrenreich, Barbara, and Deirdre English. 1973. *Witches, Midwives, and Nurses: A History of Women Healers.* New York: Feminist Press.

Eisenstein, Zillah. 1981. *The Radical Future of Liberal Feminism.* Boston, MA: Northeastern University Press.

Emmerich, Lisa. 1997. "Save the Babies!: American Indian Women, Assimilation Policy, and Scientific Motherhood." In *Writing the Range: Race, Class, and Culture in the Women's West*, edited by Elizabeth Jameson and Susan Armitage, 393–410. Norman: University of Oklahoma Press.

Erikson, Pamela. 2008. *Ethnomedicine.* Long Grove, CA: Waveland Press.

Fairchild, David, Molly Fairchild, and Shirley Stoner. 1998. "Prevalence of Adult Domestic Violence among Women Seeking Routine Care in a Native American Health Care Facility." *American Journal of Public Health* 88 (10): 1515–1517.

Faircloth, Susan, and John Tippeconnic III. 2010. *The Dropout/Graduation Rate Crisis among American Indian and Alaska Native Students: Failure to Respond Places the Future of Native Peoples at Risk.* Los Angeles, CA: Civil Rights Project/Proyecto Derechos Civiles at UCLA. Accessed July 10, 2012. www.civilrightsproject.ucla.edu.

FEMA (Federal Emergency Management Agency). 1999. "Pine Ridge Reservation Tornado Victims Receive Assistance." Accessed August 24, 2009. http://www.fema.gov/news-release/1999/07/10/pine-ridge-reservation-tornado-victims-receive-assistance.

Fifer, Susan. 1996. "Perceptions of Caring Behaviors in Health Providers." *Indian Health Service Primary Care Provider* 21 (7): 89–95.

Fiscella, Kevin. 1995. "Does Prenatal Care Improve Birth Outcome? A Critical Review." *Obstetrics and Gynecology* 85 (3): 468–479.

Fitzpatrick, Michael. 2001. *The Tyranny of Health: Doctors and the Regulation of Lifestyle.* New York: Routledge.

Forquera, Ralph. 2001. *Urban Indian Health.* Henry J. Kaiser Family Foundation. Accessed July 22, 2009. http://kff.org/disparities-policy/report/urban-indian-health/.

Foucault, Michel. 1976. *The History of Sexuality.* Vol. 1. New York: Vintage Books.

Frankford, David. 1994. "Scientism and Economics in the Regulation of Health Care." *Journal of Health Politics, Policy, and Law* 19 (4): 773–799.

Fraser, Nancy. 1989. *Unruly Practices: Power, Discourse, and Gender in Contemporary Social Theory.* Minneapolis: University of Minnesota Press.

Freeman, John Jr. 1954. "A Program for Indian Affairs: Summary of the Report of the Hoover Commission Task Force on Indian Affairs." *American Indian* 7 (Spring): 48–62.

Gallagher, Mari. 2006. *Examining the Impact of Food Deserts on Public Health in Chicago.* Chicago: Mari Gallagher Research and Consulting Group.

GAO (Government Accountability Office). 2010. *US Department of Justice Declinations of Indian Country Criminal Matters* (GAO-11–167R). Washington, DC.

———. 2013. *Capping Payment Rates for Nonhospital Services Could Save Millions of Dollars for Contract Health Services.* (GAO-13–272). Washington, DC.

Gardner, Jerry. 2007. "Preface." In *Sharing Our Stories of Survival,* edited by Sarah Deer, Bonnie Clairmont, Carrie Martell, and Maureen White Eagle, xv–xvii. Walnut Creek, CA: Alta Mira Press.

Garwick, Ann, Wendy Hellerstedt, Melanie Peterson-Hickey, and Kristine Rhodes. 2008. "Native Teen Voices: Adolescent Pregnancy Prevention Recommendations." *Journal of Adolescent Health.* 42 (1): 81–88.

Giago, Tim. 2006a. *Children Left Behind: The Dark Legacy of Indian Mission Boarding Schools.* Santa Fe: Clear Light Publishers.

———. 2006b. "Oglala Sioux President on State Abortion Law." Indianz.com, March 21. Accessed July 18, 2009. http://www.indianz.com/News/2006/013061.asp.

Ginsburg, Faye, and Rayna Rapp. 1995. "Introduction: Conceiving the New World Order." In *Conceiving the New World Order: The Global Politics of Reproduction,* edited by Faye Ginsburg and Rayna Rapp, 1–18. Berkeley: University of California Press.

Goldberg-Ambrose, Carole. 1996–1997. "Public Law 280 and the Problem of Lawlessness in California Indian Country." *UCLA Law Review.* 44: 1405–1448.

Goldberg, David Theo. 2002. *The Racial State.* Malden, MA: Blackwell Publishers.

Goldenberg, Maya. 2006. "On Evidence and Evidence-based Medicine: Lessons from the Philosophy of Science." *Social Science and Medicine* 62: 2621–2632.

Goodman, Ronald. 1992. *Lakota Star Knowledge: Studies in Lakota Stellar Theology.* Mission, SD: Sinte Gleska University.

Graham, George, Charles Rhoads, John Nichols, and Gilbert Darlington. 1948. *Report of the Committee on Indian Affairs to the Commission on Organization of the Executive Branch of the Government* (mimeographed).

Greenfeld, Lawrence, and Steven Smith. 1999. *American Indians and Crime* (NCJ 173386). Accessed January 9, 2003. http://www.bjs.gov/content/pub/pdf/aic.pdf.

Grim, Charles. 2007. "Making Medicine." Remarks at Sovereignty Symposium XX, Oklahoma City, OK. Accessed September 13, 2011. www.ihs.gov/PublicAffairs/DirCorner/2007_Statements/SovereigntySymposium2007 web.pdf.

Grosz, Elizabeth. 1994. *Volatile Bodies: Toward a Corporeal Feminism.* Bloomington: Indiana University Press.

Guerrero, M. Annette Jaimes. 2003. "Patriarchal Colonialism and Indigenism: Implications for Native Feminist Spirituality and Native Womanism." *Hypatia* 18 (2): 58–69.

Guttmacher Institute. 2009. "New Health Disparities Report: More Context for Higher Unintended Pregnancy and Abortion Rates among Women of Color." Guttmacher Institute. Accessed July 23, 2009. http://www.guttmacher.org/media/inthenews/2009/06/11/index.html.

Hancock, Trevor. 2001. "People, Partnerships, and Human Progress: Building Community Capital." *Health Promotion International* 16 (3): 275–280.

Haney, Lynn. 2000. "Feminist State Theory: Applications to Jurisprudence, Criminology, and the Welfare State." *Annual Review of Sociology* 26: 641–666.

Harding, Sandra. 2007. "Introduction: Standpoint Theory as a Site of Political, Philosophic, and Scientific Debate." In *The Feminist Standpoint Theory Reader: Intellectual and Political Controversies*, edited by Sandra Harding, 1–16. New York: Routledge.

Harjo, Joy. 1990. "Rainy Dawn." In *In Mad Love and War*, 32. Hanover, NH: Wesleyan University Press.

———. 1997. "Warrior Road." In *Reinventing the Enemy's Language*, edited by Joy Harjo and Gloria Bird, 55–61. New York: W. W. Norton.

Hart, Rebecca, and M. Alexander Lowther. 2008. "Honoring Sovereignty: Aiding Tribal Efforts to Protect Native American Women from Domestic Violence." *California Law Review* 96 (1): 185–233.

Harvard Project on American Indian Economic Development. 2008. *The State of the Native Nations: Conditions under U.S. Policies of Self-Determination.* New York: Oxford University Press.

Hatem, Marie, Jane Sandall, Declan Devane, Hora Soltani, and Simon Gates. 2008. "Midwife-led versus Other Models of Care for Childbearing Women." *In Cochrane Database of Systematic Reviews* 4. Art No.: CD004667. DOI: 10.1002/14651858.CD004667.pub2.

Healy, Andrew, Fergal Maloe, Lisa Sullivan, Flint Porter, David Luthy, et al. 2006. "Early Access to Prenatal Care: Implications for Racial Disparity in Perinatal Mortality." *Obstetrics and Gynecology* 107 (3): 625–631.

Hemminki, Elina. 1988. "Content of Prenatal Care in the United States." *Medical Care* 26 (2): 199–210.

Hernandez, Tanya. 1998. "Multiracial Discourse: Racial Classifications in an Era of Color-Blind Jurisprudence." *Maryland Law Review* 57 (1): 97–151.

HHS (Health and Human Services). 2011. "National Tribal Budget Recommendations for the Indian Health Service, Fiscal Year 2013 Budget." Accessed June 12, 2011. http://www.nihb.org/docs/03282011/FY%202013%20National%20Tribal%20Budget% 0Recommendations_Final.pdf

Huska, Chris. 2007. "Pine Ridge Reservation Will Not Get Health Clinic: Continuing the Annihilation of Native People." Party for Socialism and Liberation, August 10. Accessed August 4, 2009. http://www.pslweb.org/site/News2?page=NewsArticle&id=7173.

IHS (Indian Health Service). 2002–2003. *Trends in Indian Health 2002–2003.* Rockville, MD: Indian Health Service Office of Public Health Support Division of Program Statistics.

———. 2002–2004. *Regional Differences in Indian Health.* Rockville, MD: Indian Health Service Office of Public Health Support Division of Program Statistics.

———. 2006. *Indian Health Service: Strategic Vision 2006–2011.* Rockville, MD: Indian Health Service Office of Public Health Support Division of Program Statistics.

———. 2008. *Regional Differences in Indian Health 2002–2003 Edition.* Rockville, MD: Indian Health Service Office of Public Health Support Division of Program Statistics.

———. 2012. "General CHR Information: History and Background Development of the Program." Accessed June 24, 2012. http://www.ihs.gov/chr/index.cfm?module=history.

———. n.d. *Indian Health Service Manual.* Accessed April 29, 2009. http://www.ihs.gov/PublicInfo/Publications/IHSManual/.

IHS/MCH (Indian Health Services/Maternal and Child Health). 2010. "Did Thousands of Native American Women Undergo Forced Sterilizations in the 1970s?" Accessed September 9, 2009. http://www.ihs.gov/MedicalPrograms/MCH/M/documents/steri13705.doc (page unavailable).

Indian Health Care Improvement Act. 1976. Pub. L. No. 94–437.

Innes, Robert. 2009. "'Wait a second, who are you anyways?': The Insider-Outsider Debate and American Indian Studies." *American Indian Quarterly* 33 (4): 440–461.

Irvine, Janice. 2002. *Talk about Sex: The Battles of Sex Education in the United States.* Berkeley: University of California Press.

Iyasu, Solomon, Leslie Randall, Thomas Welty, Jason Hsia, Hannah Kinney, Frederick Mandell, Mary McClain, Brad Randall, Don Habbe, Harry Wilson, and Marian Willinger. 2002. "Risk Factors for Sudden Infant Death Syndrome among Northern Plains Indians." *Journal of the American Medical Association* 288 (21): 2717–2723.

Jennings, Francis. 1993. *The Founders of America.* New York: W. W. Norton.

Joe, Jennie, and Robert Young. 1994. *Diabetes as a Disease of Civilization: The Impact of Culture Change on Indigenous Peoples.* New York: Mouton de Gruyter.

Johansen, Bruce. 2001. "Reprise/Forced Sterilizations: Native Americans and the Last Gasp of Eugenics." In *Native American Voices,* 3rd ed., edited by Susan Lobo and Steve Talbot, 212–217. Upper Saddle, NJ: Prentice Hall.

Jones, Stacy Holman. 2005. "Autoethnography: Making the Personal Political." In *The SAGE Handbook of Qualitative Research,* edited by Norman Denzin and Yvonne Lincoln. 763–791 Thousand Oaks, CA: Sage.

Jordan, Brigitte. 1992. *Birth in Four Cultures.* Long Grove, IL: Waveland.

Kaiser Family Foundation. 2008. *Sexual Health of Adolescents and Young Adults in the United States.* September. Accessed September 4, 2009. http://www.kff.org/womenshealth/upload/3040_04.pdf

———. 2009. "Putting Women's Health Care Disparities on the Map: Examining Racial and Ethnic Disparities at the State Level." Accessed July 23, 2009. http://kff.org/disparities-policy/report/putting-womens-health-care-disparities-on-the/

Kauffman, Carol, Jennifer Desserich, Cecilia Big Crow, Bonnie Holy Rock, Ellen Keane, and Christina Mitchell. 2007. "Culture, Context, and Sexual Risk among Northern Plains American Indian Youth." *Social Science of Medicine* 64 (10): 2152–2164.

Keeler, Jacqueline. 2006. "Fire Thunder Impeachment and the Rights of Women." *Tiospaye Now.* Accessed July 18, 2009. http://tiyospayenow.blogspot.com/2006/07/fire-thunder-impeachment-and-rights-of.html.

Kelly, Maura. 2009. "Women's Voluntary Childlessness: A Radical Rejection of Motherhood?" *Women's Studies Quarterly* 37 (3/4): 157–172.

Keyes, Scott. 2013. "Top GOP Senator: Native American Juries Are Incapable of Trying White People Fairly." *Think Progress*, February 21. Accessed April 15, 2013. http://think-progress.org/justice/2013/02/21/1619501/chuck-grassley-native-americans/?mobile=nc.

Kim, Shin, Myra Tucker, Melissa Danielson, Christopher Johnson, Pelagie Snesrud, and Holly Shulman. 2008. "How Can PRAMS Survey Response Rates Be Improved among American Indian Mothers? Data from 10 States." *Maternal and Child Health Journal* 12: S119–S125.

Kornelsen, Jude. 2005. "Essences and Imperatives: An Investigation of Technology in Childbirth." *Social Science and Medicine* 61 (7): 1495–1504.

Kraus, D. Bambi. 2001. "Wealth, Success, and Poverty in Indian Country." *Poverty and Race* 10 (3): 3–4.

Krause, Neal. 1999. "Religious Support." In *Multidimensional Measurement of Religiousness/ Spirituality for Use in Health Research*, Fetzer Institute/ National Institute on Aging Working Group, 57–63. Kalamazoo, MI: Fetzer Institute.

Kravitz, Richard, Naihua Duan, and Joel Braslow. 2004. "Evidence-based Medicine, Heterogeneity of Treatment Effects, and the Trouble with Averages." *Milbank Quarterly* 82 (4): 661–687.

Krieger, Nancy. 1999. "Embodying Inequality: A Review of Concepts, Measures, and Methods for Studying Health Consequences of Discrimination." *International Journal of Health Services* 29 (2): 295–352.

Krieger, Nancy, Jarvis Chen, Pamela Waterman, David Rehkopf, and S. V. Subramanian. 2005. "Painting a Truer Picture of US Socioeconomic and Racial/Ethnic Health Inequalities: The Public Health Disparities Geocoding Project." *American Journal of Public Health* 95 (2): 312–323.

Kunitz, Stephen, and M. Tsianco. 1981. "Kinship Dependence and Contraceptive Use among Navajo Women." *Human Biology* 53 (3): 439–452.

LaDuke, Winona. 1999. *All Our Relations: Native Struggles for Land and Life*. Cambridge, MA: South End Press.

Langston, Donna Hightower. 2003. "American Indian Women's Activism in the 1960s and 1970s." *Hypatia* 18 (2): 114–132.

LaPointe, Charlene. 2008. "Sexual Violence: An Introduction to the Social and Legal Issues for Native Women." In *Sharing our Stories of Survival: Native Women Surviving Violence*, edited by Sarah Deer, Bonnie Clairmont, Carrie Martell, and Maureen White Eagle, 31–46. Walnut Creek, CA: Alta Mira Press.

Larson, Nicole I., Melissa C. Nelson, and Mary T. Story. 2009. "Neighborhood Environments: Disparities in Access to Healthy Foods in the U.S." *American Journal of Preventive Medicine* 36 (1): 74–81.

Lawrence, Charles. 1995. "The Epidemiology of Color-Blindness: Learning to Think and Talk about Race, Again." *Boston College Third World Law Journal* 15 (1): 1–18.

Lawrence, Jane. 2000. "The Indian Health Service and the Sterilization of Native American Women." *American Indian Quarterly* 24 (3): 400–419.

Lazarus, Ellen. 1994. "What Do Women Want? Issues of Choice, Control, and Class in Pregnancy and Childbirth." *Medical Anthropology Quarterly* 8 (1): 25–46.

Lazzarini, Zita. 2008. "South Dakota's Abortion Script: Threatening the Doctor-Patient Relationship." *New England Journal of Medicine* 359 (21): 2189–2191.

Leavitt, Judith. 1986. *Brought to Bed: Childbearing in America, 1750–1950*. New York: Oxford University Press.

Leeman, Lawrence, and Rebecca Leeman. 2003. "A Native American Community with a 7% Cesarean Delivery Rate: Does Case Mix, Ethnicity, or Labor Management Explain the Low Rate?" *Annals of Family Medicine* 1 (1): 36–43.

Liberty, M., D. Hughey, and R. Scaglion. 1976. "Rural and Urban Omaha Indian Fertility." *Human Biology* 48 (1): 59–71.

Lillis, Mike. 2008, "Extra Abortion Limitation for Native Americans Only." *RH Reality Check*, March 7. Accessed March 30, 2009. http://rhrealitycheck.org/article/2008/03/07/extraabortion-limitation-for-native-americans-only/.

Litoff, Judy Barrett. 1978. *American Midwives: 1860 to Present.* Westport, CT: Greenwood Press.

Liu, Lenna, Gail Slap, Sara Kinsman, and Najma Khalid. 1994. "Pregnancy among American Indian Adolescents: Reactions and Prenatal Care." *Journal of Adolescent Health* 15 (4): 336–341.

Lopez, Christina. 1999. "Norplant and Depo-Provera." *Freedom Socialist: Voice of Revolutionary Feminism.* Accessed April 9, 2012. http://www.socialism.com/drupal 6.8/?q=node/1176.

Luker, Kristin. 1984. *Abortion and the Politics of Motherhood.* Berkeley: University of California Press.

Luna, Zakiya, and Kristin Luker. 2013. "Reproductive Justice." *Annual Review of Law and Social Science* 9: 327–352.

MacDorman, Marian F., and T. J. Mathews. 2008. "Recent Trends in Infant Mortality in the United States." National Center for Health Statistics Data Brief Number 9, October. Accessed April 12, 2011. http://www.cdc.gov/nchs/data/databriefs/db09.pdf.

MacDorman, Marian F., T. J. Mathews, and Eugene Declercq. 2012. "Home Births in the United States, 1990–2009." National Center for Health Statistics, No. 84. Accessed April 2, 2013. http://www.cdc.gov/nchs/data/databriefs/db84.htm.

Malcoe, Lorraine, Bonnie Duran, and Juliann Montgomery. 2004. "Socioeconomic Disparities in Intimate Partner Violence against Native American Women: A Cross-sectional Study." *BMC Medicine* 2 (20): 1–14.

Mankiller, Wilma, and Michael Wallis. 1993. *Mankiller: A Chief and Her People.* New York: St. Martin's Griffin.

Maracle, Lee. 1996. *I Am Woman: A Native Perspective on Sociology and Feminism.* Vancouver, BC: Press Gang Publisher.

Martin, Emily. 1989. *The Woman in the Body: A Cultural Analysis of Reproduction.* Boston, MA: Beacon Press.

Matthiesson, Peter. 1991. *In the Spirit of Crazy Horse.* New York: Penguin Books.

McGreal, Chris. 2010. "Obama's Indian Problem." *Guardian.* Accessed January 4, 2011. http://www.guardian.co.uk/global/2010/jan/11/native-americans-reservations-poverty obama?

McSwain, Robert. 2009. "Renewing the Indian Health Care System." Remarks at the National Combined Councils annual meeting. Accessed May 30, 2009. http://www.ihs.gov/newsroom/includes/themes/newihstheme/displayobjects/documents/2009_Statements/NationalCombinedCouncilsAnnualMeeting%20_3.df.

Means, Russell. 1996. *Where White Men Fear to Tread.* New York: St. Martin's Griffin Press.

Menacker, Fay, and Brady Hamilton. 2010. "Recent Trends in Cesarean Delivery in the United States." National Center for Health Statistics Data Brief Number 10. Rockville, MD: U.S. Department of Health and Human Services.

Mihesuah, Devon. 1996. "Commonality of Difference: American Indian Women and History." *American Indian Quarterly* 20 (1): 15–27.

Miller, Brent, and Kristen Moore. 1990. "Adolescent Sexual Behavior, Pregnancy, and Parenting: Research through the 1980s." *Journal of Marriage and Family* 52 (4): 1025–1044.

Miller, Robert. 2006. *Native America, Discovered and Conquered: Thomas Jefferson, Lewis and Clark, and Manifest Destiny*. Westport, CT: Praeger.

Mohatt, Gerald, and Joseph Eagle Elk. 2002. *The Price of a Gift: A Lakota Healer's Story*. Lincoln: University of Nebraska Press.

Moore, Ann, Lori Frohwirth, and Elizabeth Miller. 2010. "Male Reproductive Control of Women Who Have Experienced Intimate Partner Violence in the United States." *Social Science and Medicine* 70 (11): 1737–1744.

Morgen, Sandra. 2002. *Into Our Own Hands: The Women's Health Movement in the United States, 1969–1990*. New Brunswick, NJ: Rutgers University Press.

Murry, Velma McBride, and James Ponzetti Jr. 1997. "American Indian Female Adolescents' Sexual Behavior: A Test of the Life-Course Theory." *Family and Consumer Sciences Research Journal* 26 (1): 75–95.

Mykhalovskiy, Eric, and Lorna Weir. 2004. "The Problem of Evidence-based Medicine: Directions for Social Science." *Social Science and Medicine* 59: 1059–1069.

Nagel, Joanne. 2003. *Race, Ethnicity, and Sexuality: Intimate Intersections, Forbidden Frontiers*. New York: Oxford University Press.

NAWHERC (Native American Women's Health Education Resource Center). 2002. *Indigenous Women's Reproductive Rights: The Indian Health Service and Its Inconsistent Application of the Hyde Amendment*. Lake Andes, SD: Native American Women's Health and Education Resource Center.

———. 2003. *Indigenous Women's Reproductive Rights: Roundtable Report on Access to Abortion Services through the Indian Health Service Under the Hyde Amendment*. Lake Andes, SD: Native American Women's Health Education Resource Center.

———. 2005. *Indigenous Women's Reproductive Justice: A Survey of Sexual Assault Policies and Protocols within Indian Health Service Emergency Rooms*. Lake Andes, SD: Native American Women's Health and Education Resource Center.

———. 2008. *Indigenous Women's Reproductive Justice: A Survey of the Availability of Plan B and Emergency Contraceptives within Indian Health Service*. Lake Andes, SD: Native American Women's Health and Education Resource Center.

Nelson, Jennifer. 2003. *Women of Color and the Reproductive Rights Movement*. New York: New York University Press.

Nelson, Margaret. 1983. "Working-Class Women, Middle-Class Women, and Models of Childbirth." *Social Problems* 30 (3): 284–297.

———. 1986. "Birth and Social Class." In *The American Way of Birth*, edited by Pamela S. Eakins, 142–174. Philadelphia, PA: Temple University Press.

Nies, Judith. 1996. *Native American History: A Chronology of a Culture's Vast Achievements and the Links to World Events*. New York: Ballantine Books.

Nieves, Evelyn. 2004. "On Pine Ridge, a String of Broken Promises." *Washington Post*, October 20, A01. Accessed August 24, 2009. http://www.washingtonpost.com/wpdyn/articles/A49822-2004oct20.html (page discontinued).

NIH (National Institutes of Health). 1989. *Caring for Our Future: The Content of Prenatal Care*. Bethesda, MD: National Institutes of Health (Department of Health and Human Services).

Noriega, Jorge. 1992. "American Indian Education in the United States: Indoctrination for Subordination to Colonialism." In *The State of Native America: Genocide, Colonization, and Resistance*, edited by M. Annette Jaimes, 371–402. Boston, MA: South End Press.

Norris, Tina, Paula Vines, and Elizabeth Hoeffel. 2012. *The American Indian and Alaska Native Population 2010*. Accessed April 2, 2013. http://www.census.gov/prod/cen2010/briefs/c2010br-10.pdf.

Novins, Douglas, Janette Beals, Laurie Moore, Paul Spicer, et al. 2004. "Use of Biomedical Services and Traditional Healing Options among American Indians: Sociodemographic Correlates, Spirituality, and Ethnic Identity." *Medical Care* 42 (7): 670–679.

NPAIHB (Northwest Portland Area Indian Health Board). 2009. *FY 2009 Indian Health Service Budget: Analysis and Recommendations.* Portland, OR: Northwest Portland Area Indian Health Board.

Oakley, Ann. 1980. *Women Confined: Towards a Sociology of Childbirth.* New York: Schocken Books.

Oglala Oyate Woitancan. 2008. *Empowerment Zone Strategic Plan.* Accessed August 12, 2009. http://www.rurdev.usda.gov/rbs/ezec/communit/oglala.pdf.

O'Hanlon, Katherine. 2006. "Health Policy Considerations for Our Sexual Minority Patients." *Obstetrics and Gynecology: Current Commentary* 107 (3): 709–714.

Omi, Michael, and Howard Winant. 1994. *Racial Formation in the United States from the 1960s to the 1990s.* New York: Routledge.

OSCAR. 2013. Online Submission, Consultation, and Reporting System. Accessed May 9, 2013. www.ihs.gov/OSCAR/index.cfm?module=FAQ#q1.

Owe Aku. 2011. *Crying Earth Rise Up! Environmental Justice and the Survival of a People: Uranium Mining and the Oglala Lakota People.* Manderson, SD: Owe Aku.

Pargament, Kenneth. 1999. "Religious and Spiritual Coping." In *Multidimensional Measurement of Religiousness/Spirituality for Use in Health Research*, Fetzer Institute/ National Institute on Aging Working Group, 43–56. Kalamazoo, MI: Fetzer Institute.

Parker, Jennifer. 1994. "Ethnic Differences in Midwife-Attended U.S. Births." *American Journal of Public Health* 84 (7): 1139–1141.

Payson, Kenneth E. 2003. "Check One Box: Reconsidering Directive No. 15 and the Classification of Mixed Race People." In *Mixed Race America and the Law*, edited by Kevin Johnson, 191–196. New York: New York University Press.

Pearson, J. Diane. 2003. "Lewis Cass and the Politics of Disease: The Indian Vaccination Act of 1832." *Wicazo Sa Review* 18 (2): 9–35.

———. 2004. "Medical Diplomacy and the American Indian: Thomas Jefferson, the Lewis and Clark Expedition, and the Subsequent Effects on American Indian Health and Public Policy." *Wicazo Sa Review* 19 (1): 105–130.

Perry, Steven. 2004. *American Indians and Crime—A BJS Statistical Profile 1992–2002.* Bureau of Justice Statistics, US Department of Justice, Office of Justice Programs. Accessed July 19, 2011. Available at www.bjs.gov/index.cfm?ty=pbdetail&iid=386.

Pfefferbaum, Rose, Betty Pfefferbaum, Everett Rhoades, and Rennard Strickland. 1997. "Providing for the Health Care Needs of Native Americans: Policy, Programs, Procedures, and Practices." *American Indian Law Review* 21 (2): 211–258.

Philips, Lorraine, and Win Philips. 2006. "Better Reproductive Healthcare for Women with Disabilities: A Role for Nursing Leadership." *Advances in Nursing Science* 29 (2): 134–152.

Pittman, Robert. 2006. "Point/Counterpoint: Refusal by Pharmacists to Dispense Emergency Contraception." *CCC Corner: National Council of Chief Clinical Consultants.* Accessed June 12, 2009. http://www.ihs.gov/MedicalPrograms/MCH/M/obgyn0706_AOM.cfm (page discontinued).

Portes, Alejandro. 1998. "Social Capital: Its Origins and Applications in Modern Sociology." *American Sociological Review* 24 (1): 1–24.

Powers, Marla. 1986. *Oglala Women: Myth, Ritual, and Reality.* Chicago: University of Chicago Press.

Putnam, Robert. 1993. "The Prosperous Community: Social Capital and Public Life." *American Prospect* 13: 35–42.

Ralston-Lewis, Marie. 2005. "The Continuing Struggle against Genocide: Indigenous Women's Reproductive Rights." *Wicazo Sa Review* 20 (1): 71–95.

Rapp, Rayna. 1994. "The Power of 'Positive' Diagnosis: Medical and Maternal Discourses on Amniocentesis." In *Representations of Motherhood*, edited by Donna Basin, Margaret Honey, and Meryle Kaplan, 204–219. New Haven, CT: Yale University Press.

Rappolt, S. 1997. "Clinical Guidelines and the Fate of Medical Autonomy in Ontario." *Social Science and Medicine* 44 (7): 977–987.

Reader, Tristan. 2010. *The Traditional Tohono O'odham Food System: A Short History*. Accessed on June 1, 2012. http://www.tocaonline.org/Oodham_Foods/Entries/2010/3/30_The_Health_Effects_Caused_by_the_loss_of_the_Traditional_Food_System.html.

Reilly, Philip. 1991. *The Surgical Solution: A History of Involuntary Sterilization in the United States*. Baltimore, MD: Johns Hopkins University Press.

Rhoades, Dorothy, Anthony D'Angelo, and Everett R. Rhoades. 2000. "Data Sources and Subsets of the Indian Population." In *American Indian Health: Innovations in Health Care, Promotion, and Policy*, edited by Everett R. Rhoades, 93–102. Baltimore, MD: Johns Hopkins University Press.

Roberts, Dorothy. 1997. *Killing the Black Body: Race, Reproduction, and the Meaning of Liberty*. New York: Vintage Books.

Rochelle, Dalla, and Wendy Gamble. 2001. "Teenage Mothering on the Navajo Reservation: An Examination of Intergenerational Perceptions and Beliefs." *American Indian Culture and Research Journal* 25 (1): 1–19.

Rockwell, Stephen. 2010. *Indian Affairs and the Administrative State in the Nineteenth Century*. New York: Cambridge University Press.

Rodwin, M. 2001. "The Politics of Evidence-based Medicine." *Journal of Health Politics, Policy, and Law* 26 (2): 439–445.

Rogers, Wendy. 2002. "Evidence-based Medicine in Practice: Limiting or Facilitating Patient Choice?" *Health Expectations* 5 (2): 95–103.

———. 2004. "Evidence-based Medicine and Justice: A Framework for Looking at the Impact of EBM upon Vulnerable or Disadvantaged Groups." *Journal of Medical Ethics* 30 (2): 141–145.

Rosen, Hannah. 2009. *Terror in the Heart of Freedom: Citizenship, Sexual Violence, and the Meaning of Race in the Postemancipation South*. Chapel Hill: University of North Carolina Press.

Ross, Loretta. 1992. "African-American Women and Abortion: A Neglected History." *Journal of Healthcare for the Poor and Underserved* 3 (2): 274–284.

———. 2006. "What Is Reproductive Justice?" In *Reproductive Justice Briefing Book: A Primer on Reproductive Justice and Social Change*, edited by Sistersong: Women of Color Reproductive Health Collective. Accessed May 1, 2013. http://protectchoice.org/downloads/Reproductive%20Justice%20Briefing%20Book.pdf.

Ross, Loretta, Sarah Brownlee, Dazon Diallo, Luz Rodriguez, and Sistersong Women of Color Reproductive Health Project. 2002. "Just Choices: Women of Color, Reproductive Health, and Human Rights." In *Policing the National Body: Race, Gender, and Criminalization*, edited by Jael Silliman and Anannya Bhatcharjee, 147–176. Cambridge, MA: South End Press.

Rothman, Barbara Katz. 2000. *Recreating Motherhood*. New Brunswick, NJ: Rutgers University Press.

———. 1982. *In Labor: Women and Power in the Birthplace*. New York: W. W. Norton.

Roubideaux, Yvette. 2012. *Preventing and Treating Diabetes and Its Complications in*

American Indians and Alaska Natives. Accessed June 14, 2013. http://www.ihs.gov/ newsroom/includes/themes/newihstheme/display_objects/document 2012_Speeches/ PreventingandTreatingDiabetesAIAN_UCOSpeakerSeries.pdf.

Ruzek, Sheryl Burt. 1979. *The Women's Health Movement: Feminist Alternatives to Medical Control.* New York: Praeger.

Saewyc, Elizabeth, Carol Skay, Linda Bearinger, Robert Blum, and Michael Resnick. 1998. "Sexual Orientation, Sexual Behaviours, and Pregnancy among Adolescents." *Journal of Adolescent Health* 23 (4): 238–247.

Sandefur, Gary, Ronald Rindfuss and Barney Cohen, eds. 1996. *Changing Numbers, Changing Needs: American Indian Demography and Public Health.* Washington, DC: National Academy Press.

Schaffer, Ruth. 1991. "The Health and Social Functions of Black Midwives on the Texas Brazos Bottom, 1920–1985." *Rural Sociology* 56 (1): 89–105.

Scholder v. United States, 428 F.2d. 23 (9ᵗʰ Cir. 1970), *cert. denied,* 400 U.S. 942 (1970).

Schuiling, Kerri, Theresa Sipe, and Judith Fullerton. 2010. "Findings from the Analysis of the American College of Nurse-Midwives' Membership Surveys: 2006–2008." *Journal of Midwifery and Women's Health* 55 (4): 299–307.

Schwartz, Stephanie. 2006. "The Arrogance of Ignorance." Accessed August 27, 2007. http:// silvrdrach.homestead.com/Schwartz_2006_Oct_15.html.

Scully, Judith. 2002. "Killing the Black Community: A Commentary on the United States War on Drugs." In *Policing the National Body: Race, Gender, and Criminalization,* edited by Anannya Bhattacharjee and Jael Silliman, 55–80. Cambridge, MA: South End Press.

Sequist, Thomas, Theresa Cullen, Kenneth Bernard, Shimon Shaykevich, E. John Orav, and John Ayanian. 2011. "Trends in Quality of Care and Barriers to Improvement in the Indian Health Service." *Journal of General Internal Medicine* 26 (5): 480–486.

Shaw, Shannon. 2004. "High Levels of Black Mold Found in Pine Ridge Reservation Homes." Associated Press. Accessed February 21, 2010. http://www.moldhelp.org/content/view/263/ (site discontinued).

Silliman, Jael, Marlene Gerber Fried, Loretta Ross, and Elena R. Gutierrez. 2004. *Undivided Rights: Women of Color Organize for Reproductive Justice.* Cambridge, MA: South End Press.

Simpson, Leanne. 2006. "Birthing an Indigenous Resurgence: Decolonizing Our Pregnancy and Birthing Ceremonies." In *Until Our Hearts Are on the Ground: Aboriginal Mothering and Oppression, Resistance and Rebirth,* edited by Dawn Memee Lavell-Harvard and Jeanette Corbiere Lavell, 25–33. Toronto, ON: Demeter Press.

Sistersong. 2006. *Reproductive Justice Briefing Book: A Primer on Reproductive Justice and Social Change.* Sistersong: Women of Color Reproductive Health Collective. Accessed May 13, 2010. http://www.protectchoice.org/downloads/Reproductive%20Justice%20 Briefing%20Book.pdf

Slemenda, Charles. 1978. "Sociocultural Factors Affecting Acceptance of Family Planning Services by Navajo Women." *Human Organization* 37 (2): 190–194.

Smith, Andrea. 1995. "Women of Color and Reproductive Choice: Combating the Population Paradigm." *Journal of Feminist Studies in Religion* 11 (2): 39–66.

———. 2002. "Better Dead than Pregnant: The Colonization of Native Women's Reproductive Health." In *Policing the National Body: Race, Gender, and Criminalization,* edited by Jael Silliman and Anannya Bhattacharjee, 123–146. Cambridge, MA: South End Press.

———. 2005. *Conquest: Sexual Violence and American Indian Genocide.* Cambridge, MA: South End Press.

———. 2006. "Heteropatriarchy and the Three Pillars of White Supremacy." In *The Color of Violence: The Incite! Anthology*, edited by Incite! Women of Color against Violence, 66–73. Cambridge, MA: South End Press.

Smith, Dorothy. 1990. *The Conceptual Practices of Power: a Feminist Sociology of Knowledge*. Boston, MA: Northeastern University Press.

———.1987. *Everyday World as Problematic: A Feminist Sociology*. Boston, MA: Northeastern University Press.

———. 1992. "Sociology from Women's Experience: A Reaffirmation." *Sociological Theory* 10 (1): 88–98.

———. 1999. *Writing the Social: Critique, Theory, and Investigations*. Toronto, ON: University of Toronto Press.

———. 2004. Writing the Social: Critique, Theory, and Investigations. Toronto, ON: University of Toronto Press.

Smith, Linda Tuhiwai. 2002. *Decolonizing Methodologies: Research and Indigenous Peoples*. London: Zed Books.

Smith, Paul Chaat, and Robert Warrior. 1997. *Like a Hurricane: The Indian Movement from Alcatraz to Wounded Knee*. New York: New Press.

Snipp, Matthew. 1991. *American Indians: The First of This Land*. New York: Russell Sage Foundation.

Snyder Act.1921. Pub. L. No. 67–85, 25 U.S.C. §13.

Soliday, Elizabeth. 2009. "Intensive Mothering, Intensive Visiting: How Mothers View Prenatal Care Schedules." *Journal of the Association for Research on Mothering* 11 (1): 49–58.

Solis, Hilda. 2012. *Labor Force Characteristics by Race and Ethnicity 2011*. U.S. Department of Labor. Report 1036.

South Dakota Department of Health Office of Data, Statistics, and Vital Records. 2008. *South Dakota Health Data by County*. Pierre, SD: Office of Health Statistics.

Spelman, Elizabeth. 1988. *Inessential Woman: Problems of Exclusion in Feminist Thought*. Boston, MA: Beacon Press.

Stack, Carol. 1974. *All Our Kin: Strategies for Survival in a Black Community*. New York: Basic Books.

Stannard, David. 1992. *American Holocaust*. New York: Oxford University Press.

Starr, Paul. 1982. *The Social Transformation of American Medicine*. New York: Basic Books.

Steele, John Yellow Bird. 2007. "Testimony of the Honorable John Yellow Bird Steele, President of the Oglala Sioux Tribe." Oversight Hearing on Indian Housing before the Senate Committee on Indian Affairs. Accessed July 9, 2012. http://www.indian.senate.gov/public/_files/Steele032207.pdf.

Stiffarm, Lenore, and Phil Lane Jr. 1992. "The Demography of Native North America: A Question of American Indian Survival." In *The State of Native American: Genocide, Colonization, and Resistance*, edited by M. Annette Jaimes and Theresa Halsey, 23–54. Cambridge, MA: South End Press.

St. Pierre, Mark, and Tilda Long Soldier. 1995. *Walking in a Sacred Manner: Healers, Dreamers, and Pipe Carriers—Medicine Women of the Plains Indians*. New York: Simon and Schuster.

Strong, Thomas Jr. 2003. *Expecting Trouble: The Myth of Prenatal Care in America*. New York: New York University Press.

Stubblefied, Anna. 2007. "Beyond the Pale: Tainted Whiteness, Cognitive Disability, and Eugenic Sterilization." *Hypatia* 22 (2):162–181.

Tapahonso, Luci. 1987. "A Breeze Swept Through." In *A Breeze Swept Through*. 2–6. Albuquerque, NM: West End Press.

Tasina Ska Win. 2003. "A Natural Way of Life Is Returning, Remembering, Reviving." *Indigenous Woman* 4 (3): 42–47.

Taylor, Alan. 2002. *American Colonies*. Vol. 1 of *The Penguin History of the United States*. New York: Penguin Books.

Thunder Valley. 2009. "Who We Are." Accessed July 29, 2009. http://www.Thunder Valley. org/.

Tjaden, Patricia, and Nancy Thoennes. 2000. *Prevalence, Incidence, and Consequences of Violence against Women: Findings from the National Violence against Women Survey, NIJ, Center for Disease Control and Prevention* (NCJ 172837). Washington, DC: U.S. Department of Justice, National Institute of Justice. Accessed January 7, 2003. www.ncjrs.gov/pdffiles/172837.pdf.

Torpy, Sally. 2000. "Native American Women and Coerced Sterilization: On the Trail of Tears in the 1970s." *American Indian Culture and Research Journal* 24 (2): 1–22.

Trask, Haunani Kay. 1993. *From a Native Daughter: Colonialism and Sovereignty in Hawai'i*. Honolulu: University of Hawai'i Press.

———. 2006. "The Color of Violence." In *Color of Violence: The Incite! Anthology*, edited by Incite! Women of Color against Violence, 81–87. Cambridge, MA: South End Press.

Trujillo, Michael. 1996. *Testimony on Oversight Hearing on the President's Proposed Indian Health Service*. Department of Health and Human Services. Accessed July 11, 2009. http://www.hhs.gov/asl/testify/t960419b.html.

Twetten, Daniel. 2000. "Public Law 280 and the Indian Gaming Regulatory Act: Could Two Wrongs Ever Be Made into a Right?" *Journal of Criminal Law and Criminology* 90 (4): 1317–1352.

UIHP (Urban Indian Health Program) 2009. *Urban Indian Health Service Program Overview*. Accessed May 30, 2009. http://www.ihs.gov/NonMedicalPrograms/Urban/Overview.asp (page discontinued).

Ulrich, Laurel Thatcher. 1982. *Good Wives: Image and Reality in the Lives of Women in Northern New England 1650–1750*. New York: Knopf.

———. 1991. *A Midwife's Tale: the Life of Martha Ballard Based on Her Diary 1785–1812*. New York: Vintage Books.

US Commission on Civil Rights. 2003. *A Quiet Crisis: Federal Funding and Unmet Needs in Indian Country*. Washington, DC.

———. 2004. *Broken Promises: Evaluating the Native American Healthcare System*. Washington, DC.

US Census Bureau. 2000. "American Factfinder: Pine Ridge Reservation Total Demographics." Accessed June 12, 2010. http://factfinder2.census.gov/faces/nav/jsf/pages/searchresults.xhtml?refresh=t#none.

———. 2010. "Small Area Income and Poverty Estimates." Accessed April 4, 2012. http://www.census.gov/did/www/saipe/data/statecounty/maps/2010.html.

Ventura, Stephanie, T. J. Matthews, and Brady Hamilton. 2001. "Births to Teenagers in the United States, 1940–2000." *National Vital Statistics Report* 49:10. Washington, DC: National Center for Health Statistics.

Veracini, Lorenzo. 2010. *Settler Colonialism: A Theoretical Overview*. New York: Palgrave Macmillan.

Volscho, Thomas. 2010. "Sterilization Racism and Pan-ethnic Disparities of the Past Decade: The Continued Encroachment on Reproductive Rights." *Wicazo Sa Review* 25 (1): 17–31.

Wagner, Marsden. 2008. *Born in the USA: How a Broken Maternity System Must Be Fixed to Put Women and Children First*. Berkeley: University of California Press.

Wahab, Stephanie, and Lenora Olson. 2004. "Intimate Partner Violence and Sexual Assault in Native American Communities." *Trauma, Violence, and Abuse* 5 (4): 353–366.

Walters, Karina, and Jane Simoni. 2002. "Reconceptualizing Native Women's Health: An 'Indigenist' Stress-Coping Model." *American Journal of Public Health* 92 (4): 520–524.

Ward, Martha C. 1995. "Early Childbearing: What Is the Problem and Who Owns It." In *Conceiving the New World Order: The Global Politics of Reproduction*, edited by Faye Ginsburg and Rayna Rapp, 140–158. Berkeley: University of California Press.

Wendland, Claire. 2007. "The Vanishing Mother: Cesarean Section and 'Evidence-Based Obstetrics.'" *Medical Anthropology Quarterly* 21 (2): 218–233.

Wennberg, David. 1998. "Variation in the Delivery of Health Care: The Stakes Are High." *Annals of Internal Medicine* 128 (10): 866–868.

Wertz, Richard, and Dorothy Wertz. 1989. *Lying In: A History of Childbirth in America*. New Haven, CT: Yale University Press.

Wessman, Jeff, and Neil Harvey. 2000. "An Interview with Katsi Cook." *Talking Leaves* 10 (1): n.p.

Wilkie, Laurie. 2003. *The Archaeology of Mothering: An African-American Midwife's Tale*. New York: Routledge.

Wilkins, David. 2002. *American Indian Politics and the American Political System*. New York: Rowman and Littlefield.

Wilson, Shawn. 2001. "What Is an Indigenous Research Methodology?" *Canadian Journal of Native Education* 25 (2): 175–179.

———. 2008. *Research Is Ceremony: Indigenous Research Methods*. Halifax: Fernwood Publishing.

Wingood, Gina, and Ralph DiClemente. 1997. "The Effects of an Abusive Primary Partner on the Condom Use and Sexual Negotiation Practices of African-American Women." *American Journal of Public Health* 87 (6): 1016–1018.

Wolfe, Patrick. 1999. *Settler Colonialism and the Transformation of Anthropology: The Politics and Poetics of an Ethnographic Event*. New York: Cassell.

———. 2011. "After the Frontier: Separation and Absorption in US Indian Policy." *Settler Colonial Studies* 1 (1): 13–51.

Worldnet Weekly. 2006. "Indian Tribe Challenges Abortion Law with Clinic." *World Net Daily*, April 1. Accessed January 1, 2012. http://www.wnd.com/2006/04/35526/.

Woster, Kevin. 2010. "Tribal Officials Say Safe Housing Key to Maintaining Fabric of Life on a Reservation." *Rapid City Journal*, August 25. Accessed January 21, 2011. http://rapidcityjournal.com/news/tribal-officials-say-safe-housing-key-to-maintaining-fabric-of/article_4325a19a-b074-11df-98a0-001cc4c03286.html.

Yee, Jessica. 2010. "Native + Sex = Strong, Sexy, Powerful, and Unapologetic." *First-People's Blog*. Accessed October 11, 2011. http://www.firstpeoplesnewdirections.org/blog/?p=1881.

Young Bear, Severt, and R. D. Theisz. 1996. *Standing in the Light: A Lakota Way of Seeing*. Lincoln: University of Nebraska Press.

Zimmerman, Mark, Jesus Ramirez-Valles, Kathleen Washienko, Benjamin Walter, and Sandra Dyer. 1996. "The Development of a Measure of Enculturation for Native American Youth." *American Journal of Community Psychology* 24 (2): 295–310.

Index

About the Author

Barbara Gurr is an assistant professor in residence in the Women's, Gender, and Sexuality Studies Program at the University of Connecticut.

CPSIA information can be obtained
at www.ICGtesting.com
Printed in the USA
FFOW02n1256170317
33617FF

9 780813 564685